10th Edition

STUDY GUIDE

COST ACCOUNTING
PLANNING AND CONTROL

Edward J. VanDerbeck
Xavier University
Cincinnati, Ohio

COLLEGE DIVISION South-Western Publishing Co.

CINCINNATI   DALLAS   LIVERMORE

Sponsoring Editor: Mark R. Hubble
Developmental Editor: Sara E. Bates
Production Editor: Sharon L. Smith
Production House: Special Press, Inc.
Cover Designer: Joseph M. Devine

ISBN: O-538-80926-4

1 2 3 4 5 6 7 DH 5 4 3 2 1 0

Printed in the United States of America

CONTENTS

CHAPTER 1
THE MANAGEMENT CONCEPT AND THE FUNCTION OF THE CONTROLLER

REVIEW SUMMARY

1. The three basic management functions are planning, organizing, and controlling. *Planning* refers to the construction of a detailed operating program for all phases of operations. Planning is the process of sensing external opportunities, determining objectives, and employing resources to accomplish these objectives. *Organizing* is the establishment of the framework within which required activities are to be performed. Organizing involves the establishment of functional divisions, departments, sections, or branches. *Controlling* is management's systematic effort to compare performance to plans. Actual results are measured against plans; if significant differences are noted, remedial action is taken.

2. The larger the business organization the greater the problems of planning, and the more involved the process of controlling the activities of individual units scattered throughout the world. Authority and responsibility is assigned to middle and operating management to assure the success and control of management's plans. *Authority* originates with executive management, which delegates it to the various managerial levels. *Responsibility* arises in the superior–subordinate relationship due to the fact that the superior has the authority to require specified work from the subordinates. Another aspect of responsibility is *accountability*—reporting results achieved back to higher authority.

3. An *organization chart* sets forth each principal management position and helps to define authority, responsibility, and accountability. It is essential to the development of a cost system and cost reports that parallel the responsibility of individuals for implementing management plans. An organization chart based on the *line-staff concept* categorizes all positions as to either "line" or "staff." An organization chart based on the *functional-team concept* categorizes positions as resources functions, processes functions, or human interrelations functions.

4. The controller is the executive manager who is responsible for a company's accounting function. The controller coordinates management's participation in the planning and control phases, in determining the effectiveness of policies, and in creating organizational structures and procedures. The controller also aids in the control of business operations by issuing performance reports that advise management of activities that require corrective action. Concentrating on the activities that deviate significantly from the plan is called *management by exception.*

5. The cost department, under the direction of the controller, is responsible for keeping records of a company's manufacturing and nonmanufacturing activities. It must issue significant control reports and other decision-making data to those managers who assist in controlling and improving costs and operations. The collection, presentation, and analysis of cost data should help management accomplish the following: (1) creating and executing plans and budgets for operating under expected competitive and economic conditions; (2) establishing costing methods and procedures that permit control, reduction, or improvements of costs; (3) creating inventory values for costing and pricing purposes; (4) determining company costs and profit for an accounting period; and (5) choosing from among two or more alternatives that might increase revenues or decrease costs.

6. The Certified Management Accountant (CMA) is the professional certification that recognizes professional competence and educational achievement in the field of management accounting. Requirements for the CMA certificate include passing a five-part examination and completing two years of professional experience. The *Standards of Ethical Conduct for Management Accountants* presents fifteen responsibilities of the management accountant, grouped under the headings of competence, confidentiality, integrity, and objectivity. The standards also outline procedures for management accountants to follow if they have knowledge of, or think they are being asked to do, something unethical.

7. In the public sector, financial reporting has been influenced significantly by the Securities and Exchange Commission (SEC), the Internal Revenue Service (IRS), and the Cost Accounting Standards Board (CASB). In the private sector, financial reporting has been influenced by the American Institute of Certified Public Accountants (AICPA), which sponsored the formation of the Financial Accounting Standards Board (FASB); the National Association of Accountants (NAA); the American Accounting Association (AAA); the Financial Executives Institute (FEI); and the International Accounting Standards Committee (IASC).

8. The federal government, through the actions of the SEC and other regulatory agencies, is showing an increased interest and influence in companies' external reports. In its publication, *Regulation S-X,* the SEC sets forth the requirements for financial statements filed with the Commission. IRS regulations influence financial reporting and cost accounting methods, in that the income tax consequences of various alternatives are weighed heavily in the decision-making process. The Cost Accounting Standards Board promulgated the cost and profit requirements to be followed by businesses in connection with government contracts.

PART 1

Instructions: *Place a check mark in the appropriate column to indicate whether each of the following statements is **True** or **False**.*

	True	False
1. Control is basically an executive management responsibility.	_____	_____
2. In practice, planning and control are interrelated functions that are not easily separated.	_____	_____
3. Participation in the budgeting process has been shown to have positive effects on managers' attitudes toward their jobs.	_____	_____
4. The accounting function should plan and act independently of the management function.	_____	_____
5. The CASB's pronouncements are in general harmony with sound accounting concepts and techniques and with generally accepted accounting principles.	_____	_____
6. Decentralization of planning and control functions results in the delegation of more authority to individual managers.	_____	_____
7. Executive management delegates responsibility to the various managerial levels.	_____	_____
8. Accountability is the act of reporting results achieved by individual managers back to executive management.	_____	_____
9. An organization chart is necessary for the development of an effective cost system.	_____	_____
10. Line gives advice and performs technical functions for employees classified as staff.	_____	_____
11. The resources, processes, and human interrelations functions are position categories under the functional-teamwork concept of management.	_____	_____
12. The controller's most important contribution to planning is to coordinate information for management's use.	_____	_____
13. The control phase of cost accounting consists of comparing current results with predetermined standards.	_____	_____
14. Cost accounting is applicable only to manufacturing operations.	_____	_____
15. All levels of management should be involved in creating the budget program.	_____	_____

PART 2

Instructions: *In the blank space at the left of each of the following items, place the letter from the right-hand column that identifies the term that best matches the statement in the column on the left. No letter should be used more than once.*

_____ 1. The process of sensing external opportunities and threats, determining desirable objectives, and employing resources to accomplish these objectives.

_____ 2. The process of establishing the framework within which required activities are to be performed.

_____ 3. Originates with executive management, which delegates it to the various managerial levels.

_____ 4. Arises in the superior-subordinate relationship, but can't be delegated.

_____ 5. Reporting results achieved back to higher authority.

_____ 6. That group of workers who make decisions and perform the true management functions.

_____ 7. That group of workers who give advice or perform any technical function.

_____ 8. Sets forth each principal management position and helps to define authority, responsibility, and accountability.

_____ 9. Based on the fundamental assumption that all positions or functional divisions can be categorized into two groups.

_____ 10. An organizational concept that groups business functions around resources, processes, and human interrelations.

_____ 11. Management's systematic effort to achieve objectives by comparing performance to plans and taking corrective action, if necessary.

_____ 12. Predetermined costs for direct materials, direct labor, and factory overhead that are established by using information accumulated from past experience and from scientific research.

_____ 13. Established by the NAA in response to the need to have a formal means to recognize professional competence in management accounting.

_____ 14. Responsible for the functions of planning and decision processes, special managerial cost analysis, cost accounting, and general accounting.

_____ 15. Concentrating on the significant deviation of actual results from predetermined plans.

_____ 16. Activities such as product design, research and development, purchasing, manufacturing, and marketing.

_____ 17. Address issues related to competence, confidentiality, integrity, and objectivity, as well as outline procedures to follow in resolving ethical conflicts.

_____ 18. Relies upon accounting, budgeting, and related reports in scheduling case requirements and expectations.

_____ 19. Directs the company's efforts in relation to the behavior of people outside and inside the organization.

_____ 20. Innovative technology such as this is drastically changing the nature of costs through lower inventory levels, decreased use of labor, and increased fixed costs.

a. planning
b. controller
c. line
d. management by exception
e. staff
f. processes functions
g. line-staff concept
h. organization chart
i. control
j. CMA
k. standard costs
l. treasury department
m. accountability
n. responsibility
o. authority
p. organizing
q. *Standards of Ethical Conduct for Management Accountants*
r. flexible manufacturing systems
s. functional-teamwork concept
t. human interrelations function

PART 3

Instructions: *In the blank space at the left of each of the following items, place the letter of the choice that most correctly completes each item.*

_____ 1. In a business organization, a structure of individuals composed of foremen and supervisors is called the:
   a. executive management group   d. middle management group
   b. line-staff management group   e. controllership group
   c. operating management group

_____ 2. The comparison of actual performance with predetermined plans and the measurement of the extent to which objectives were reached is that facet of responsibility called:
   a. accountability   d. authority
   b. obligation   e. securing results
   c. delegation

_____ 3. The organizational group that makes decisions and performs the true management functions is the:
   a. staff   d. line
   b. function   e. team
   c. executive management

_____ 4. In the functional-teamwork concept of management, the business function that directs the company's effort toward the behavior of people inside and outside the company is the:
   a. executive function   d. resources function
   b. staff   e. human interrelations function
   c. processes function

_____ 5. The level of management that most requires data for purposes of long-range planning is:
   a. executive management   d. scientific management
   b. middle management   e. exception management
   c. operating management

_____ 6. The group that promulgated the cost and profit requirements to be followed by businesses in connection with government contracts is the:
   a. Cost Accounting Standards Board   d. Securities and Exchange Commission
   b. Financial Accounting Standards Board   e. Federal Trade Commission
   c. Financial Executives Institute

_____ 7. The smallest organizationally independent segment of a company that has been charged by management with profit and loss responsibility is the:
   a. cost center   c. investment center
   b. profit center   d. service center

_____ 8. A function, organizational subdivision, contract, or other work unit for which cost data are desired is a(n):
   a. cost objective   c. department
   b. organizational unit   d. division

_____ 9. Pretermined costs for direct materials, direct labor, and factory overhead that are established by using information accumulated from past experience and scientific research are:
   a. budgets   c. normal costs
   b. actual costs   d. standard costs

_____ 10. A written expression of management's plans for the future is a(n):
   a. organization chart   c. charter
   b. performance report   d. budget

PART 4

Instructions: *Define, describe, or explain each of the following:*

1. The five tasks that the collection, presentation, and analysis of cost data should help management accomplish

_____

_____

_____

_____

2. The three Cost Accounting Standards that have the potential for impact far beyond the government contracting area

_____

_____

_____

_____

_____

3. Line-staff concept of management _____

_____

_____

_____

_____

_____

4. The differences between short-range plans and long-range plans _____

_____

_____

_____

5. Management by exception _____

_____

_____

_____

_____

_____

6. Explain the procedures that an accountant is to follow in resolving an ethical conduct problem according to *The Standards of Ethical Conduct for Management Accountants.* _____

_____

_____

_____

_____

CHAPTER 2
COST CONCEPTS AND THE COST ACCOUNTING SYSTEM

REVIEW SUMMARY

1. It is important to distinguish between the terms "cost" and "expense," particularly since they are often used interchangeably. *Cost* is an exchange price, a forgoing, a sacrifice made to secure benefit. *Expense* is the measured overflow of goods and services that is matched with revenue to determine income. A request for cost data must be accompanied by a description of the situation in which the data are to be used. For planning purposes, for example, the accountant must often abandon recorded past costs and deal with future, imputed, differential, or opportunity costs.

2. Once a cost object is selected, measurement of costs depends heavily on the traceability of costs to the cost object. A common way of characterizing costs is to label them as either direct or indirect costs of a particular cost object, as if there were only two degrees of traceability. In fact, degrees of traceability exist along a continuum, with costs that can be physically or contractually identified with the cost object at one extreme and costs that can be identified with the cost object only by the most arbitrary allocations at the other extreme. The traceability of costs is as important for decision making in service businesses as it is in manufacturing, regardless of whether there is a need to determine the cost of inventories for external reporting.

3. A cost accounting information system must correspond to an organization's division of authority so that an individual manager can be held accountable for the departmental cost incurred. A system must reflect the manufacturing and administrative processes of the company for which it was designed. It should provide prompt and meaningful cost reports to management. In determining the degree of sophistication needed, the cost of the system should be compared to its prospective value to management.

4. A company's *chart of accounts* provides control accounts for the recognized elements of cost and all expenses. Accounting coding in the form of numbers, letters, and other symbols is essential to facilitate the processing of information.

5. *Data processing* is the accumulation, classification, analysis, and summary reporting of large quantities of information. *Electronic data processing* is a system for recording repetitive data. *Programming* involves the analysis of the job to be converted to electronic data processing, the preparation of flowcharts, the instruction coding for the computer, the debugging process, and trial runs.

6. It is vital that cost accounting systems be in harmony with the manufacturing methods in current usage. Robotics, just-in-time inventory systems, intensified competition, and other changes in the manufacturing environment have created a need to broaden the range of information that accountants deal with and has led to increased attention to *nonfinancial performance measures*. Nonfinancial performance measures use simple physical data rather than allocated accounting data, are not connected to the general financial accounting system, and are selected to measure one specific aspect of performance rather than to be "all things for all purposes."

7. Costs are classified by the nature of the cost element. *Manufacturing cost* consists of direct materials, direct labor, and factory overhead. *Commercial expenses* consist of marketing expenses and administrative expenses. *Marketing expenses* are the expenses of making sales and delivering products. *Administrative expenses* are incurred in the direction, control, and administration of the organization. *Prime cost* consists of direct materials and direct labor, while *conversion cost* consists of direct labor and factory overhead.

8. Costs are classified by their relation to the product. *Direct materials* are all materials that form an integral part of the finished product. *Direct labor* is labor applied directly to the materials composing the finished product. *Factory overhead* includes all manufacturing costs except direct materials and direct labor.

9. Costs are classified by their tendency to vary with volume or activity. *Variable costs* vary directly in relation to changes in the volume of production, remain constant on a per-unit basis within a relevant range, are reasonably easy to assign to operating departments, and are the responsibility of the supervisor of the department in which they were incurred. *Fixed costs* are fixed in amount within a relevant range, decrease on a per-unit basis when output is increased, are often assigned to departments by arbitrary methods, and in most cases executive management is responsible for incurring them. *Semivariable costs* contain both fixed and variable elements.

10. Costs are classified by their relation to manufacturing departments. For product costing, the factory is divided into departments, cost centers, or cost pools. *Producing departments* are those whose costs may be charged to the product because they contribute directly to its production. *Service departments* are not directly engaged in production but render services for the benefit of other departments. Factory overhead cost is considered a *direct cost* to a specific department if it is readily identifiable with that department. It is classified as an *indirect* or *common cost* if it is incurred for the benefit of several departments and must be allocated to those departments.

11. Costs are classified as to their nature as common or joint costs. *Common costs* are costs of facilities or services employed in the output of two or more operations, commodities, or services. *Joint costs* occur when the production of one product is possible only if one or more other products are manufactured at the same time.

12. Costs are classified with respect to the accounting period in which they apply. A *capital expenditure* is expected to benefit future periods and is classified as an asset. A *revenue expenditure* benefits the current period and is termed an expense.

PART 1

Instructions: *Place a check mark in the appropriate column to indicate whether each of the following statements is True or False.*

	True	False
1. Expense is the measured outflow of goods and services that is matched with revenue to determine income.	____	____
2. The accountant primarily uses past costs for planning purposes.	____	____
3. Indirect materials would include factory supplies and lubricants.	____	____
4. Direct labor would include the wages of assemblers and finishers.	____	____
5. Fixed factory overhead would include fuel costs and receiving costs	____	____
6. Variable factory overhead would include straight-line depreciation and property taxes	____	____
7. Factory overhead includes all manufacturing costs except direct materials and direct labor	____	____
8. Expenses such as rent and depreciation are examples of common costs	____	____
9. The allocation of joint costs to joint products is a very precise process.	____	____
10. A common way of characterizing costs is to label them as direct or indirect as to a particular cost object, because there are only two degrees of traceability.	____	____
11. Manual data processing is a system for recording and processing information without rerecording repetitive data.	____	____
12. A manufacturing process that heavily utilizes robotics would be more apt to use direct labor hours than machine hours as a base for allocating factory overhead.	____	____
13. The traceability of costs is as important for decision making in service businesses as it is in manufacturing.	____	____
14. Variable costs are thought of as the costs of being in business, whereas fixed costs are the costs of doing business.	____	____
15. Cost accounting information should be restricted to information that is measured in dollars.	____	____

PART 2

Instructions: *In the blank space at the left of each of the following items, place the letter from the right-hand column that identifies the term that best matches the statement in the column on the left. No letter should be used more than once.*

_____ 1. A product, job order, contract, project, or department for which an arrangement is made to accumulate and measure cost.

_____ 2. Composed of direct materials, direct labor, and factory overhead.

_____ 3. The costs of making sales and delivering products.

_____ 4. There is a trend toward relying on this as the most important basis for classifying and understanding costs.

_____ 5. Expected to benefit future periods and classified as an asset.

_____ 6. Benefits the current period and termed an expense.

_____ 7. Remains constant on a per-unit basis within a relevant range.

_____ 8. Decreases on a per-unit basis when output is increased.

_____ 9. Contains both fixed and variable elements.

_____ 10. Includes all materials that form an integral part of the finished product.

_____ 11. Includes all manufacturing costs except direct materials and direct labor.

_____ 12. Any individual operating unit for which costs are accumulated.

_____ 13. A cost that was incurred for the benefit of several departments and that must be allocated to those departments.

_____ 14. A cost that occurs when the production of one product is possible only if one or more other products are manufactured at the same time.

_____ 15. Examples of these would include number of defective units produced, hours of machine downtime, and weight of scrap materials produced.

_____ 16. A prerequisite for efficiently collecting, identifying, and coding data for recording in journals and posting to ledger accounts.

_____ 17. Seeks to reduce dramatically the investments in direct materials and work in process inventories by ordering on an as-needed basis only.

_____ 18. The consumption of these is so minimal or so complex that attempting to identify them with individual products would be futile.

_____ 19. Expensed factory labor that does not directly affect the construction or the composition of the finished product.

_____ 20. Work applied directly to the materials composing the finished product.

a. direct labor
b. direct materials
c. indirect labor
d. semivariable cost
e. indirect materials
f. fixed cost
g. just-in-time inventory system
h. variable cost
i. chart of accounts
j. revenue expenditure
k. traceability
l. capital expenditure
m. joint cost
n. nonfinancial performance measures
o. common cost
p. marketing expenses
q. cost center
r. manufacturing cost
s. factory overhead
t. cost object

PART 3

Instructions: *In the blank space at the left of each of the following items, place the letter of the choice that most correctly completes each item.*

_____ 1. Factory overhead includes:
  a. all manufacturing costs
  b. all manufacturing costs, except direct materials and direct labor
  c. indirect materials but not indirect labor
  d. indirect labor but not indirect materials
  e. none of the above
                                                      (AICPA adapted)

_____ 2. The term "fixed costs" refers to:
  a. all costs that are likely to respond to the amount of attention devoted to them by a specified manager
  b. all costs that are associated with marketing, shipping, warehousing, and billing activities
  c. all costs that do not change in total for a given period of time and relevant range, but become progressively smaller on a per-unit basis as volume increases
  d. all costs that fluctuate in total in response to small changes in the rate of utilization of capacity
  e. none of the above
                                                      (ICMA adapted)

_____ 3. Inventoriable costs are:
  a. manufacturing costs incurred to produce units of output
  b. all costs associated with manufacturing, other than direct labor and raw materials
  c. costs associated with marketing, shipping, warehousing, and billing activities
  d. the sum of direct labor and factory overhead
  e. none of the above
                                                      (ICMA adapted)

_____ 4. The term "conversion cost" refers to:
  a. manufacturing cost incurred to produce units of output
  b. all costs associated with manufacturing, other than direct labor and raw materials
  c. the sum of direct labor and all factory overhead
  d. the sum of direct materials and direct labor
  e. none of the above
                                                      (ICMA adapted)

_____ 5. From the following, the best example of a variable cost is:
  a. property taxes   d. straight-line depreciation
  b. interest charges   e. none of the above
  c. corporate president's salary
                                                      (ICMA adapted)

_____ 6. From the following, the best example of a fixed cost is:
  a. receiving costs   d. fuel
  b. salaries of production executives e. none of the above
  c. hauling within the plant

_____ 7. A typical indirect factory overhead cost is:
  a. postage   d. freight out
  b. power   e. all of the above
  c. stationery and printing

_____ 8. From the following, the best example of a semivariable cost is:
  a. maintenance and repairs of machinery and   c. depreciation
     equipment   d. insurance
  b. property tax   e. none of the above

_____ 9. A typical administrative expense is:
  a. freight and cartage out   d. auditing expenses
  b. entertainment   e. all of the above
  c. sales salaries

_____ **10.** A typical marketing expense is:

    a. legal expenses   **d.** office salaries

    b. advertising   **e.** all of the above

    c. uncollectible accounts

PART 4

Instructions: *Place a check mark in the appropriate column to indicate whether the following costs are variable, fixed, or semivariable.*

Item	Variable	Fixed	Semivariable
1. Direct materials			
2. Units-of-production depreciation			
3. Property tax			
4. Small tools			
5. Payroll taxes			
6. Direct labor			
7. Fuel			
8. Reclamation expenses			
9. Rent			
10. Salaries of production executives			
11. Health and accident insurance			
12. Supervision			
13. Wages of security guards			
14. Property insurance			
15. Straight-line depreciation			
16. Receiving costs			
17. Royalties			
18. Overtime premium			
19. Factory office services			
20. Machinery maintenance			

PART 5

Instructions: *Place a check mark in the appropriate column to indicate the proper classification of each of the following costs.*

Item	Indirect Materials	Indirect Labor	Other Indirect Factory Costs	Marketing Expenses	Administrative Expenses
1. Legal fees					
2. Fire and liability insurance on factory buildings					
3. Lubricants					
4. Supervision					
5. Office salaries					
6. Uncollectible accounts expense					
7. Freight out					
8. Samples					
9. Payroll taxes on factory wage					
10. Small tools					
11. Overtime premium for factory workers					
12. Experimental work by engineers					
13. Glue and nails in finished product					
14. Cleaning compound for factory					
15. Sales commissions					
16. Entertainment of clients					
17. Audit fees					
18. Employer payroll taxes on president's salary					
19. Inspection					
20. Idle time due to assembly line breakdown					

PART 6

The estimated unit costs for Rijo Rotors, when operating at a production and sales level of 5,000 units, are as follows:

Cost Item	Estimated Unit Cost
Steel	$ 25
Direct labor	6
Variable factory overhead	9
Fixed factory overhead	15
Variable marketing	3
Fixed marketing	5

Instructions:

1. Calculate the estimated conversion cost per unit.

2. Calculate the estimated prime cost per unit.

3. Calculate the estimated variable manufacturing cost per unit.

4. Calculate the estimated total variable cost per unit.

5. Calculate the total cost that would be incurred in a month that had a production level of 5,000 units and a sales level of 4,500 units.

REVIEW SUMMARY

1. To assure the flow of cost information into control accounts and subsidiary records, a transaction must be account-classified and coded. Properly approved transaction documents generate the flow of accounting events into the accounting system. The *journal voucher control system*, consisting of journal vouchers supported by the original transaction documents, facilitates the flow of accounting information. The *journal voucher* should include the voucher number, the date, coded accounts, the amounts to be debited and credited, and the signed approval.

2. A knowledge of a flow of products throught the various productive steps determines the nature of the cost accumulation procedures to be used. Direct materials, direct labor, and applied factory overhead are charged to Work in Process during the accounting period. The total cost of goods completed is transferred from the Work in Process account to the Finished Goods account. The cost of goods sold during that period is transferred from the Finished Goods account to the Cost of Goods Sold account. At the end of each accounting period, Cost of Goods Sold is closed to Income Summary.

3. Costs may be accumulated using an *actual cost system* or a *standard cost system*. In an actual cost system, the job or the process is charged with the actual costs of material used and labor expended, whereas factory overhead is usually charged on the basis of a predetermined overhead rate. In a standard cost system, the actual costs are being charged in the accounts, and any differences between standard and actual costs are recorded in variance accounts. Costs allocated to units of production may include all manufacturing costs, *full absorption costing* or only the variable manufacturing costs, *direct* or *variable costing*. Generally accepted accounting principles require that full absorption costing be used for external financial reporting.

4. In a *job order cost system*, the costs of various jobs or contracts are kept separate during their manufacture or construction. The system is used in industry when it is possible to physically identify the jobs produced and to charge each with its own cost. *Process costing* is used in industries when units are not distinguishable from one another during the manufacturing process. Many companies use both the job order and the process cost method; for example, where different units have very different direct material costs, but all units undergo identical conversion in large quantities.

5. *Flexible Manufacturing Systems* (FMS) consist of an integrated collection of automated production processes, automated materials movement, and computerized systems controls to efficiently manufacture a highly flexible variety of products. FMS impacts upon many of the factors that management should consider in evaluating a system, such as planning and control of materials and work in process inventories. Although an FMS may seem attractive, there is the need to consider the substantial capital investment and the knowledgeable personnel required to run such systems.

6. In recent years, some manufacturing facilities have so successfully implemented the *just-in-time philosophy of inventory management* that their average elapsed time between receipt of raw materials and production of finished work has been reduced to a matter of hours. This results in a very small amount of work in process inventory at any time and makes the tracking of production costs to work in process unimportant. *Backflush costing* is a way to accumulate manufacturing costs in a factory in which processing systems are fast. The purpose of backflush costing is to reduce the number of cost accounting entries that must be made. The Work in Process account is not adjusted throughout the accounting period to reflect all of the costs of units in process, but rather its balance is corrected by means of a single end-of-period adjusting entry and no subsidiary records are kept for work in process. Backflush costing determines the elements of the cost of completed work only after the work is completed. The cost of the completed work is then subtracted from the balance in the Work in Process account in a step called *post-deduction*.

PART 1

Instructions: *Place a check mark in the appropriate column to indicate whether each of the following statements is True or False.*

	True	False
1. The journal voucher control system is another name for the voucher register.		
2. The journal voucher should include the amounts to be debited and credited.		
3. At the end of an accouting period, Cost of Goods Sold is closed to Income Summary		
4. In an actual cost system, factory overhead is usually charged on the basis of an actual overhead rate.		
5. In a standard cost system, any differences between standard and actual costs are recorded in variance accounts.		
6. Process systems are most frequently used in industries such as breweries and flour mills.		
7. Job order costing is used in industries where it is physically impossible to identify individual jobs.		
8. For tax reporting, the Tax Reform Act of 1986 requires certain purchasing and storage costs to be allocated to inventory.		
9. Process costing is applicable to service businesses that have only a small number of engagements underway at one time such as accounting and architectural firms.		
10. In automated manufacturing systems, manufacturing changes can be made more efficiently than in labor-intensive systems.		
11. A company cannot use both the job order and the process cost accumulation systems in the same factory.		
12. In Flexible Manufacturing Systems, a group of related machines is coordinated by a computer.		
13. In a firm using the just-in-time philosophy, the accurate assignment of costs to work in process inventory is more important than ever.		
14. In backflush costing, the Work in Process account is not adjusted throughout the accounting period to reflect all of the costs of units in process.		
15. Some manufacturers have so successfully implemented the just-in-time philosophy that their average elapsed time from receipt of raw materials to production of finished goods has been reduced to a matter of hours.		

PART 2

Instructions: *In the blank space at the left of each of the following items, place the letter from the right-hand column that identifies the term that best matches the statement in the column on the left. No letter should be used more than once.*

_____   1. A general ledger account that is supported by a number of subsidiary accounts or records.

_____   2. The basis for the preparation of journal entries that record the transactions for a given period.

_____   3. Prepared using data from the income statement and balance sheet and from elsewhere in the company records.

_____   4. Collects costs as they occur but delays the presentation of results until manufacturing operations have been performed.

_____   5. System in which unit costs are predetermined in advance of production.

_____   6. System that presupposes the possibility of physically identifying the lots produced and charging each with its own cost.

_____   7. System used when units are not distinguishable from one another during one or more of the manufacturing processes.

_____   8. Production processes that are traditionally labor intensive are being automated through the use of this.

_____   9. The requirement for tax reporting that certain purchasing and storage costs be allocated to inventory.

_____ 10. An integrated collection of automated production processes, automated materials movement, and computerized systems controls to effectively manufacture a variety of products.

_____ 11. Designed to reduce the number of cost accounting entries that must be measured and routinely recorded in a factory where processing speeds are extremely fast.

_____ 12. In backflush costing, means of subtracting the cost of completed work from the balance of the Work in Process account.

_____ 13. Inventory system in which materials are delivered by the supplier at the time the factory is ready to use them.

_____ 14. Source documents used to track labor costs.

_____ 15. Source documents used to track materials costs.

a. historical cost system
b. just-in-time (JIT)
c. journal voucher
d. process cost system
e. time tickets
f. statement of cash flows
g. journal voucher
h. postdeduction
i. control account
j. flexible manufacturing systems
k. standard cost system
l. robotics
m. backflush costing
n. super absorption
o. job order cost system

Instructions: *In the blank space at the left of each of the following items, place the letter of the choice that most correctly completes each item.*

_____ 1. The best accumulation procedure to use when there is continuous mass production of like units is:
  a. actual   d. process
  b. standard   e. none of the above
  c. job order   (AICPA adapted)

_____ 2. Of the following production operations, the most likely to employ job cost manufacturing is:
  a. soft-drink manufacturing   d. candy manufacturing
  b. printing   e. none of the above
  c. crude oil refining   (AICPA adapted)

_____ 3. Which of the following would not be used in job order costing?
  a. Standards   d. Factory overhead allocation based on direct labor
  b. Averaging of direct labor and material rates   hours applied to the job
  c. Direct costing   e. None of the above   (AICPA adapted)

_____ 4. One feature of a historical cost system is that:
  a. factory overhead is usually allocated on the basis of a predetermined rate
  b. unit costs are predetermined in advance of production
  c. differences between actual and standard costs are collected in separate accounts
  d. products, operations, and processes are costed using standards for both quantity and dollar amounts
  e. none of the above

_____ 5. An industry that would most likely use process costing procedures is:
  a. office equipment   d. pharmaceuticals
  b. musical instrument manufacturing   e. none of the above
  c. aircraft manufacturing

_____ 6. The best cost accumulation procedure to use when products manufactured within a department or cost center are heterogeneous is:
  a. actual   d. process
  b. standard   e. none of the above
  c. job order

_____ 7. Which of the following consists of an integrated collection of automated production procedures, automated materials movement, and computerized systems controls to effectively manufacture a variety of products?
  a. Flexible manufacturing system   d. Direct costing system
  b. Just-in-time inventory system   e. None of the above
  c. Absorption costing system

_____ 8. Which of the following manufacturing systems is characterized by one kind of product, a large range of viable production volumes, and tightly constrained production qualities?
  a. Manual systems   d. Process cost systems
  b. Fixed automation systems   e. Job order cost systems
  c. Flexible manufacturing systems

_____ 9. Which of the following manufacturing systems is characterized by many kinds of products, a substantial learning curve effect, and long lead times?
  a. Manual systems   d. Process cost systems
  b. Fixed automation systems   e. None of the above
  c. Flexible manufacturing systems

_____ 10. Which of the following manufacturing systems is characterized by several kinds of products, middle-range production volumes, and consistent product quality?
  a. Manual systems   d. Process cost systems
  b. Fixed automation systems   e. Job order cost system
  c. Flexible manufacturing systems

PART 4

During the past month, the Murphy Company incurred these costs: direct labor, $180,000; factory overhead, $90,000; and direct materials purchases, $75,000. Inventories were costed as follows:

	Beginning	Ending
Finished goods	$30,000	$25,000
Work in process	55,000	45,000
Materials	20,000	17,000

Instructions:

1. Calculate the cost of goods manufactured.

2. Calculate the cost of goods sold.

PART 5

Selected transactions of the Lee Company for a recent month are as follows:

a. Materials purchased and received on account: $70,000.

b. Materials requisitioned: $52,000 for production and $6,300 for factory supplies.

c. Total gross payroll was $180,000, with 7.5% FICA tax and 15% income tax withheld.

d. The payroll was distributed as follows: direct labor, $75,000; indirect factory labor, $40,000; marketing salaries, $30,000; administrative salaries, $35,000.

e. Employer payroll taxes were: FICA tax, 7.5%; federal unemployment tax, 0.8%; state unemployment tax, 3%.

f. Depreciation of $25,000 and expired insurance of $2,500 related to factory operations were recorded.

g. Other factory overhead costs of $12,500 were recorded as a liability.

h. Accounts payable of $76,000 and the accrued payroll and payroll taxes, except for unemployment taxes, were paid.

i. Amounts received from customers in payment of their accounts totaled $315,000.

j. Work completed and transferred to finished goods, $151,000.

k. Finished goods costing $140,000 were sold on account for $285,000.

Instructions: *Using the ruled form on page 20, prepare journal entries to record these transactions.*

Account	Debit	Credit

PART 6

The Raiderville Manufacturing Company uses a Raw and In Process (RIP) inventory account. At the end of each month, all inventories are counted, their conversion cost components are estimated, and inventory account balances are adjusted accordingly. Raw material cost is backflushed from RIP to finished goods. The following information is for the month of August:

Beginning balance of RIP account, including $2,500 of conversion cost .... $ 23,000
Raw materials received on credit 162,000
Ending RIP inventory per physical count, including $1,400 conversion cost estimate 18,900

Instructions: *On the form provided below, prepare the journal entries involving the Raw and In Process Account for the month of August.*

Account	Debit	Credit

REVIEW SUMMARY

1. In job order costing, the cost of each order produced or the cost of each lot to be placed in stock is recorded on a *job order cost sheet*. The cost sheet indicates the materials, labor, and factory overhead applied to each order or lot. Cost sheets are subsidiary records and are controlled by the Work in Process account.

2. When materials are purchased, the account debited is Materials or Materials Inventory. Additionally, each purchase is also recorded on an individual *materials ledger card*. Materials necessary for production are issued to the factory on the basis of *materials requisitions* prepared by production scheduling clerks. Each requisition of direct materials results in a debit to Work in Process and a credit to Materials, as well as an entry to the materials section of the appropriate cost sheet. When indirect materials are issued, the requisitions are charged to the factory overhead control account and are also recorded on a *factory overhead analysis sheet*.

3. To compute the direct labor cost of a given order, the time spent on each job during a day must be recorded on each worker's time ticket. At regular intervals, the labor time and the labor cost for each job are entered on the job order cost sheets. Indirect labor is also accounted for through the use of time tickets and is entered on factory overhead analysis sheets. Payroll taxes for both direct and indirect labor are treated as factory overhead.

4. Factory overhead is entered on the job cost sheets on the basis of a predetermined overhead rate. A causal relationship between two factors such as direct labor hours and factory overhead is used as a basis for charging factory overhead to jobs. An applied factory overhead account is often used to keep applied costs and actual costs in separate accounts. Actual factory overhead is charged to Factory Overhead Control and to the factory overhead analysis sheets as the actual expenses become known. If actual overhead expenses exceed applied overhead, the overhead is said to be underapplied; if applied exceeds actual, it is overapplied. A relatively small balance in the under- or overapplied factory overhead account is usually charged or credited to Cost of Goods Sold, whereas significant balances are allocated to inventory accounts and Cost of Sales.

5. When jobs are completed, cost sheets are moved from the in-process category to the finished work file. Completion of a job for stock results in a debit to Finished Goods and a credit to Work in Process. If the completed job is a component used in a subsequent manufacturing process, Ma-terials is debited. If the job is produced for a specific customer, Cost of Goods Sold is debited at the time the job is completed.

6. The amount realized from the sale of scrap and waste may be shown on the income statement under Other Income or it may be credited to Factory Overhead Control, thus reducing factory overhead expense and cost of goods manufactured. If spoilage is normal and happens at any time and at any stage of the productive process, its cost should be treated as factory overhead, included in the predetermined factory overhead rate, and prorated over all production of a period. If normal spoilage is caused by exacting specifications, difficult processing, and so on, it should be charged to that specific job or order, and an allowance for normal spoilage should *not* be included in the predetermined factory overhead rate used to charge overhead to that specific job. Abnormal spoilage should always be charged to factory overhead. If defective work is experienced in regular manufacturing, the additional cost to correct defective units should be included in predetermined factory overhead, based on previous experience, and all units produced during the period should be charged with a portion of the rework cost as overhead is applied to production. Defective work resulting from special orders may be charged directly to the specific job, and the factory overhead rate should be reduced by the allowance for reworking defective units because the rework cost is to be charged directly to the job instead of to factory overhead.

7. Many job order settings involve a complex product line with products that can be produced in several sizes, grades, and configurations. As a result, reliable product cost data cannot be obtained using any single predetermined overhead rate. One approach is to divide overhead costs into two or more overhead cost pools and to calculate an overhead rate for each pool. In determining the cost of a job, the result would be a multiple-part overhead cost calculation within a single responsibility center.

8. In service businesses, such as legal, architectural, and accounting services, several varieties of job order costing are used. The predetermined overhead rate is usually based on direct labor cost because direct labor is often the largest cost. It is also common to combine the labor cost rate with the predetermined overhead rate; thus the amount charged to a job for each hour of labor time also represents overhead. The only remaining costs to be charged to the job are the directly traceable costs other than labor, such as travel, meals, and photocopying.

PART 1

Instructions: *Place a check mark in the appropriate column to indicate whether each of the following statements is True or False.*

	True	False
1. In job order costing, the sheet on which direct materials, direct labor, and applied factory overhead are summarized for a job is called a *job order cost sheet.*	_____	_____
2. A departmentalized job cost sheet will indicate the materials, labor, and overhead cost incurred in each department.	_____	_____
3. Job cost sheets are subsidiary records that are controlled by the factory overhead account...........	_____	_____
4. If a job is produced for a specific customer, the cost of the completed job is debited directly to Materials...	_____	_____
5. When indirect materials are issued, the requisitions are charged to the Work in Process account.	_____	_____
6. Time tickets are a basic source document in the computation of labor cost.	_____	_____
7. Payroll taxes for direct and indirect labor are treated as factory overhead........................	_____	_____
8. When actual overhead expenses are greater than applied overhead, the overhead is said to be over-applied.	_____	_____
9. The Applied Factory Overhead account is closed to the Actual Factory Overhead account by debiting Factory Overhead Control and crediting Applied Factory Overhead...............................	_____	_____
10. Completion of a job for stock results in a debit to Cost of Goods Sold and a credit to Work in Process.	_____	_____
11. Service industries do not use job order costing because they provide a service rather than a product. .	_____	_____
12. Separate overhead rates are only appropriate if a company has two or more departments.	_____	_____
13. To reduce accounting for scrap to a minimum, often no entry is made until the scrap is actually sold.	_____	_____
14. Normal spoilage should always be charged to factory overhead.................................	_____	_____
15. If defective work is experienced in regular manufacturing operations, the additional cost to correct defective units should be considered in determining the factory overhead rate.	_____	_____

PART 2

Instructions: *In the blank space at the left of each of the following items, place the letter from the right-hand column that identifies the term that best matches the statement in the column on the left. No letter should be used more than once.*

_____	1. Imperfections that arise in the manufacturing process due to faults in materials, labor, and machines.
_____	2. If this is caused by exacting specifications, difficult processing, or other unexpected factors, its cost should be charged to the specific order.
_____	3. Represent the difference between actual and standard costs.
_____	4. To reduce accounting for this to a minimum, often no entry is made until it is sold.
_____	5. If this is attributable to an event that is not expected to recur, the cost of the units in excess of their net realizable value should be charged to Factory Overhead Control.
_____	6. It may be a ton of coal, barrel of oil, dozen of shirts, etc.
_____	7. A record on which the cost of each order produced for a given customer is recorded.
_____	8. Each is an accounting unit to which materials, labor, and factory overhead is assigned.
_____	9. Each purchase of direct materials is also entered on one of these.
_____	10. The individual who is usually responsible for issuing materials requisitions.
_____	11. The individual who assembles the materials called for on the requisitions.
_____	12. A subsidiary ledger for the recording of factory overhead items.
_____	13. This item is accounted for through the use of time tickets and clock cards and is entered in the Factory Overhead Control account.
_____	14. This tax is composed of equal contributions by employer and employee.
_____	15. Traditionally labor-intensive production processes are being automated through the use of this.
_____	16. It is determined based on the relationship of one factor to another.
_____	17. The account in which estimated factory overhead is recorded.
_____	18. The account in which actual factory overhead is recorded.
_____	19. Factory overhead is said to be this when actual expenses exceed applied expenses.
_____	20. Factory overhead is said to be this when applied expenses exceed actual expenses.

a. storekeeper
b. Factory Overhead Control
c. scrap
d. underapplied
e. factory overhead rate
f. job cost sheet
g. overapplied
h. variances
i. factory overhead analysis sheets
j. cost unit
k. normal spoilage
l. robotics
m. ledger card
n. FICA tax
o. defective work
p. Applied Factory Overhead
q. job
r. indirect labor
s. abnormal spoilage
t. production scheduling clerk

Instructions: *In the blank space at the left of each of the following items, place the letter of the choice that most correctly completes each item.*

_____ **1.** In job order costing, the basic document to accumulate the cost of each order is the:

    a. invoice

    b. purchase order

    c. materials requisition

    d. job cost sheet

    e. none of the above

_____ **2.** In job order costing, payroll taxes paid by the employer for factory employees are preferably accounted for as:

    a. direct labor

    b. factory overhead

    c. indirect labor

    d. administrative costs

    e. none of the above

_____ **3.** The tie-in between general accounts and cost accounts is often discussed in connection with accounting procedures. An example of a general account is:

    a. Work in Process

    b. Finished Goods

    c. Factory Overhead Control

    d. Accumulated Depreciation

    e. none of the above

_____ **4.** Cost of Goods Sold is debited and Finished Goods is credited for a:

    a. purchase of goods account

    b. transfer of completed production to the finished goods storeroom

    c. transfer of completed goods out of the factory

    d. transfer of materials to the factory

    e. none of the above

_____ **5.** Dalton Processing Co. paid its March payroll, withholding $15,000 in federal income tax and $7,500 in FICA tax. There were no unemployment taxes due on this payroll. The total amount to be remitted to the federal government is:

    a. $15,000

    b. $7,500

    c. $22,500

    d. -0-

    e. none of the above

_____ **6.** When normal spoilage occurs as a result of exacting specifications or difficult processing, any loss is charged to:

    a. extraordinary losses

    b. the specific job in which the spoilage occurred

    c. administrative expenses

    d. factory overhead control

    e. none of the above

_____ **7.** In contrast to normal spoilage, abnormal spoilage:

    a. is considered part of good production

    b. arises under efficient operating conditions

    c. is controllable in the short run

    d. is not an inherent result of the particular manufacturing process

    e. none of the above   (CIA adapted)

_____ **8.** In a process costing system, the cost of abnormal spoilage should be:

    a. prorated between units transferred out and ending inventory

    b. included in the cost of units transferred out

    c. treated as a loss in the period incurred

    d. ignored

    e. none of the above   (CIA adapted)

_____ **9.** A manufacturer of electric motors expects 4% of output to be rejected at the final inspection point. These rejected units are sold through specific channels at less than 10% of normal selling price. The proper assignment of the costs associated with these defective units is to:

    a. charge to the cost of inspection

    b. charge to general factory overhead

    c. charge as an unfavorable material usage variance

    d. accumulate and add to the cost of good units completed during the period

    e. none of the above   (CIA adapted)

_____ **10.** Assume 550 units were worked on during a period in which a total of 500 good units were completed. Normal spoilage consisted of 30 units; abnormal spoilage, 20 units. Total production costs were $2,200. The company accounts for abnormal spoilage separately on the income statement as loss due to abnormal spoilage. Normal spoilage is not accounted for separately. What is the cost of the good units produced?

    a. $2,000

    b. $2,080

    c. $2,100

    d. $2,200

    e. none of the above

                                                                                         (CIA adapted)

Instructions: *Complete the job cost sheet shown below, using the following data. (Round all totals to the nearest dollar.)*

	Week Ending 3/12	Week Ending 3/19
Materials used, Cutting Dept.	$3,600 (Req. #6281)	$1,800 (Req. #6299)
Direct labor rate, Cutting Dept.	$10.80 per hour	$10.80 per hour
Labor hours used, Cutting Dept.	400	220
Materials used, Assembly Dept.	$240 (Req. #6288)	$360 (Req. #6308)
Direct labor rate, Assembly Dept.	$9.50	$9.50
Labor hours used, Assembly Dept.	200	300
Machine hours, Cutting Dept.	300	160
Applied factory overhead, Cutting Dept.	$7.50 per machine hour	$7.50 per machine hour
Applied factory overhead, Assembly Dept.	$6.00 per direct labor hour	$6.00 per direct labor hour

Marketing and administrative costs are charged to each order at a rate of 40% of the cost to manufacture. The sales price of the order is $50,000.

OTTO OFFICE SUPPLY, INC.   Job Order No. 1215

For: Erman Engineering   Date Ordered: 3/5/19—

Product: File Cabinets   Date Started: 3/7/19—

Specifications: Attached   Date Completed: 3/19/19—

Quantity: 20

Direct Materials

Date	Department	Req. No.	Cost	Total

Direct Labor

Date	Department	Hours	Hourly Rate	Cost	Total

Factory Overhead Applied

Date	Department	Rate of Application	Hours	Cost	Total

Direct materials .... $_____	Sales price	$_____
Direct labor .... _____	Factory cost	$_____
Factory overhead applied .... _____	Marketing and administrative	
	expenses	_____
	Cost to make and sell..........	_____
	Profit	$_____

PART 5

Konstantine Corporation uses job order costing. At the beginning of March, two jobs were in process:

	Job 101	Job 103
Materials	$3,000	$ 800
Direct labor	6,000	2,250
Applied factory overhead	6,000	2,250

There was no inventory of finished goods on March 1. During the month, Jobs 105 through 110 were started. Materials requisitions for March totaled $25,000; direct labor cost, $30,000; and actual factory overhead, $31,500. Factory overhead is applied at a rate of 100% of direct labor cost. The only job still in process at the end of March is No. 110, with costs of $2,300 for materials and $1,500 for direct labor. Job 107, the only finished job on hand at the end of March, has a total cost of $9,000.

Instructions: *Using the T accounts below, record all of the information above, including the determination of the cost of goods manufactured, the cost of goods sold, and the closing of over- or underapplied factory overhead to Cost of Goods Sold.*

Work in Process

Finished Goods

Factory Overhead Control

Cost of Goods Sold

Applied Factory Overhead

PART 6

Mountain Products, Inc. provided the following data for May:

Materials and supplies
    Inventory, May 1 .... $10,000
    Purchases on account 25,000

Labor
    Paid monthly on the last day of the month 33,000
    [Deductions from gross earnings are 15% for income tax and 7.5% for FICA tax. Payroll taxes include federal
    unemployment tax (0.8%) and state unemployment tax (4%).]

Factory overhead costs
    Supplies (issued from materials) 2,500
    Indirect labor 5,500
    Depreciation 1,000
    Other factory overhead costs (all from outside suppliers on account) 10,000

Work in process

	Job 101	Job 102	Job 103	Total
Work in process, May 1	$ 4,000	—	—	$ 4,000
Job costs during May:				
Direct materials	9,000	$12,200	$ 8,000	29,000
Direct labor	7,500	12,000	8,000	27,500
Applied factory overhead (100% of direct labor cost)	7,500	12,000	8,000	27,500

Job 101—started in April, finished during May, and sold to a customer for $40,000 cash.
Job 102—started in May, not yet finished.
Job 103—started in May, finished during May, and now in the finished goods warehouse awaiting customer's disposition.

Finished goods inventory, May 1 .... -0-

Instructions: *Using the ruled form on the following two pages, prepare journal entries, with detail for the respective job orders and factory overhead subsidiary records, to record the following transactions for May:*

(1) Purchases of materials on account.
(2) Liability for the monthly payroll.
(3) Payment of the payroll.
(4) Labor cost distribution.
(5) Liability for payroll taxes.
(6) Materials issued.
(7) Depreciation for the month.
(8) Acquisition of other overhead costs on credit.
(9) Overhead applied to production.
(10) Jobs completed and transferred to finished goods.
(11) Sales revenue.
(12) Cost of goods sold.
(13) Applied factory overhead closed to the Factory Overhead Control account.
(14) The balance in the Factory Overhead Control account closed to Cost of Goods Sold.

Account	Subsidiary Record	Debit	Credit

Account	Subsidiary Record	Debit	Credit

PART 7

Suarez Company produced 1,000 units in a recent production run and discovered that 50 were defective and required reworking as follows:

Rework cost per unit:
Materials .... $ 5
Labor 10
Factory overhead 10
Total $25
Normal production cost per unit:
Materials $10
Labor 25
Factory overhead 25
Total $60

Instructions:

1. Using the journal form provided below, prepare journal entries to record the rework costs and to transfer the job cost to finished goods, assuming that rework costs are to be charged to all production.

Account	Subsidiary Record	Debit	Credit

2. Using the journal form provided below, prepare the same journal entries as in (1), assuming that rework costs are to be charged to the specific job.

Account	Subsidiary Record	Debit	Credit

REVIEW SUMMARY

1. Process costing is used when products are manufactured under conditions of continuous processing or under mass production methods. The cost of a completed unit is computed by dividing total cost incurred during a period by total units completed. Separate departmental Work in Process accounts are used to charge each department for the materials, labor, and factory overhead used to complete its share of a manufacturing process. Departmental total and unit costs are determined by the use of a cost of production report.

2. Each item manufactured goes through the same set of operations in a *sequential product flow* format. In a *parallel product flow*, certain portions of the work are done simultaneously and then brought together for completion. When the initial product moves to different departments within the plant, depending upon the desired final product, this is called a *selective product flow* format.

3. The details involved in process costing for materials requisitions are usually fewer than those in job order costing because materials are charged to departments rather than jobs. The cost of materials used can be determined at the end of the period either by *inventory difference procedures* (beginning inventory + purchases – ending inventory), or by *consumption reports* that state the cost or quantity of materials put into process by various departments. The entry to charge direct materials to production consists of a debit to Work in Process—Department X and a credit to Materials.

4. Daily time tickets or weekly time clock cards are used to identify labor costs with departments in process costing. The entry to charge labor costs to production consists of debits to the various departmental work in process accounts and a credit to Payroll.

5. Factory overhead expenses should be accumulated in a factory overhead control account by means of an entry debiting Factory Overhead Control and crediting the various prepaid items, liabilities, etc. The use of a factory overhead control account requires a subsidiary ledger consisting of departmental expense analysis sheets for both service and producing departments. The entry charging applied overhead to production consists of a debit to the various work in process accounts and a credit to Applied Factory Overhead. In highly automated manufacturing environments where direct labor is a relatively small proportion of total manufacturing costs, the trend is to combine the direct labor and factory overhead cost elements when computing the overhead rate that is used for charging costs to jobs.

6. A departmental cost of production report shows all costs chargeable to a department. Total cost is broken down by cost elements for each department head responsible for the costs incurred. The cost section of the report is divided into two parts: one showing total costs for which the department is accountable; the other showing the disposition of those costs.

7. Computation of individual unit costs requires an analysis of the ending work in process inventory to determine its stage of completion. To assign costs equitably to in-process units and transferred units, units still in process must be restated in terms of completed units. To determine *equivalent units of production*, restated partially completed units are added to units actually completed during the period. Materials, labor, and overhead costs are then divided by the appropriate equivalent production figure to determine unit costs for each of these elements.

8. Continuous processing leads to the possibility of waste, shrinkage, and other factors that cause loss or spoilage of production units. The only effect of losing units in the first department is that it increases the unit cost of the remaining good units. A method by which the accountant can reconcile quantities put into production with quantities reported as completed or lost is to compute a *process yield*, indicating the finished production that should result from processing various materials. Such a figure is useful to management for controlling materials consumption.

9. The cost of production reports for departments other than the first department must include additional information as follows: (a) costs received from the preceding departments, (b) adjustment of preceding departments' unit cost due to lost units, and (c) costs received from the preceding departments to be included in the cost of the ending work in process inventory. If units are lost in departments subsequent to the first department, the lost unit cost can be computed by one of two methods. One method determines a new unit cost for work done in the preceding department and subtracts the preceding department's old unit cost figure from the adjusted unit cost figure. The difference between the two figures is the additional cost due to lost units. The other method determines the lost unit's share of total cost and allocates this cost to the remaining good units. If units are lost at the beginning of or during a process, the cost is spread over the units completed and the units in process. When units are lost at the end of a process, the cost of the lost units is charged to completed units only.

10. The cost of units lost due to normal spoilage is spread over the remaining good units. The cost of units lost due to abnormal spoilage is charged either to Factory Overhead or directly to a current period expense and reported as a separate item in the cost of goods sold statement. *Normal spoilage* is uncontrollable spoilage that occurs in the production process under efficient operating conditions. *Abnormal spoilage* is due to inefficient operating conditions that could have been avoided, given better control over production. Any cost necessary to correct *defective work* is simply reported as additional cost of materials, labor, and factory overhead, provided the rate of defectives is within normal limits; otherwise, it would be expensed in the current period.

11. When added materials do not increase the number of units but increase total cost and unit costs, a materials unit cost must be computed for the department and a materials cost must be included in the work in process inventory. When additional materials result in additional units, the greater number of units causes a decrease in unit cost, which necessitates an adjustment of the preceding department's unit cost.

12. When additional materials increase the number of units being processed, it is still possible to have lost units. If increased and lost units both occur, no separate computation is required for lost units. Only the net units added are used.

PART 1

Instructions: *Place a check mark in the appropriate column to indicate whether each of the following statements is True or False.*

	True	False
1. In process costing, the cost of a completed unit is determined by dividing total costs incurred during the period by equivalent total units completed	____	____
2. A single Work in Process account is used for materials, labor, and factory overhead, regardless of the number of producing departments	____	____
3. In a selective product flow, certain portions of the work are done simultaneously and then brought together in a final process.	____	____
4. When additional materials result in additional units, the preceding department's unit cost must be adjusted.	____	____
5. In highly automated manufacturing environments, direct labor is usually a higher percentage of manufacturing costs than it is in more traditional manufacturing settings.	____	____
6. The cost to correct defective work is always reported as an additional cost of materials, labor, and overhead on the job.	____	____
7. When additional units increase the number of units being processed, it is still possible to have lost units.	____	____
8. Departmental expense analysis sheets serve as the subsidiary ledger for the Work in Process account.	____	____
9. In process costing, all costs chargeable to a department are summarized in a departmental cost of production report.	____	____
10. Equivalent production is determined by subtracting partially completed units in process from completed units.	____	____
11. The process yield indicates the finished production that should result from processing various materials.	____	____
12. The only effect of losing units in the first department is to increase the unit cost of the remaining good units.	____	____
13. When units are lost at the end of a process, the cost of the lost units is spread over the units completed and the units still in process.	____	____
14. The cost of normal spoilage is spread over the remaining good units.	____	____
15. When computing the cost of the ending work in process inventory of any department subsequent to the first, costs received from preceding departments must be omitted.	____	____

PART 2

Instructions: *In the blank space at the left of each of the following items, place the letter from the right-hand column that identifies the term that best matches the statement in the column on the left. No letter should be used more than once.*

_____   1. Often referred to as continuous or mass production costing.

_____   2. The addition of these in departments subsequent to the first may increase the number of units and also cause a change in the unit cost.

_____   3. A product flow format in which the product moves to different departments, depending upon the desired final product.

_____   4. A product flow format in which each item manufactured goes through the same set of operations.

_____   5. Indicates the cost or quantity of materials put into process by various departments.

_____   6. The method of determining the cost of materials used by adding purchases to beginning inventory and then deducting ending inventory.

_____   7. If this is your goal, any loss of units is considered abnormal.

_____   8. Often included in the computation of the overhead rate in highly automated manufacturing environments.

_____   9. Compose a subsidiary ledger for factory overhead.

_____   10. When overhead is applied in process costing, the predetermined rates are multiplied by this.

_____   11. A section of the cost of production report that indicates the disposition of the units started in process.

_____   12. Represents the number of units for which sufficient materials, labor, and overhead were issued to enable completion.

_____   13. A figure representing the finished production that should result from processing various materials.

_____   14. When units are lost at the end of a process, the cost of the lost units is charged to this.

_____   15. Added to departmental units costs to arrive at the unit cost at the end of the department's operations.

_____   16. Spoilage considered with acceptable tolerance limits for people and machines.

_____   17. Spoilage that is not expected to arise under efficient operating conditions.

_____   18. An account to which the cost of abnormal spoilage may be debited.

_____   19. An account that must be reduced by the cost of abnormal spoilage

_____   20. A schedule showing quantities and costs chargeable to a department.

a. zero defects
b. abnormal spoilage
c. Work in Process
d. sequential product flow
e. cost of production report
f. process yield
g. inventory difference procedures
h. completed units
i. consumption reports
j. equivalent production
k. departmental expense analysis sheets
l. adjusted cost from preceding department
m. processing cost
n. Factory Overhead Control
o. direct labor cost
p. quantity schedule
q. materials
r. normal spoilage
s. actual activity base
t. selective product flow

PART 3

Instructions: *In the blank space at the left of each of the following items, place the letter of the choice that most correctly completes each item.*

_____ 1. In a process costing system, if units are lost at the beginning or during the process of production and the loss is normal, the determination of equivalent units should:
   a. ignore the units lost
   b. assign the cost of units lost to units transferred out
   c. use all of the units lost in the computation
   d. none of the above

_____ 2. When lost units occur at the end of a process and the loss is normal and the company's process costing system is designed to account for this possibility, the cost of lost units is:
   a. charged to units still in process only
   b. charged to units completed only
   c. prorated over units in process and completed units
   d. ignored
   e. none of the above

_____ 3. For a process costing system, procedures must be designed to:
   a. value inventory of work still in process
   b. determine a unit cost for each department
   c. accumulate materials, labor, and factory overhead costs by departments
   d. all of the above

_____ 4. A cost of production report for a department shows all of the following except:
   a. total and unit costs transferred from a preceding department
   b. the cost per job
   c. unit costs added by the department
   d. costs transferred to a subsequent department or to finished goods
   e. all of the above

_____ 5. Costs should be charged against revenue in the period in which costs are incurred except:
   a. for factory overhead costs for a product manufactured and sold in the same accounting period
   b. when the costs will not benefit any future period
   c. for costs from idle manufacturing capacity resulting from an unexpected plant shutdown
   d. for costs of normal shrinkage and scrap incurred for the manufacture of a product in inventory
   e. none of the above

_____ 6. Which of the following is a characteristic of process costing?
   a. Work in process inventory is restated in terms of completed units.
   b. Costs are accumulated by order.
   c. It is used by a company manufacturing custom machinery.
   d. Standard costs are not applicable.
   e. None of the above.   (AICPA adapted)

_____ 7. An error was made in computing the percentage of completion of the current year's ending work in process inventory. The error resulted in assigning a higher percentage of completion to each component of the inventory than actually was the case. The effect of this error on (a) computation of equivalent units in total, (b) computation of costs per equivalent unit, and (c) costs assigned to cost of goods completed for the period is:

	(a)	(b)	(c)
a.	understate	overstate	overstate
b.	understate	understate	overstate
c.	overstate	understate	understate
d.	overstate	overstate	understate

(AICPA adapted)

_____ 8. In process cost accumulation, transferred-in cost denotes:
   a. labor that is transferred from another department within the same plant instead of hiring temporary workers from the outside
   b. cost of the production of a previous internal process that is subsequently used in a succeeding internal process
   c. supervisory salaries that are transferred from a service cost center to a production cost center
   d. ending work in process inventory of a previous period that will be used in a succeeding process
   e. none of the above   (AICPA adapted)

_____ 9. Premier Products transferred 15,000 units to one department. An additional 5,000 units of materials were added in the department. At the end of the month, 12,000 units were transferred to the next department, while 6,000 units remained in the work in process inventory. There was no beginning inventory, and lost units occurred throughout the production process. The costs for units transferred in would be effectively allocated over:
   a. 21,000 units   d. 20,000 units
   b. 15,000 units   e. none of the above
   c. 12,000 units   (AICPA adapted)

_____ 10. Kew Co. had 3,000 units in work in process at April 1 which were 60% complete as to conversion cost. During April, 10,000 units were completed. At April 30, 4,000 units remained in work in process; they were 40% complete as to conversion cost. Direct materials are added at the beginning of the process. How many units were started during April?
   a. 9,900   d. 11,000
   b. 9,800   e. none of the above
   c. 10,000   (AICPA adapted)

PART 4

During June, 80,000 units were transferred from Department A to Department B at a cost of $240,000. Materials cost of $40,000 and conversion cost of $115,000 were added in Department B. On June 30, Department B had 30,000 units of work in process, 1/4 complete as to conversion costs. Materials are added at the beginning of the process in Department B.

Instructions: *Complete the three schedules below for Department B.*

1. *Quantity Schedule*

Units received from Department A . . . .   ==========

Units transferred to finished goods . . . .

Units still in process . . . .   _____   ==========

2. *Equivalent Production*

	Transferred in from Department A	Materials	Conversion
Transferred to finished goods			
Ending inventory	_____	_____	_____
	==========	==========	==========

3. Cost per equivalent unit for materials cost and for conversion costs in Department B . . . .   _____   _____

PART 5

Reina Inc. uses process costing. The costs for Department B for June were:

Cost from preceding department		$ 90,000
Cost added by department:		
Materials...................................	$57,500	
Labor	68,750	
Factory overhead...........................	34,375	160,625

The following information was obtained from the department's quantity schedule:

Units received...	15,000
Units transferred out...	13,125
Units still in process	1,875

The degree of completion of the work in process as to costs originating in Department B was 2/3 complete as to materials costs and 1/3 complete as to conversion costs.

Instructions: *Complete the following June cost of production report for Department B.*

Reina Inc
Department B
Cost of Production Report
For the Month of June, 19–

Quantity Schedule

Units received from preceding department..........		
Units transferred to next department		
Units still in process..........................		

Cost Charged to the Department	Total Cost	Unit Cost
Cost from preceding department:		
Transferred in during the month	$	$
Cost added by department:		
Materials...................................	$	$
Labor		
Factory overhead...........................		
Total cost added	$	$
Total cost to be accounted for	$	$

Cost Accounted for as Follows

Transferred to next department...................		$
Work in process—ending inventory:		
Cost from preceding department	$	
Materials...................................		
Labor		
Factory overhead...........................		
Total cost accounted for		$

Additional Computations:

Equivalent production:

PART 6

For May, Zabricki Industries Inc. reported the following production data for Department B:

Transferred in from Department A 20,000

Transferred out to Department C 16,000

In process at end of May (with 50% labor and factory overhead) 3,000

All materials were put into process in Department A.

The Cost Department collected these figures for Department B:

Unit cost for units transferred in from Department A .... $ 12,350

Labor cost in Department B 105,000

Applied factory overhead 78,750

(Any loss of units is considered to be within the normal tolerance limits and to have occurred throughout the production process.)

Instructions: *Complete the May cost of production report below for Department B.*

Zabricki Industries Inc
Department B
Cost of Production Report
For the Month of May, 19–

Quantity Schedule

Units received from preceding department ....

Units transferred to next department ....

Units still in process ....

Units lost in process ....

Cost Charged to the Department	Total Cost	Unit Cost
Cost from preceding department:		
Transferred in during the month	$_____	$_____
Adjusted cost from preceding department		$_____
Cost added by department:		
Labor	$	$
Factory overhead	_____	_____
Total cost added	$_____	$_____
Total cost to be accounted for	$_____	$_____

Cost Accounted for as Follows

Transferred to next department .... $

Work in process—ending inventory:

Cost from preceding department .... $

Labor ....

Factory overhead .... _____   _____

Total cost accounted for .... $_____

Additional Computations:

Equivalent production:

PART 7

During July, the Cooking Department received 16,000 units from the Blending Department at a unit cost of $5. Costs added in the Cooking Department were: materials, $27,900; labor, $84,000; and factory overhead, $56,000. There was no beginning inventory. Of the 16,000 units received, 12,000 were transferred out; 3,000 units were in process at the end of the month (all materials, 50% converted); 1,000 lost units were 50% complete as to materials and conversion costs. The entire loss is considered abnormal and is to be charged to factory overhead.

Instructions: *(1) Complete the July cost of production report for the Cooking Department appearing on page 41.*
(2) Prepare the journal entry to record the spoilage, using the journal paper provided below.

Account	Debit	Credit

Cooking Department
Cost of Production Report
For the Month of July, 19–

Quantity Schedule

    Units received from preceding department . . . .

    Units transferred to next department . . . .

    Units still in process (all materials - ½ labor and

    factory overhead . . . .

    Units lost in process (abnormal - ½ materials, labor,

    and factory overhead) . . . .

	Total Cost	Unit Cost
Cost Charged to the Department		
Cost from preceding department:		
Transferred in during the month	$_____	$_____
Cost added by department:		
Materials	$	$
Labor		
Factory overhead	_____	_____
Total cost added	$_____	$_____
Total cost to be accounted for	$_____	$_____
Cost Accounted for as Follows		
Transferred to next department		$
Transferred to factory overhead:		
From preceding department	$	
Materials		
Labor		
Factory overhead	_____	
Work in process—ending inventory:		
From preceding department	$	
Materials		
Labor		
Factory overhead	_____	_____
Total cost accounted for		$_____

Additional Computations:

  Equivalent production:

  Unit costs:

CHAPTER 6
PROCESS COSTING: AVERAGE AND FIFO COSTING

REVIEW SUMMARY

1. If the *average costing method* is used to account for beginning inventory costs, these costs are added to the costs of the new period. In the first department, the cost of materials already in process would be added to the materials cost for the period before dividing by the equivalent production figure. In a subsequent department, the portion of the work in process inventory representing the cost of work done in preceding departments is added to the cost of transfers received from the preceding department during the current period. A weighted average unit cost for work done in preceding departments is then computed. The other portion of the work in process inventory, representing costs added by the department under consideration, is entered as a departmental cost to be added to other departmental costs incurred during the period before dividing by the equivalent production figure.

2. Using average costing, the lost unit cost adjustment figure is computed on the assumption that units lost cannot be identified as coming from units in process at the beginning or from units received during the period. The units are assumed to have been lost from both sources, and the adjustment is computed by dividing total preceding department cost by the remaining good units and then subtracting the previous average unit cost figure.

3. In first-in, first-out costing, beginning work in process costs are kept separate from the additional new costs incurred in the next period, thus giving separate unit costs for beginning work in process units completed and for units started and finished in the new period. In the first department, the cost of completing units in process at the beginning of the period is computed first, followed by the computation of the cost of units started and finished within the period. Units in process at the beginning will usually have a completed unit cost that is different from the unit cost for work started and finished during the period. In departments subsequent to the first, the procedure is the same, except that the unit cost of units transferred into these departments is shown only as one figure, determined by dividing total units received into total costs received.

4. In fifo costing, lost units must be identified as either beginning work in process units or new units started during the period. This identification is needed to determine which unit cost should be adjusted.

5. The principal disadvantage of fifo costing is that if several unit cost figures are used at the same time, extensive detail is required within the cost of production report. In firms where production is continuous and more or less uniform and appreciable fluctuations in unit costs are rare, average costing is preferable due to its simplicity.

6. Difficulties associated with the use of process costing include (a) the determination of an accurate estimate for stage of completion; (b) the determination of accurate materials cost figures when materials prices are based on fluctuating market quotations; (c) determining at what point shrinkage, spoilage, or evaporation actually occurred; and (d) allocating joint processing cost.

PART 1

Instructions: *Place a check mark in the appropriate column to indicate whether each of the following statements is True or False.*

	True	False

1. If the average costing method is used, the cost of labor already in process would be added to the labor cost for the month before dividing by the equivalent production figure. . . . . _____ _____

2. In fifo costing, the portion of the work in process inventory representing the cost of work done in preceding departments is kept separate from the cost of transfers received from the preceding department during the current period. . . . . _____ _____

3. A weighted average unit cost is computed by adding two separate unit costs and dividing the sum by two. . . . . _____ _____

4. In average costing, the lost unit cost adjustment figure is computed on the assumption that units lost cannot be identified as coming exclusively from either beginning units in process or from units received during the period. . . . . _____ _____

5. In fifo costing, beginning work in process costs are combined with the costs incurred in the current period. . . . . _____ _____

6. In fifo costing, the cost of units started and finished within the period are computed first, followed by the computation of the cost of completing the beginning units in process. . . . . _____ _____

7. When average costing is used, beginning units in process will usually have a completed unit cost that is different from the unit cost of work started and completed during the period. _____ _____

8. The averaging process that is used to cost units transferred into subsequent departments is consistent with the principles of fifo costing. . . . . _____ _____

9. In average costing, there is a need to identify whether lost units come from beginning work in process units or from units started during the period. . . . . _____ _____

10. In firms where production is continuous and uniform and fluctuations in unit costs are rare, average costing is preferable due to its simplicity. . . . . _____ _____

11. A major difficulty associated with the use of process costing is obtaining an accurate estimate of the stage of completion of in-process inventories. . . . . _____ _____

12. Some companies use both job order and process costing procedures. . . . . _____ _____

13. When units are lost by shrinkage, spoilage, or evaporation, the time when the loss occurs is relevant to final cost calculations. . . . . _____ _____

14. Industries using job cost procedures are usually of the multiple product type. . . . . _____ _____

15. When materials prices are influenced by fluctuating market conditions, the materials cost may not even be entered on the cost of production report. . . . . _____ _____

Instructions: *In the blank space at the left of each of the following items, place the letter of the choice that most correctly completes each item.*

_____ 1. The fifo method of process costing differs from the average method in that the fifo method:

  a. considers the state of completion of beginning work in process inventory in computing equivalent units of production, but the average method does not

  b. does not consider the stage of completion of beginning work in process inventory in computing equivalent units of production, but the average method does

  c. is applicable only to those companies using the fifo inventory pricing method, but the average method may be used with any inventory pricing method

  d. allocates costs based on whole units, but the average method uses equivalent units

  e. none of the above

  (AICPA adapted)

_____ 2. When using the fifo process costing method, the correct equivalent units of production for use in computing unit costs is equal to the number of units:

  a. started into process during the period, plus the number of units in work in process at the beginning of the period

  b. in work in process at the beginning of the period, plus the number of units started during the period, plus the number of units remaining in work in process at the end of the period times the percentage of work necessary to complete these units

  c. in work in process at the beginning of the period times the percentage of work necessary to complete the items, plus the number of units started and completed during the period, plus the number of units remaining in work in process at the end of the period times the percentage of work performed on these units during the period

  d. transferred out during the period, plus the number of units remaining in work in process at the end of the period times the percentage of work necessary to complete the units

  e. none of the above

  (AICPA adapted)

_____ 3. A condition in which the fifo process costing method will produce the same cost of goods manufactured as the average method is:

  a. when goods produced are homogeneous in nature

  b. when there is no beginning inventory

  c. when there are no lost units

  d. when beginning and ending inventories are each 50 percent complete

  e. none of the above

  (AICPA adapted)

_____ 4. Paki Inc. had 8,000 units of work in process in its Department M on March 1. These units were 50% complete as to conversion costs. Materials are introduced at the beginning of the process. During March, 17,000 units were started, 18,000 units were completed, and there were 2,000 units of normal spoilage. Paki had 5,000 units of work in process at March 31 which were 60% complete as to conversion costs. Under Paki's cost accounting procedures, normal spoilage units reduce the number of units over which total cost is spread. Using the average costing method, the equivalent units of production for March for conversion costs were:

  a. 17,000   **d.** 20,000

  b. 19,000   **e.** none of the above

  c. 21,000

  (AICPA adapted)

_____ 5. Trigger Company manufactures Product H in a two-stage production cycle in Departments A and B. Materials are added at the beginning of the process in Department B. Trigger uses the average process costing method. Conversion costs for Department B were 50% complete as to the 6,000 units in the beginning work in process inventory and 75% complete as to the 8,000 units in the ending work in process inventory. A total of 12,000 units were completed and transferred out of Department B during February. An analysis of the costs relating to February 1 work in process and to February production activity in Department B is:

	Costs		
	Transferred In	Materials	Conversion
Work in process, February 1	$12,000	$2,500	$1,000
February production activity	29,000	5,500	5,000

  The total Product H cost per equivalent unit transferred out for February, rounded to the nearest cent, was:

  a. $2.75   **d.** $3.00

  b. $2.78   **e.** none of the above

  c. $2.82

  (AICPA adapted)

6. Information for May concerning Department A, the first stage of Cee Corporation's production cycle, is as follows:

	Materials	Conversion Costs
Work in process, beginning	$ 4,000	$ 3,000
Current costs	20,000	16,000
Total cost	$ 24,000	$ 19,000
Equivalent units based on average method	100,000	95,000
Average unit cost	$ .24	$ .20
Goods completed	90,000 units	
Work in process, ending	10,000 units	

Materials are added at the beginning of the process. The ending work in process is 50% complete as to conversion costs. Using the average costing method, the total costs accounted for would be distributed to goods completed and ending work in process, respectively, as follows:

a. $39,600; $3,400

b. $39,600; $4,400

c. $44,000; $0

d. $44,000; $3,400

e. none of the above

(AICPA adapted)

7. Larkin Company adds materials in the beginning of the process in the Shaping Department, which is the first of two stages of its production cycle. Information concerning the materials used in the Shaping Department in October is as follows:

	Units	Materials Cost
Work in process as of October 1	6,000	$ 3,000
Units started during October...............	50,000	25,560
Units completed and transferred to next department during October	44,000	

Using the average costing method, and assuming that there were no spoiled units, the materials cost of work in process at October 31 is:

a. $3,600

b. $5,520

c. $6,000

d. $3,060

e. none of the above

(AICPA adapted)

8. Protein Products transferred 15,000 units to one department. An additional 5,000 units of materials were added in the department. At the end of the month, 12,000 units were transferred to the next department, while 7,000 units remained in work in process inventory. There was no beginning inventory, and the lost units occurred throughout the production process. The costs for units transferred in would be effectively allocated over:

a. 19,000 units

b. 15,000 units

c. 12,000 units

d. 20,000 units

e. 25,000 units

9. Difficulties encountered in the use of process cost accounting procedures include all of the following except:

a. determination of production quantities and their stage of completion

b. determination of materials cost

c. allocation of joint processing cost

d. different assumptions as to the time that lost units occur

e. determination as to the job to which departmental costs should be charged

10. Paducah Processing Co. uses the average costing method and reported a beginning inventory of 3,000 units that were 40% complete with respect to materials in one department. During the month, 18,000 units were started; 14,000 units were finished; ending inventory amounted to 7,000 units that were 80% complete with respect to materials. Total materials cost during the period for work in process should be spread over:

a. 15,400 units

b. 21,000 units

c. 19,600 units

d. 18,000 units

e. none of the above

PART 3

Lindner Company operates two producing departments whose quantity reports appear as follows:

	Department A	Department B
Beginning inventory	500	600
Department A—all materials, 75% conversion cost		
Department B—all materials, 50% conversion cost		
Started in process	3,000	2,500
	3,500	3,100
Transferred out	2,500	2,600
Ending inventory	1,000	500
Department A—all materials, 25% conversion cost		
Department B—all materials, 50% conversion cost		
	3,500	3,100

Instructions:

1. Using the form provided below, compute equivalent production figures for each department, using the average method.

	Materials Units	Conversion Units
Department A:		
Transferred out		
Ending inventory	_____	_____
Equivalent production	_____	_____

	Units from Preceding Dept.	Conversion Units
Department B:		
Transferred out		
Ending inventory	_____	_____
Equivalent production	_____	_____

2. Using the form provided below, compute equivalent production figures for each department, using the fifo method.

	Materials Units	Conversion Units
Department A:		
Transferred out		
Less beginning inventory (all units)	_____	_____
Started and finished this period		
Add beginning inventory (work this period)		
Add ending inventory (work this period)	_____	_____
Equivalent production	_____	_____

	Units from Preceding Dept.	Conversion Units
Department B:		
Transferred out		
Less beginning inventory (all units)	_____	_____
Started and finished this period		
Add beginning inventory (work this period)		
Add ending inventory (work this period)	_____	_____
Equivalent production	_____	_____

PART 4

C. Maldonado, Production Manager of Montgomery Company, requested the ending work in process inventory figured on (1) the average cost basis and (2) the first-in, first-out basis. The data are:

Units in beginning inventory, 10,000; 75% materials, 50% labor and overhead.
Cost of beginning inventory: materials, $7,500; labor, $9,125; and overhead, $9,125.
Placed in process, 40,000 units. Cost: materials, $120,000; labor, $80,000; overhead, $80,000.
Units completed and transferred, 35,000.
Units in process at the end, 15,000, 50% materials, 25% labor and overhead.

Instructions: *Using the form provided below, determine the information requested by Maldonado. (Carry unit costs to three decimal places.)*

1. Average costing:

Materials . . . . $

Labor . . . .

Overhead . . . .   _____

Work in process inventory . . . . $_____

Computations

2. Fifo costing:

Materials . . . . $

Labor . . . .

Overhead . . . .   _____

Work in process inventory . . . . $_____

Computations

PART 5

Palm Springs Supply Company manufactures a single product on a continuous plan in three departments. On June 1, the work in process in Department B was:

Cost in preceding department	$30,000
Materials—Department B	–0–
Labor—Department B	$ 2,000
Factory overhead—Department B	$ 1,000
Units in process	5,000

Costs in Department B during June were:

Labor	$25,000
Factory overhead	$12,500

During June, 45,000 units were received from Department A at a unit cost of $5; 40,000 units were completed in Department B, of which 38,000 were transferred to Department C and 2,000 units were on hand in Department B at the end of the month. There were 8,000 units still in process, estimated to be one half complete as to labor and factory overhead. The balance was lost within the department; its cost is to be absorbed by all the finished and unfinished production of the department.

Instructions: *Complete the following cost of production report for Department B, using the average costing method for beginning work in process inventories. (Round all costs to three decimal places.)*

Palm Springs Supply Company
Department B
Cost of Production Report
For the Month of June, 19–

Quantity Schedule

Units in process at beginning . . . .

Units received from preceding department . . . .

Units transferred to next department . . . .

Units completed and on hand . . . .

Units still in process . . . .

Units lost in process . . . .

Cost Charged to the Department	Total Cost	Unit Cost
Cost from preceding department:		
Work in process—beginning inventory	$	$
Transferred in during period	_____	
Total...	$_____	$_____
Adjusted cost from preceding department		$_____
Cost added by department:		
Work in process—beginning inventory:		
Labor	$	
Factory overhead		
Cost added during period:		
Labor	$	$
Factory overhead	_____	_____
Total cost added..	$_____	$_____
Total cost to be accounted for	$_____	$_____

Cost Accounted for as Follows

	Total Cost	Unit Cost
Transferred to next department		$
Work in process—ending inventory:		
Completed and on hand		
Still in process:		
Cost from preceding department		
Labor		
Factory overhead		_____
Total cost accounted for		$_____

Additional Computations:

Equivalent production—labor & overhead:

Units transferred to next department	
Units completed and on hand	
Units in process	_____
	_____

PART 6

Chomyszak Chemical Company operates three producing departments—Mixing, Refining, and Finishing. During May, the Refining Department transferred 40,000 units to the Finishing Department, lost 2,000 units, and had 5,000 units in process at the end of May. There were 10,000 units in process on May 1 in the Refining Department. The remaining units started in the Refining Department during May were received from the Mixing Department. The costs incurred in the Refining Department during May were labor, $50,000, and factory overhead, $40,000. The work in process inventory on May 1 was $10,000. The costs transferred to the Refining Department from the Mixing Department amounted to $120,000. The Refining Department work in process inventory was one half complete on May 1 and three fourths complete on May 31.

Instructions: *Complete the following May cost of production report for the Refining Department, using the first-in, first-out method of accounting for beginning inventories. (Carry unit cost computations to three decimal places.)*

Chomyszak Chemical Company
Refining Department
Cost of Production Report
For the Month of May, 19–

Quantity Schedule

Units in process at beginning ....

Units received from preceding department .... _____   ═══════════════

Units transferred to next department ....

Units still in process ....

Units lost in process .... _____   ═══════════════

Cost Charged to the Department	Total Cost	Unit Cost
Work in process—beginning inventory	$_____	
Cost from preceding department:		
Transferred in during the month	$_____	$_____
Adjusted cost from preceding department		$_____
Cost added by the department:		
Labor...	$	$
Factory overhead	_____	_____
Total cost added	$_____	$_____
Total cost to be accounted for	$_____	$_____

Cost Accounted for as Follows

Transferred to next department

From beginning inventory:

Inventory cost .... $

Labor added ....

Factory overhead added .... $

From current production:

Units started and finished ....   _____ $

Work in process—ending inventory:

Adjusted cost from preceding

department .... $

Labor ....

Factory overhead ....   _____   _____

Total cost accounted for .... $_____

Additional computations:
Equivalent production:

REVIEW SUMMARY

1. *By-products* are one or more products of relatively small total value that are produced simultaneously with a product of greater total value. By-products are classified into two groups according to their marketable condition at the split-off point: (a) those sold in their original form without need of further processing and (b) those that require further processing in order to be salable.

2. *Joint products* are produced simultaneously by a common process or series of processes, with each product posessing more than nominal value. A *joint cost* arises from the common processing or manufacturing of products. It is incurred prior to the point at which separately identifiable products emerge from the same process.

3. The accepted methods for costing by-products are:
   (a) A joint product cost is not allocated to the by-product. Any revenue resulting from sales of the by-product is credited either to income or to cost of the main product.
   (b) Some portion of the joint production cost is allocated to the by-product.
   The specific accounting methods used for (a) above are as follows:
   (1) Revenue from sales of the by-product is listed on the income statement either as other income, additional sales revenue, a deduction from the cost of goods sold of the main product, or a deduction from the total production cost of the main product.
   (2) Revenue from sales of the by-product less its marketing and adminstrative expenses and additional processing costs is shown on the income statement as in (1) above.
   (3) The cost assigned to the by-product is the purchase or replacement cost existing in the market.
   The specific accounting method used for (b) above is the market value (reversal cost) method, which reduces the manufacturing cost of the main product by an estimate of the by-product's market value at the time of recovery. This estimate is determined by subtracting from the ultimate market value of the by-product the total of the by-product's estimated gross profit, its marketing and administrative expenses, and its estimated production costs after split-off.

4. The allocation to joint products of the joint production cost incurred up to the split-off point can be made by one of the following methods:
   (a) The *market* or *sales value method* prorates the joint cost of the items produced on the basis of their respective market values at the split-off point. For products that have no market value at the split-off point, a hypothetical market value must be computed by subtracting the after-split-off processing costs from the ultimate sales value of the product. If it is desired to make every joint product equally profitable, an overall gross profit percentage for all joint products is used to compute the gross profit for each product. The gross profit is then deducted from the ultimate sales value to find the total cost, which in turn is reduced by each product's further processing cost to determine the joint cost allocation to each product.
   (b) The *quantitative unit method* distributes the total joint cost on the basis of some unit of measurement, such as pounds, gallons, or tons.
   (c) The *average unit cost method* apportions total joint production cost to the various products on the basis of an average unit cost obtained by dividing total joint production cost by the total number of units produced.
   (d) The *weighted average method* multiplies finished production by weight factors to apportion the total joint cost to individual units. Weight factors include the size of the unit, difficulty of manufacture, time consumed in making the unit, and amount of materials used.

5. Federal income tax regulations state that the tax payer may use "allocated cost as a basis for pricing inventories, provided such allocation bears a reasonable relation to the respective selling values of the different kinds, sizes, or grades of product."

6. The method chosen to allocate joint product cost determines the degree of profitability of the various individual products. For profit planning, management should consider a product's contribution margin after separate or individual costs are deducted from sales.

PART 1

Instructions: *Place a check mark in the appropriate column to indicate whether each of the following statements is True or False.*

	True	False
1. To be classified as a by-product, a product must have more than nominal value.	____	____
2. The unit cost of a by-product or a joint product is difficult to determine because a true joint cost is indivisible.	____	____
3. A joint product is a product of relatively small total value that is produced simultaneously with a product of greater value.	____	____
4. An acceptable method of accounting for a by-product is to credit any revenue resulting from its sale to the cost of the main product.	____	____
5. The replacement cost method of accounting for by-products is especially popular with firms that use the by-product within their own plant.	____	____
6. In the market value method of accounting for by-products, the manufacturing cost of the main product is reduced by an estimate of the by-product's market value at the point of recovery.	____	____
7. If joint products have no market value at the split-off point, the market value method of prorating joint costs cannot be used.	____	____
8. An overall gross profit percentage for all joint products may be used for purposes of making each joint product equally profitable.	____	____
9. The quantitative unit method distributes the total cost on the basis of some unit of measurement such as pounds or gallons.	____	____
10. The weighted average method apportions total joint production cost to the various products on the basis of a predetermined standard or index of production.	____	____
11. An average unit cost may be obtained by dividing total joint production cost by the hypothetical market value.	____	____
12. Variables such as unit size, time needed to manufacture, and amount of materials consumed may be used as weight factors in allocating joint costs.	____	____
13. Federal income tax regulations imply that the market value method is the preferred method for allocating by-product and joint product costs.	____	____
14. Tax laws have solved the problem of costing joint products and by-products for the accountant and the manufacturer.	____	____
15. The cost incurred up to the split-off point should be the key figure used by management in determining whether a particular joint product should continue to be marketed.	____	____

PART 2

Instructions: *In the blank space at the left of each of the following items, place the letter from the right-hand column that identifies the term that best matches the statement in the column on the left. No letter should be used more than once.*

_____ 1. The cost that arises from the common processing or manufacturing of products produced from the same process.

_____ 2. Produced simultaneously by a common process, with each product posessing more than nominal value.

_____ 3. Products of relatively small total value that are produced simultaneously with a product of greater total value.

_____ 4. Using this method, sales of the by-product are listed on the income statement as other income, additional sales revenue, a deduction from the cost of goods sold of the main product, or a deduction from the total manufacturing cost of the main product.

_____ 5. Remelted scrap steel would be credited to the cost of finished steel at the market cost of equivalent grades purchased if this method of accounting for by-products were used.

_____ 6. This method of costing by-products is commonly known as the market value method.

_____ 7. Using this method, the allocation of joint production cost is based on the relative sales values of the individual products.

_____ 8. To determine this, the after-split-off processing costs are deducted from the ultimate market value.

_____ 9. This method of joint product costing attempts to distribute the total joint cost on the basis of some unit of measurement such as pounds, gallons, or tons.

_____ 10. Under this method, the total joint production cost is apportioned to the various products on the basis of a predetermined standard or index of production.

_____ 11. This is irrelevant to a decision as to whether to sell a product at the split-off point or process it further.

_____ 12. Under this method, finished production of every kind is multiplied by certain factors to apportion the total joint cost to individual units.

_____ 13. It argues for the recording of by-product inventory in the period of production at an amount approximating its cost to produce, provided there is a market for the by-product.

_____ 14. A digest of legal viewpoints on such matters as acceptable methods of joint cost allocation is given in these.

_____ 15. Under this method, revenue from the sale of the by-product, less the costs of placing the by-product on the market and less any additional processing costs of the by-product, is shown on the income statement.

a. quantitative unit method
b. reversal cost method
c. joint production cost
d. by-products
e. weighted average method
f. joint products
g. asset recognition concept
h. replacement cost method
i. hypothetical market value
j. average unit cost method
k. joint cost
l. market value method
m. Federal Income Tax Regulations
n. recognition of gross revenue method
o. recognition of net revenue method

PART 3

Instructions: *In the blank space at the left of each of the following items, place the letter of the choice that most correctly completes each item.*

_____ 1. Joint product costs generally are allocated using:
  a. relative sales values at split-off
  b. additional costs after split-off
  c. relative profitability
  d. direct labor hours
  e. contribution margin

_____ 2. Costing difficulty because of indivisibility is encountered in dealing with:

	By-Products	Joint Products
a.	yes	yes
b.	yes	no
c.	no	yes
d.	no	no	(AICPA adapted)

_____ 3. One of the accepted methods of accounting for a by-product is to recognize the cost of the by-product as it is produced. Under this method, inventory costs for the by-product would be based on:
  a. an allocation of some portion of joint costs but not any subsequent processing costs
  b. neither an allocation of some portion of joint costs nor any subsequent processing costs
  c. subsequent processing costs less an allocation of some portion of joint costs
  d. an allocation of some portion of joint costs plus any subsequent processing costs
  e. none of the above
  (AICPA adapted)

_____ 4. The components of production allocable as joint costs when a single manufacturing process produces several salable products are:
  a. materials, labor, and factory overhead
  b. materials and labor only
  c. labor and factory overhead only
  d. factory overhead and materials only
  e. factory overhead and commercial expenses
  (AICPA adapted)

_____ 5. If two or more products share a common process before they are separated, the joint costs should be allocated in a manner that:
  a. assigns a proportionate amount of the total cost to each product by means of a quantitative basis
  b. maximizes total earnings
  c. minimizes variations in a unit of production cost
  d. does not introduce an element of estimation into the process of accumulating costs for each product
  e. none of the above
  (AICPA adapted)

_____ 6. Which of the following is not an accepted method by which to allocate joint cost?
  a. market value
  b. weighted average method
  c. relative weight, volume, or linear measure
  d. average unit cost
  e. none of the above
  (AICPA adapted)

_____ 7. Tobin Company manufactures Products C and R from a joint process. The total cost is $60,000. The market value is $75,000 for 8,000 units of Product C and $50,000 for 2,000 units of Product R. Assuming that the total joint cost is allocated using the market value method, what was the joint cost allocated to Product C?
  a. $48,000
  b. $12,000
  c. $24,000
  d. $36,000
  e. none of the above
  (AICPA adapted)

_____ 8. Sullivan Company manufactures two products, Erin and Braugh. Initially, they are processed from the same raw material and then, after split-off, they are further processed separately. Additional information is as follows:

	Erin	Braugh	Total
Final sales price	$9,000	$6,000	$15,000
Joint costs prior to split-off point	?	?	6,600
Costs after split-off point	3,000	3,000	6,000

Using the market value method, the assigned joint costs of Erin and Braugh, respectively, are:
  a. $3,300 and $3,300
  b. $3,960 and $2,640
  c. $4,400 and $2,400
  d. $4,560 and $2,040
  e. none of the above
  (AICPA adapted)

_____ **9.** Missouri Corporation manufactures liquid chemicals A and B from a joint process. Joint cost is allocated on the basis of the market value at the split-off point. It costs $4,560 to process 500 gallons of A and 1,000 gallons of B to the split-off point. The market value at split-off is $10 per gallon for A and $14 for B. Product B requires an additional process beyond split-off at a cost of $2 per gallon if it is to be sold at the most profitable price. The resulting cost to produce 1,000 gallons of B is:

    a. $3,360   **d.** $2,000

    b. $4,560   **e.** none of the above

    c. $5,360   (AICPA adapted)

_____ **10.** Mill Company operates in three different industries, each of which is appropriately regarded as a reportable segment. Segment No. 1 contributed 40% of Mill Company's total sales. Sales for Segment No. 1 were $900,000 and traceable cost was $400,000. Total common cost for Mill was $600,000. Mill allocates common cost based on the ratio of a segment's sales to total sales, an appropriate method of allocation. What should be the operating profit presented for Segment No. 1 for 19A?

    a. $140,000   **d.** $540,000

    b. $260,000   **e.** none of the above

    c. $500,000   (AICPA adapted)

PART 4

The following data relate to the sale of a main product and by-product by the Franco Company for September:

Main product:

Sales (10,000 units @ $1.50)	$15,000
Beginning inventory (5,000 units @ $.75)	3,750
Total production cost (9,000 units @ $.75)	6,750
Marketing and administrative expense	3,000

By-product:

Revenue from sale of product	$ 750

Instructions: *Prepare answers to the following:*

1. If by-product revenue is treated as other income, determine (a) the gross profit and (b) the income before income tax.

2. If by-product revenue is treated as additional sales revenue, determine (a) the gross profit and (b) the income before income tax.

3. If by-product revenue is treated as a deduction from the cost of goods sold, determine (a) the gross profit and (b) the income before income tax.

4. If by-product revenue is deducted from production cost, determine (a) the new average unit cost for the main product (round to three decimal places) and (b) the dollar amount of the ending inventory.

PART 5

Labreque Laminators Inc. manufactures one main product and two by-products. Data for July are:

	Main Product	By-Product Lam	By-Product Nate
Sales	$80,000	$12,000	$6,000
Manufacturing cost before separation	40,000	–	–
Manufacturing cost after separation	15,000	5,000	2,500
Marketing and administrative expense	8,000	2,000	750

Instructions: *Complete the income statement below. Assume no beginning or ending inventories and use the market value method for the by-products, allowing a 25% operating profit for Lam and a 20% operating profit for Nate.*

Labreque Laminators Inc.
Income Statement
For the Month of July, 19—

	Main Product	By-Product Lam	By-Product Nate	Total
Sales	$	$	$	$
Cost of goods sold:				
Manufacturing cost before separation:				
Costs assigned:				
Operating profit		$	$	
Marketing and administrative expense				
Manufacturing cost after separation				
Total		$	$	
Cost before separation	$	$	$	$
Manufacturing cost after separation				
Cost of goods sold	$	$	$	$
Gross profit	$	$	$	$
Marketing and adminstrative expense				
Operating profit	$	$	$	$

PART 6

Grimm Chemicals Inc. manufactures three chemicals that are processed through a joint refining process—Inkin, Blinkin, and Nodd. Five gallons of input result in 1 unit of Inkin, 3 units of Blinkin, and 5 units of Nodd. The total joint processing cost is $60.75 for 5 gallons of input. Outputs are complete at the end of the joint refining process. During January, 10,000 gallons were inputted to the process. There were no beginning inventories. Sales of the outputs were:

	Units Sold	Sales
Inkin	1,500	$ 15,000
Blinkin	5,000	60,000
Nodd	8,000	56,000
Total		$131,000

Instructions: *On the form provided below, prepare the allocation of joint cost to Inkin, Blinkin, and Nodd, using the market or sales value method. (Carry the joint cost allocation percentage to two decimal places.)*

Grimm Chemicals Inc.
Allocation of Joint Cost
For January, 19—

Chemical	Units Produced (1)	Units Sold	Units in Ending Inventory	Unit Sales Price (2)	Market Value of Production	Joint Cost Allocated (3)	Cost of Sales (4)	Ending Inventory
Inkin				$	$	$	$	$
Blinkin ...								
Nodd								
					$	$	$	$

Computations:
(1)

(2)

(3)

(4)

PART 7

Celestial Products Inc. produces Darth and Vader from its centrifuge. For each gallon of Spock placed in process, three fourths of a gallon of Darth and one fourth of a gallon of Vader are produced. Darth is sold at $10 per gallon, while Vader is sold at $15 per gallon. During April, the total cost of the centrifuge operation was $1,012,500, and 300,000 gallons of Spock were processed. There were no inventories at either the beginning or end of April. No other processing was required for Darth or Vader.

Instructions:

1. Complete the schedule below, showing the unit cost of sales and the unit gross profit for Darth and Vader, using the quantitative unit method. (Round to the nearest tenth of a percent or tenth of a cent.)

Celestial Products Inc.
Quantitative Unit Method
For April, 19—

	Units Produced and Sold	Joint Cost Allocated*	Unit Market Value	Unit Cost of Sales	Unit Gross Profit
Darth		$	$	$	$
Vader					

Computations:
  *

2. Complete the schedule below, showing the unit cost and the unit gross profit for Darth and Vader, using the relative sales value method.

Celestial Products Inc.
Relative Sales Value Method
For April, 19—

	Units Produced and Sold	Unit Market Value	Total Market Value	Joint Cost Allocation	Unit Cost of Sales	Unit Gross Profit
Darth		$	$	$	$	$
Vader						
			$	$		

Computations:

REVIEW SUMMARY

1. The purchase of all materials is usually made by the purchasing department, although in small companies department heads sometimes have this authority. The purchasing department receives purchase requisitions; keeps informed as to sources of supply, prices, and shipping shedules; prepares and places purchase orders; and arranges for reports between Purchasing, Receiving, and Accounting. Supplies, services, and repairs should be purchased in a similar manner.

2. The *purchase requisition* informs the purchasing agent concerning the quantity and type of materials needed. The *purchase order* is a written authorization to a vendor to supply specified quantities of described goods at agreed terms and at a designated time and place. Paperwork savings are enhanced by the use of *Electronic Data Interchange* (EDI), which is the exchange of documents and transactions by a computer in one company with the computer of another company. Modern inventory management, especially in a JIT environment, emphasizes reducing the number of vendors, improving the quality of procurements, and developing long-term vendor relationships rather than seeking short-run price breaks. The *receiving report* certifies quantities received and may report results of inspection and testing for quality.

3. If the vendor's invoice is correct, the invoice clerk approves it, attaches it to the purchase order and the receiving report, and sends these papers to another clerk for the preparation of the voucher. The voucher data are entered in the purchases journal, the subsidiary records, and then the cash payments journal. The treasurer mails a check with the original voucher to the vendor, files a voucher copy, and returns one voucher to the accounting department.

4. Upon receipt of the invoice in an electronic data processing system, the data are directly input from the invoice to the computer and are edited, audited, and merged with the purchase order and receiving order data that are stored in the computer data bank. When in agreement, the cost data are entered into the accounts payable computer file with a date for later payment. It is equally important to post the invoice data in quantities and dollar values to the materials inventory file in the EDP system.

5. Materials are commonly carried at the invoice price paid the vendor, through all acquisition costs and price adjustments affect the materials cost. Acquisition costs are generally charged to factory overhead when it is not practical to follow a more accurate costing procedure. If it is decided that the materials cost should include incoming freight charges and other acquisition costs, an applied rate may be added to each invoice instead of charging these costs directly to factory overhead.

6. The storekeeper is responsible for safeguarding the materials by placing them in bins or other storage areas and by seeing that they are taken from the storeroom only when properly requisitioned. The *materials requisition* is the authorization for the storeroom to issue materials to departments. Preparation of the materials requisition results in entries to the Issued section of the materials ledger cards and in postings to the job order cost sheets, production reports, or the various expense analysis sheets for individual departments. The *materials ledger cards* record the receipt and the issuance of each class of materials and provide a perpetual inventory record. The *materials requisition journal*, a form of materials summary, greatly facilitates the posting of materials withdrawals to the proper ledger control accounts. The *bill of materials*, a kind of master requisition, is a printed form that lists all the materials and parts necessary for a typical job or production run. *Materials Requirements Planning (MRP)* is a computer simulation module that enters the items to be produced and their due dates, accesses the bill of materials, materials delivery lead times, and on-hand and on-order inventory balances; determines the component part requirements; and projects the time-phased production demands on various work centers.

7. Even with a perpetual inventory system, periodic physical counts are necessary to discover and eliminate discrepancies between the actual count and the balances on materials ledger cards. When the inventory count differs from the balance on the materials ledger card, the ledger card is adjusted to conform to the actual count.

8. The *fifo method* of costing issued materials assumes that materials are issued from the oldest supply in stock and that the cost of those units when placed in stock is the cost of those same units when issued. The *average costing method* assumes that each batch of materials taken from the storeroom is composed of uniform quantities from each shipment in stock at the date of issue. Some companies establish a month-end average cost for each type of material on hand and use this cost for all issues during the following month. The *lifo method* of costing materials is based on the premise that units issued should carry the cost of the most recent purchase, because it is most significant in matching cost with revenue for income determination. Under the *dollar-value lifo method*, similar inventory items are grouped into a pool and layers are determined, based on the pool's total dollar changes. The *market price at date of issue method* substitutes replace-

ment cost for incurred cost and has the advantage of charging materials into production at current prices. The *standard cost method* charges issued materials at a predetermined or estimated price reflecting a normal or expected future price.

9. The AICPA position in regard to inventory valuation is as follows:
   a. In principle, inventories are to be valued at cost.
   b. Where cost cannot be recovered upon sale in the ordinary course of business, a lower figure should be used.
   c. This lower figure is normally market replacement cost, except that the amount should not exceed the expected sales price less a deduction for costs yet to be incurred in making the sale. On the other hand, this lower market figure should not be less than the amount to be realized in the sale of the goods, reduced by a normal profit margin.

   The application of the lower of cost or market price to individual inventory items results in the lowest inventory value. However, application to inventory groups or to the inventory as a whole usually provides a sufficiently conservative valuation with less effort. Instead of adjusting materials ledger cards for departures from cost, companies create an inventory valuation account. Use of the valuation retains the cost of the inventory and at the same time reduces the materials inventory for statement purposes to the desired cost or market valuation, whichever is lower, without disturbing the materials ledger cards.

10. The amount realized from the sale of scrap and waste may be shown on the income statement under Other Income or it may be credited to Factory Overhead Control, thus reducing factory overhead expense and cost of goods manufactured. If spoilage is normal and happens at any time and at any stage of the productive process, its cost should be treated as factory overhead, included in the predetermined factory overhead rate, and prorated over all production of a period. If normal spoilage is caused by exacting specifications, difficult processing, and so on, it should be charged to that specific job or order. Abnormal spoilage should always be charged to factory overhead. If defective work is experienced in regular manufacturing, the additional cost to correct defective units should be included in predetermined factory overhead, based on previous experience. Defective work resulting from special orders may be charged directly to the specific job.

PART 1

Instructions: *Place a check mark in the appropriate column to indicate whether each of the following statements is True or False.*

	True	False
1. With EDI, transactions are machine readable and computers can transfer data between companies without extensive paperwork.	___	___
2. The purchase order contains all necessary information regarding price, discount agreement, and delivery information.	___	___
3. The receiving report is usually signed by the purchasing agent, and the original and an acknowledgement copy are sent to the vendor.	___	___
4. One copy of the receiving report is sent to the accounting department, where it is matched with the purchase order and the vendor's invoice and then paid.	___	___
5. Materials acquisition costs are generally charged to factory overhead when it is not practical to follow a more accurate costing procedure.	___	___
6. In a just-in-time inventory environment, the emphasis is on increasing the number of vendors and suppliers.	___	___
7. Bin cards are not an integral part of the accounting records because they do not include unit prices.	___	___
8. In an EDP system, the computer program would produce a materials summary similar to the materials requisitioned journal.	___	___
9. An advantage of lifo costing is that inflationary prices of recent purchases are charged to operations.	___	___
10. An advantage of using standard costs for materials costing is that it eliminates the erratic costing inherent in actual cost methods.	___	___
11. The application of the lower of cost or market rule to the inventory on an item-by-item basis results in the lowest inventory value.	___	___
12. If a perpetual inventory system is used, periodic physical counts are unnecessary.	___	___
13. To reduce accounting for scrap to a minimum, often no entry is made until the scrap is actually sold.	___	___
14. Normal spoilage should always be charged to factory overhead.	___	___
15. If defective work is experienced in regular manufacturing operations, the additional cost to correct defective units should be considered in determining the factory overhead rate.	___	___

PART 2

Instructions: *In the blank space at the left of each of the following items, place the letter from the right-hand column that identifies the term that best matches the statement in the column on the left. No letter should be used more than once.*

_____ 1. Provides the master plan from which details concerning materials requirements are eventually developed.

_____ 2. The exchange of documents and transactions by a computer in one company with the computer of another company.

_____ 3. Authorizes appropriate quantities to be delivered at specified dates.

_____ 4. Certifies quantities received and may report results of inspection and testing for quality.

_____ 5. Notifies the storeroom or warehouse to deliver specified types and quantities of materials to a given department.

_____ 6. Records the receipt and the issuance of each class of materials and provides a perpetual inventory record.

_____ 7. Materials purchased for stock would be debited to this general ledger control account.

_____ 8. Materials purchased for a particular job or department would be debited to this general ledger control account.

_____ 9. The purchase of factory services or repairs would be debited to this general ledger control account.

_____ 10. Any balance in Freight In at the end of a period is usually closed to this account.

_____ 11. Requires a fundamental philosophical change resulting in developing long-term vendor relationships rather than seeking short-term price breaks.

_____ 12. Used to facilitate the posting of the materials withdrawals to the proper ledger control accounts.

_____ 13. A printed or duplicated form that lists all the materials and parts necessary for a particular job or production run.

_____ 14. An inventory costing method in which similar inventory items are grouped into a pool and layers are determined, based upon the pool's total dollar changes.

_____ 15. A materials costing method that charges issued materials at a predetermined price reflecting an expected future price.

_____ 16. An inventory valuation principle that is generally justified on the grounds of conservatism.

_____ 17. The estimated selling price in the ordinary course of business, less reasonably predictable costs of completion and disposal.

_____ 18. Imperfections that arise in the manufacturing process due to faults in materials, labor, or machines.

_____ 19. If this is caused by exacting specifications, difficult processing, or other unexpected factors, its cost should be charged to the specific order.

_____ 20. Inform the purchasing agent about the quantity and type of materials needed.

a. purchase order
b. Work in Process
c. lower of cost or market
d. normal spoilage
e. materials requisitioned journal
f. just-in-time (JIT) inventory system
g. materials ledger card
h. dollar-value lifo
i. Factory Overhead
j. receiving report
k. Electronic Data Interchange (EDI)
l. net realizable value
m. purchase requisition
n. standard cost
o. production budget
p. bill of materials
q. Cost of Goods Sold
r. defective work
s. Materials
t. materials requisition

PART 3

Instructions: *In the blank space at the left of each of the following items, place the letter of the choice that most correctly completes each item.*

_____ 1. A company offers terms of 2/10, n/60. The true interest cost for these terms, assuming a 360-day year, is:
   a. 2%   **b.** 12%   **c.** 14.4%   **d.** 28.8%   **e.** none of the above

_____ 2. The AICPA limits the highest value for "market" to be used in inventory valuation to:
   a. selling price
   b. replacement cost
   c. selling price less expenses to sell and less an allowance for normal profit
   d. selling price less expenses to complete and sell
   e. none of the above

_____ 3. When normal spoilage occurs as a result of exacting specifications or difficult processing, any loss is charged to:
   a. extraordinary losses
   b. the specific job in which the spoilage occured
   c. administrative expenses
   d. factory overhead control
   e. none of the above

_____ 4. The inventory method that assumes that the cost of the latest purchased merchandise or materials is assignable to inventory is:
   a. average costing
   b. lifo costing
   c. next in, first-out costing
   d. fifo costing
   e. none of the above

_____ 5. An auditor tests the quality of materials charged to work in process by tracing these quantities to:
   a. cost ledgers
   b. perpetual inventory records
   c. receiving reports
   d. materials requisitions
   e. none of the above

_____ 6. When evaluating materials inventory at cost or market, whichever is lower, the term "market" means:
   a. net realizable value
   b. net realizable value less a normal profit margin
   c. replacement cost
   d. discounted present value
   e. none of the above

(AICPA adapted)

_____ 7. If inventory levels are stable or increasing, an argument that is not in favor of the lifo method as compared to fifo is:
   a. income tax tends to be reduced in periods of rising prices
   b. cost of goods sold tends to be stated at approximately current cost in the income statement
   c. cost assignments typically parallel the physical flow of goods
   d. income tends to be smoothed as prices change over a period of time
   e. none of the above

_____ 8. An item of inventory purchased this period for $15 has been written down to its current replacement cost of $10. It sells for $30, with a disposal cost of $3 and a normal profit of $12. Which of the following statements is not true?
   a. The cost of goods sold of the following year will be understated.
   b. The current year's income is understated.
   c. The ending inventory of the current year is understated.
   d. Income of the following year will be understated.
   e. None of the above

_____ 9. Which statement is not valid as it applies to inventory costing methods?
   a. If inventory quantities are to be maintained, part of the earnings must be invested (plowed back) in inventories when fifo is used during a period of rising prices.
   b. Lifo tends to smooth out the income pattern, since it matches the current cost of goods sold with current revenue, and inventories remain at constant quantities.
   c. When a firm using the lifo method fails to maintain its usual inventory position (reduces stock on hand below customary levels), there may be a matching of old costs with current revenue.
   d. Unlike lifo, the use of fifo permits some control by management over the amount of income for a period through controlled purchases.
   e. None of the above

(AICPA adapted)

_____ **10.** A company's balance sheet inventory cost using fifo was lower than using lifo. Assuming no beginning inventory, the direction of movement of the cost of purchases during the period was:

a. up   **c.** steady

b. down   **d.** undeterminable

PART 4

Yogi Manufacturing Inc. makes the following purchases and issues of a new material during July:

July 2 Received 200 lbs. @ $4.50; total cost, $900.
      8 Received 60 lbs. @ $5; total cost, $300.
   18 Issued 100 lbs.
   24 Received 240 lbs. @ $6; total cost, $1,400.
   31 Issued 200 lbs.

Instructions: *Using a perpetual inventory system and materials ledger cards provided below and on the following page, state the cost of materials consumed and the cost assigned to the inventory at the end of July. (Round unit costs to three decimal places.)*

1. First-in, first-out costing

Date	Received			Issued			Balance		
	Quantity	Unit Cost	Amount	Quantity	Unit Cost	Amount	Quantity	Unit Cost	Amount

Cost of materials consumed .... $_____

Cost assigned to inventory .... $_____

2. Last-in, first-out costing

Date	Received			Issued			Balance		
	Quantity	Unit Cost	Amount	Quantity	Unit Cost	Amount	Quantity	Unit Cost	Amount

Cost of materials consumed .... $_____

Cost assigned to inventory .... $_____

3. Average costing

Date	Received			Issued			Balance		
	Quantity	Unit Cost	Amount	Quantity	Unit Cost	Amount	Quantity	Unit Cost	Amount

Cost of materials consumed . . . . $_____

Cost assigned to inventory . . . . $_____

PART 5

Assume that a certain commodity sells for $10, the marketing expense is $2.50, and the normal profit is $1.50.

Instructions:

1. Determine the inventory value for each of the independent cases in the schedule appearing below, using the AICPA lower of cost or market rule.

Case	Cost	Replacement Cost	Floor	Ceiling	Market	Lower of Cost or Market
A	$4.00	$5.00	$	$	$	$
B	7.00	6.50				
C	6.50	5.50				
D	5.00	5.50				
E	6.50	8.25				
F	7.25	7.50				

2. Assume in Case B above that 1,000 units were in work in process inventory. Prepare the journal entry to record the decline of inventory to market.

Account	Subsidiary Record	Debit	Credit

PART 6

Lorrie Company produced 1,000 units in a recent production run and discovered that 50 units were defective and required reworking as follows:

Rework costs per unit:
Materials	$ 5
Labor	10
Factory overhead...............................	10
Total	$25

Normal production costs per unit:
Materials	$10
Labor	25
Factory overhead...............................	25
Total	$60

Instructions:

1. Using the journal form provided below, prepare the journal entries to record the rework costs and to transfer the job costs to finished goods, assuming that rework costs are to be charged to all production.

Account	Subsidiary Record	Debit	Credit

2. Using the journal form provided below, prepare the same journal entries as in (1), assuming that rework costs are to be charged to the specific job.

Account	Subsidiary Record	Debit	Credit

REVIEW SUMMARY

1. To plan manufacturing requirements, every stock item must be analyzed periodically to forecast demand, determine acquisition lead time, plan usage during lead time, establish quantity on hand, place units on order, and determine reserve or safety stock requirements. *Lead time* is the time between the order and the delivery of an item. *Safety stock* is the desired inventory cushion or supply, expressed as days, weeks, or months.

2. The *economic order quantity* (EOQ) is the amount of inventory to be ordered at one time for purposes of minimizing annual inventory cost. The quantity to order at a given time must be determined by balancing two factors: (a) the cost of possessing (carrying) materials and (b) the cost of acquiring (ordering) materials. Costs of carrying inventory include interest expense, property tax and insurance, handling and storage, and deterioration and obsolescence of the items. Costs of not carrying enough inventory include extra purchasing, handling, and transportation costs; higher prices due to small order quantities; frequent stockouts resulting in disruption of production schedules; inflation-oriented increases in prices when inventory purchases are deferred; and lost sales and loss of customer goodwill.

3. The formula for the economic order quantity in units is:

$$\sqrt{\frac{2 \times \text{Annual required units} \times \text{Cost per order}}{\text{Cost per unit of material} \times \text{Carrying cost percentage}}}$$

The formula for the economic order quantity in dollars is:

$$\sqrt{\frac{2 \times \text{Annual required units} \times \text{Cost per unit} \times \text{Cost per order}}{\text{Carrying cost percentage}}}$$

The EOQ formula is equally appropriate in computing the optimum size of a production run in units:

$$\sqrt{\frac{2 \times \text{Annual required units} \times \text{Setup cost per run}}{\text{Variable manufacturing cost} \times \text{Carrying cost percentage}}}$$

4. The question of when to order is controlled by the time needed for delivery, the rate of inventory usage, and the safety stock. A safety stock is often the least costly device for protecting against a *stockout*. The optimum safety stock is that quantity that results in minimal total annual cost of stockouts and safety stock carrying cost. The annual cost of stockouts depends upon the probability of their occurrence and the actual cost of each stockout. The *order point* is reached when inventory on hand and quantities due in are equal to the lead time usage quantity plus the safety stock quantity (I + QD = LTQ + SSQ). Two statistical techniques used for safety stock calculations are (1) variability in demand, and (2) deviations from forecast demand.

5. The following forecasting techniques are used to predict the materials needed for a future period. *Factor listing* involves enumerating the favorable and unfavorable conditions likely to influence sales and relies upon the forecaster's judgment to evaluate the degree of the influence factor. *Barometric methods* result in systematized factor listing. *Statistical methods* describe historical patterns in time series and are used for the purpose of revealing patterns that have occurred in the past and projecting them into the future. *Regression analysis* usually employs the least squares method to determine economic relationships between a dependent variable and one or more independent variables, such as sales territory or family incomes. *Forecasting surveys* are made in order to determine consumer buying intentions, opinions, or feelings about the business outlook, and capital investment plans.

6. Purchasing and production managers are primarily interested in unit control of inventory. Financial managers are concerned that dollars invested in inventory are utilized effectively as measured by an adequate return on capital employed. Materials control is commonly centralized in one department called the materials management or materials control department.

7. A materials control method that examines periodically the status of quantities on hand of each class of items is the *order cycling* or *cycle review method*. Under the *min-max method*, a maximum quantity for each item is established and a minimum level provides the margin of safety nec-

essary to prevent stockouts during a reorder cycle. The *two-bin* system separates each stock item into two bins: the first bin contains enough stock to satisfy usage that occurs between receipt of an order and the placing of the next order; the second bin contains the normal amount used from order date to delivery date plus safety stock. Under the *order point system*, when the quantity on hand drops to the established order point, the materials cards are automatically machine-sorted and are routed to order clerks who activate orders for the quantity specified. A *just-in-time inventory system* (JIT) requires coordination with suppliers so that materials arrive immediately prior to their use.

8. The *ABC plan*, also known as *control by importance and exception (CIE)*, is an analytical approach based on statistical averages. "A", or high-value items, are under the tightest control, whereas "C" items would be under simple physical controls such as the two-bin system.

PART 1

Instructions: *Place a check mark in the appropriate column to indicate whether each of the following statements is True or False.*

	True	False
1. The cost of carrying inventory and the cost of inadequate carrying are two conflicting kinds of costs .	___	___
2. Costs of carrying inadequate inventory include frequent stockouts, additional clerical costs, and higher prices due to small order quantities.	___	___
3. Of all the methods used to calculate safety stock, the traditional rules of thumb, such as a two-week supply, furnish management with the soundest basis for determining the level of safety stock.	___	___
4. In determining the economic order quantity, only the variable costs of procuring an order should be included.	___	___
5. It is not unusual for order costs to amount to $20 or more per order and for carrying costs to amount to as much as 35% of the average inventory investment.	___	___
6. The ideal order size is the point where the total cost curve is at its lowest.	___	___
7. The ideal order size is the point where the annual carrying charges exceed the ordering charges.	___	___
8. If lead time or usage is more than expected during an order period, the new materials will arrive before the existing stock is consumed, thus adding to the cost of carrying inventory.	___	___
9. The optimum safety stock is that quantity that results in maximum total annual cost of stockouts and safety stock carrying cost.	___	___
10. The order point is reached when inventory on hand and quantities due in are equal to the lead time usage quantity plus the safety stock quantity.	___	___
11. It is usually possible to forecast exactly the materials needed for a future period, but it is difficult to estimate the time required to receive the materials.	___	___
12. Examples of independent variables as used in regression analysis include sales territories and family incomes.	___	___
13. JIT focuses on individual materials or operations rather than emphasizing minimum inventory levels and integrated manufacturing processes.	___	___
14. For JIT to operate properly, machine setup time must be kept short and production flows through the various work station must be uniform.	___	___
15. Under the ABC plan of materials control, items are classified and ranked in descending order on the basis of the annual dollar value of each item.	___	___

PART 2

Instructions: *In the blank space at the left of each of the following items, place the letter from the right-hand column that identifies the term that best matches the statement in the column on the left. No letter should be used more than once.*

_____ 1. The time between the order and the delivery of materials.

_____ 2. Represents the amount of inventory to be ordered at one time for purposes of minimizing annual inventory cost.

_____ 3. Only this type of cost of procuring an order should be included in the determination of order quantities.

_____ 4. A statistical technique in which the safety stock calculation is based on the variability in forecasting errors.

_____ 5. Result in disruption of production schedules, overtime, and extra setup time.

_____ 6. Expressed as a percentage of the average inventory investment.

_____ 7. Expressed as a dollar amount per occurrence.

_____ 8. $\sqrt{\dfrac{2 \times RU \times CO}{CU \times CC}}$

_____ 9. $\sqrt{\dfrac{2 \times RU \times CU \times CO}{CC}}$

_____ 10. Result in a lower cost per unit and may alter the economic order quantity.

_____ 11. Another term for inventory cushion.

_____ 12. Determined by multiplying the probability of a stockout at a specific level of safety stock by the number of annual orders.

_____ 13. Based on usage during the time necessary to requisition, order, and receive materials, plus an allowance for protection against stockout.

_____ 14. Involves enumerating the favorable and unfavorable conditions likely to influence sales.

_____ 15. $\sqrt{\dfrac{P}{P - D}}$

_____ 16. A computer simulation module that offers a modern method of dealing with each product's bill of materials, inventory status, and manufacturing process.

_____ 17. $\dfrac{\text{Process Time}}{\text{Process Time} + \text{Wait Time} + \text{Move Time} + \text{Inspection Time}}$

_____ 18. Made in order to determine consumer buying intentions, feelings about the business outlook, and capital investment plans.

_____ 19. Concentrates on important stock items and is also known as "control by importance and exception."

_____ 20. Method of materials control based on the premise that the quantities of most stock items are subject to definable limits.

a. stockouts
b. expected annual stockouts
c. forecasting surveys
d. inventory carrying cost
e. Materials Requirement Planning (MRP)
f. EOQ formula in dollars
g. factor listing
h. deviation from forecast demand
i. order points
j. EOQ formula in units
k. economic order quantity
l. min-max method
m. quantity price discounts
n. ABC plan
o. ordering cost
p. EOQ production run correction factor
q. lead time
r. manufacturing cycle efficiency formula
s. safety stock
t. variable cost

PART 3

Instructions: *In the blank space at the left of each of the following items, place the letter of the choice that most correctly completes each item.*

_____ 1. The Joshua Company requires 40,000 units of Product Q for the year. It costs $60 to place an order and $10 annually to carry a unit in inventory. The economic order quantity in units is:

    a. 400   **b.** 490   **c.** 600   **d.** 693   **e.** none of the above   (AICPA adapted)

_____ 2. Fun Inc. manufactures dolls. The cost of carrying one doll in inventory for one year is $.60. Fun manufactures 6,000 dolls evenly throughout the year. Using the EOQ approach, the optimal production run would be 200 when the setup cost is:

    a. $2.00   **b.** $3.00   **c.** $3.50   **d.** $4.00   **e.** none of the above   (AICPA adapted)

_____ 3. The following information is available for Hornsby Company's Material Y:

Annual usage in units	10,000
Working days per year	250
Normal lead time in working days	30
Maximum lead time in working days	90

Assuming that the units of Material Y will be required evenly throughout the year, the order point would be:

    a. 600   **b.** 1,800   **c.** 1,200   **d.** 2,400   **e.** none of the above   (AICPA adapted)

_____ 4. A relevant factor in determining economic order quantity is:

    a. physical plant insurance costs   **d.** physical plant depreciation charges
    b. warehouse supervisory salaries   **e.** none of the above
    c. variable costs of processing a purchase order

    (AICPA adapted)

_____ 5. A company buys a certain part for its manufacturing process. To determine the optimum size of a normal purchase order, the formula for the economic order quantity is used. In addition to the annual demand, other information necessary to complete the formula is:

    a. cost of placing an order and annual cost of carrying a unit in stock.
    b. cost of the part and annual cost of carrying a unit in stock
    c. cost of placing an order
    d. cost of the part
    e. none of the above

_____ 6. If Wonder Company orders raw materials in quantities larger than the optimum quantity obtained using the basic EOQ model in order to obtain a quantity discount, the company will experience:

    a. ordering costs higher than if the optimum quantity were ordered
    b. ordering costs the same as if the optimum quantity were ordered
    c. carrying costs higher than ordering costs
    d. ordering costs higher than carrying costs
    e. none of the above

    (ICMA adapted)

_____ 7. The level of safety stock is affected by:

    a. the amount of idle cash that management believes it has to invest in safety stock
    b. the speed with which the inventory will turn over
    c. the level of uncertainty that management is willing to accept with respect to an out-of-stock condition
    d. the firm's ability to come close to full capacity utilization
    e. none of the above

    (ICMA adapted)

_____ **8.** A sales office has developed the following probabilities for daily sales of a perishible product:

Daily Sales	Probabilities
150 units	.25
225	.50
300	.20
375	.05
	1.00

The product is restocked at the start of each day. If the company desires a 2% probability of satisfying sales demand, the initial stock balance for each day should be:

a. 225   **b.** 338   **c.** 300   **d.** 375   **e.** none of the above   (AICPA adapted)

_____ **9.** A company's treasurer complains about an excessive investment in inventories. At the same time, the purchasing agent states that large inventory balances are necessary to take advantage of supplier discounts, and the production manager complains that production often is delayed by inventory shortages. The quantitative technique most relevant to this situation is:

a. economic order quantity models   **d.** probability analysis

b. linear programming   **e.** none of the above

c. payback analysis   (AICPA adapted)

_____ **10.** Ignoring safety stocks, a valid computation of the order point is:

a. the economic order quantity

b. the economic order quantity multiplied by the anticipated demand during lead time

c. the anticipated demand during lead time

d. the square root of the anticipated demand during the lead time

e. none of the above   (AICPA adapted)

PART 4

On January 1, the materials analyst for Schoolkraft Company is asked to determine the number of units of Material A to order for March delivery. The production schedule calls for 10,000 units of this material for January operations, 13,500 units in February, and 14,800 units in March. On January 1, the inventory shows 8,000 units on hand, 12,000 units on order for January delivery, and 13,000 units on order for February delivery. A 7,500-unit minimum reserve inventory is maintained.

Instructions:

1. Determine the quantity to order for March delivery.

2. Determine the number of units on hand on (a) March 1 and (b) on March 31, if the planned usage occurs and outstanding orders are received on expected delivery dates.

PART 5

Julian Products Inc. uses 180,000 units of Material 101 annually in its production. Order costs consist of $20 for placing a long-distance call to make the order and $60 for delivering the order by truck to the company warehouse. Each 101 costs $400, and the carrying cost is estimated at 20% of the inventory cost.

Instructions: *Compute the optimal order quantity in units for 101 and the total order cost and carrying cost for the year.*

PART 6

Magic Manufacturing Inc. uses an item for which it places 100 orders per year. The cost of a stockout is $100, and the carrying cost is $2 per unit. The following probabilities of a stockout have been estimated for various levels of safety stock:

Probability	Safety Stock Level
50%	0 units
30	200
10	400
5	800

Instructions: *Determine the total carrying cost and stockout cost at each level of safety stock and indicate the optimum level of safety stock.*

Safety Stock Level	Expected Annual Stockouts	Total Stockout Cost	Total Carrying Cost	Total Stockout and Carrying Cost
0				
200				
400				
800				

PART 7

The Formosa Corporation has obtained the following costs and other data pertaining to one of its materials:

Working days per year	250
Normal use per day	100 units
Maximum use per day	150 units
Minimum use per day	50 units
Lead time	10 days
Variable cost of placing one order	$25
Variable carrying cost per unit per year	$ 5

Instructions:

1. Determine the economic order quantity in units.

2. Determine the maximum safety stock.

3. Determine the order point.

4. Determine the normal maximum inventory.

5. Determine the absolute maximum inventory.

6. Determine the average inventory, assuming normal lead time and unsage.

PART 8

Purple Mountain Co. has ten items in its inventory, with total units used per year and unit costs as follows:

Item	Units	Unit Cost
A	3,000	$ .21
B	600	8.00
C	1,500	.50
D	200	55.00
E	1,300	.40
F	750	2.40
G	500	9.60
H	100	200.00
I	300	16.70
J	1,750	.40

Instructions:

1. Complete the schedule below, showing the relationships between the percentage of units and the percentage of total annual materials costs. Arrange the items in terms of total cost, listing first the item with the highest total cost. (Round percentages to one decimal place.)

Item	Units	% of Total	Unit Cost	Total Cost	% of Total

2. Prepare a grapic illustration to be presented to management for instituting an ABC inventory control plan. Plot the cumulative percentage of total units (horizontal axis) against the cumulative percent of annual dollar usage. Do not divide the graph into A, B, or C categories.

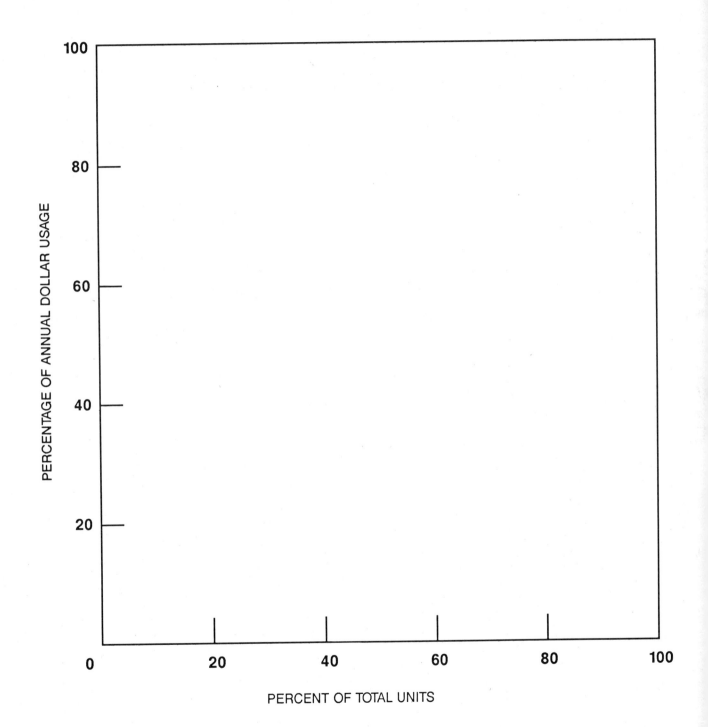

PART 9

Because of erratic customer demand, Garfield Company has been experiencing stockouts on one of its important inventory items, even though deliveries arrive on a dependable schedule—one month from the date of an order. Records provide the usage forecast and the actual consumption on this item for the past nine months. The sum of the deviations squared is 5,000 and the sum of the forecast minus units consumed is zero. A 95% protection against stockout is desired.

Instructions:

1. Compute the safety stock, using the Student's t table.
2. Determine the order point if average usage is 250 units per month.
3. Calculate the safety stock for 95% protection if four months are required from order to delivery.

CHAPTER 10
LABOR:
CONTROLLING AND ACCOUNTING FOR COSTS

REVIEW SUMMARY

1. Labor cost represents an important cost factor. The basic pay for work performed is called the *base rate* or *job rate*. *Fringe benefits* also form a substantial element of labor cost and include such items as the employer's share of FICA tax, holiday pay, overtime premium pay, and pension costs. In recent years, employment costs—wages, salaries, and fringes—have risen more than output per labor hour, leading to higher prices to meet higher unit labor costs. To curtail the wage-price spiral requires labor cost increases that do not exceed the unit cost reduction resulting from increased productivity.

2. *Labor productivity* is the measure of production performance using the expenditure of human effort as a yardstick. Setting a standard of labor performance is not easy. The pace at which an observed employee is working is referred to as a *rating* or *performance rating*. Normal or standard time is the time that it should take a person working at a normal pace to do a job, with allowances for rest periods. The *productivity-efficiency ratio* measures the output of an individual, relative to the performance standard.

3. Four fundamental assumptions of human resource management are: (1) workers are best qualified to improve their work; (2) decisions should be made at the lowest possible level in the organization; (3) worker participation increases job satisfaction; and (4) there is a vast pool of ideas in the workforce. Quality-of-conformance costs consist of (1) *prevention costs,* the costs of designing, implementing and maintaining the quality system; (2) *appraisal costs,* the costs of ensuring that materials and products meet quality standards; (3) *internal failure costs,* which occur when materials and products fail to meet quality standards; and (4) *external failure costs,* which result from shipping inferior products to customers. The accounting system should aid in measuring these costs for control purposes.

4. An incentive wage plan should reward workers in direct proportion to their increased output. To be successful, an incentive wage plan should (a) be applied to situations in which a worker can increase output, (b) provide for proportionately more pay for output above standard, (c) set fair standards so that extra effort will result in bonus pay, and (d) provide immediate rewards each payday. The *straight piecework plan* pays wages above the base rate for production above the standard. Under the *100 percent bonus plan*, a standard time is allowed to complete a job or unit, and the worker is paid for the standard time at the hourly rate if the job or unit is completed in standard time or less. *Group bonus plans* depend upon the superior productive performance of an entire department or factory. In *organizational incentive plans* employee suggestions are the heart of these *gainsharing plans* and the incentive equation is based on some ratio of labor costs to the value that is added to sales as a result of improved productivity.

5. Learning curve theory may be used in determining time standards. *Learning curve theory* stipulates that every time the cumulative quantity of units produced is doubled, the cumulative average time per unit is reduced by a given percentage. In highly automated manufacturing situations, the learning curve is not operative, because the speed of the production process is machine controlled.

6. Labor cost control is based on pertinent and timely information submitted to management. It begins with an adequate production planning schedule supported by labor-hour requirements and accompanying labor costs, determined well in advance of production runs. The departments that should cooperate in this process include personnel, production planning, timekeeping, payroll, and cost.

7. The chief function of the personnel department is to provide an efficient labor force. The production planning department is responsible for scheduling work, releasing job orders to producing departments, and dispatching work in the factory. The timekeeping department gathers and collects total and specific time worked on a job, product, process, or in a department. A *clock card* shows the time a worker started and stopped work each day, with overtime or other premium hours clearly indicated. The *time ticket* provides information as to the type of work performed and the job on which it was performed. The payroll department determines the gross and net amount of earnings of each worker, computes the total payroll, and keeps earnings records for each employee. The cost department charges jobs, products, processes, or departments with the applicable costs as evidenced by the payroll distribution.

8. *Labor performance reports* are designed to compare budgets and standards with actual results attained, thereby pointing to variances from planned performance. *Plantwide labor cost reports* are sent to executive and plant management to indicate the trend of direct and indirect la-

bor cost in the various departments, and the actual cost compared with the estimated cost figures. *Daily performance reports for labor* and *daily idle time reports* combine three types of daily labor reports: (a) employee performance, (b) departmental performance, and (c) idle time.

9. Payroll procedures were among the first to be programmed for computers. Computerized labor accounting begins the day an employee is hired, and the pertinent data are entered in the employee master file. Computerized payroll procedures can be used to produce the types of reports that have been mentioned above.

PART 1

Instructions: *Place a check mark in the appropriate column to indicate whether each of the following statements is* **True** *or* **False**.

	True	False
1. Labor cost control begins with an adequate production planning schedule.	____	____
2. The marginal revenue associated with the additional output and the marginal cost of administering an incentive wage plan are two factors that may influence management's decision to install a plan	____	____
3. Fringe costs are generally accounted for as direct labor costs.	____	____
4. Quality costs as a percentage of sales dollars are much lower in Japan than in the United States......	____	____
5. Effective control of labor costs is best achieved by comparisons between actual performance and predetermined standards.	____	____
6. In recent years, output per labor hour has risen less than employment costs.	____	____
7. The chief function of a payroll department is to provide an efficient labor force.	____	____
8. Replacement hiring usually requires authorization by executive management.	____	____
9. The cost accounting records include a record of the time each worker spends on each job or process or in each department.	____	____
10. In comparing the accounting for labor with the accounting for materials, the job ticket is comparable to the materials invoice, whereas the clock card is comparable to the materials requisition.	____	____
11. A fundamental assumption of human resource management is that people who perform the work are best qualified to improve it.	____	____
12. By utilizing a special payroll bank account, only one check, drawn on the general bank account, appears in the cash payments journal each payroll period.	____	____
13. An incentive wage plan should reward workers in direct proportion to their increased high-quality output.	____	____
14. A production planning department is responsible for the scheduling of work, the release of job orders to the producing departments, and the dispatching of work in the factory.	____	____
15. Learning curve theory is more applicable to simple, repetitive tasks than to complex tasks.	____	____

PART 2

Instructions: *In the blank space at the left of each of the following items, place the letter from the right-hand column that identifies the term that best matches the statement in the column on the left. No letter should be used more than once.*

_____ 1. Developed a productivity measure that considers the use of capital, raw materials, energy, and labor related to a plant's output.

_____ 2. Under this, the company sets a predetermined formula; if improvement above a certain amount occurs, all employees including management participate in the bonus.

_____ 3. Factor based on the pace at which an observed employee is working.

_____ 4. The time it should take a person working at a normal pace to do the job, with allowances for rest periods, possible delays, etc.

_____ 5. Inherent in these is an employee-centered management style that places great emphasis on the involvement and participation of all employees.

_____ 6. Unquestionable evidence of the employee's presence in the plant.

_____ 7. The costs associated with inferior quality products being shipped to customers.

_____ 8. Items such as FICA tax, pension costs, and vacation pay.

_____ 9. Designed to compare budgets and standards with actual results attained.

_____ 10. Sent to executive and plant management to indicate the trends of direct and indirect labor costs in various departments.

_____ 11. Shows the specific use that has been made of the labor purchased and is comparable to the materials requisition.

_____ 12. A phase of production where no further learning takes place.

_____ 13. Its chief function is to provide an efficient labor force.

_____ 14. Starts with a labor requisition sent to the personnel department by a department head or supervisor.

_____ 15. Requires authorization by executive management, resulting from its approval of the labor requirements of a production schedule.

_____ 16. Is responsible for the scheduling of work, the release of job orders to the departments, and the dispatching of work in the factory.

_____ 17. The costs associated with materials and products that fail to meet quality standards and result in manufacturing losses.

_____ 18. Under this, a standard time is allowed to complete a unit, and the worker is paid for the standard time at the hourly rate if the unit is completed in standard time or less.

_____ 19. Under this, the production standard is computed in minutes per piece and is then translated into money per piece.

_____ 20. Stipulates that every time the cumulative quantity of units produced is doubled, the cumulative average time per unit is reduced by a given percentage.

a. standard time
b. time ticket
c. labor performance reports
d. steady-state condition
e. replacement hiring
f. external failure costs
g. internal failure costs
h. expansion hiring
i. plant-wide labor cost reports
j. fringe costs
k. performance rating
l. straight piecework plan
m. learning curve theory
n. 100 percent bonus plan
o. American Standards for Productivity Measurement
p. production planning department
q. clock card
r. personnel department
s. organizational incentive plans
t. Scanlon plan

PART 3

Instructions: *In the blank space at the left of each of the following items, place the letter of the choice that most correctly completes each item.*

_____ 1. Effective internal control over the payroll function includes:
   a. reconciling total time recorded on clock cards to job reports by employees responsible for those specific jobs
   b. supervising payroll department employees by personnel department management
   c. maintaining employee personnel records by payroll department employees
   d. comparing total time spent on jobs with total time indicated on clock cards
   e. all of the above

_____ 2. An 80% learning curve was in effect for a certain industry. The first time the task was performed required a time of 100 minutes. When the task was performed for the fourth time, the cumulative average time per task unit equaled:
   a. 100 minutes   d. 144 minutes
   b. 80 minutes   e. none of the above
   c. 64 minutes

_____ 3. In (2) above, the total estimated minutes that would have been required to perform the task four times would be:
   a. 400   d. 256
   b. 144   e. none of the above
   c. 320

_____ 4. The document that provides evidence of an employee's total time in the plant is the:
   a. time ticket   d. requisition
   b. daily performance report   e. none of the above
   c. clock card

_____ 5. The incentive program that bases a department's bonus on meeting an objective that has been stated in terms of time per output unit is the:
   a. group straight piecework plan   d. 100 percent group bonus plan
   b. Emerson efficiency system   e. none of the above
   c. group learning curve plan

_____ 6. In the process of setting labor standards, the rate or speed at which a person is working is the:
   a. performance rating   d. physical output per labor hour
   b. standard time   e. none of the above
   c. base rate

_____ 7. An example of a fringe cost is:
   a. the direct labor wage rate   d. overtime premium pay
   b. withheld taxes   e. none of the above
   c. union dues paid by the employee

_____ 8. A type of labor report that shows significant differences between a worker's usual efficiency and the efficiency attained in the current period is the:
   a. physical report for labor   d. employee performance report—significant adverse
   b. labor time ticket   changes
   c. idle time report   e. all of the above

_____ 9. If prices are to be kept from rising, it is necessary that:
   a. increased productivity must be reflected in lower prices rather than higher wages
   b. unit cost increases must be greater than wage increases
   c. direct labor cost increases must be in the form of fringe benefits
   d. productivity increases must be met by corresponding wage increases
   e. none of the above

_____ 10. The company division that is responsible for recording the direct labor costs on the appropriate job cost sheets and indirect costs on the departmental expense analysis sheet is the:
   a. payroll department   d. production planning department
   b. timekeeping department   e. none of the above
   c. cost department

PART 4

Instructions: *Complete the following table, assuming that standard production is 20 units per hour and the 100 percent bonus plan is in use. (When the efficiency ratio is less than 100, no bonus is earned.) Round all computations to the nearest cent.*

Worker	Hours Worked	Output Units	Standard Units	Efficiency Ratio	Base Rate	Base × Efficiency Ratio	Total Earned	Labor Cost per Unit	Overhead per Hour	Overhead per Unit	Conversion Cost per Unit
Adams	40	840			$15.00				$20.00		
Burley	40	800			15.00				20.00		
Condon	40	880			15.00				20.00		
Dow	36	750			10.00				20.00		
Evert	40	720			7.50				20.00		

PART 5

D. Garcia, an employee of the Ponce Co., submitted the following data for work activities last week:

Day	Units Produced Each Day
Monday	30
Tuesday	32
Wednesday	46
Thursday	28
Friday	34

During the week, Garcia worked 8 hours each day. The company guarantees a flat hourly wage of $12 of its straight piecework plan. Standard production is 4 units per hour. Wages are computed on a daily basis.

Instructions: *Complete the schedule below. (Round labor cost per unit to two decimal places.)*

Day	Units Produced	Daily Earnings	Labor Cost per Unit Produced Each Day
Monday		$	$
Tuesday			
Wednesday			
Thursday			
Friday			

PART 6

Cavendish Company uses labor standards in manufacturing its products. Based upon past experience, the company considers the effect of an 80% cumulative average time learning curve when developing standards for direct labor costs.

The company is planning the production of an item that requires the assembly of purchased components. Production is planned in lots of 10 units each. A steady-state production phase with no further increases in labor productivity is expected after the eighth lot. The first production lot of units requires 150 hours of direct labor time at a standard rate of $20 per hour.

Instructions:

1. Complete the schedule below demonstrating the 80% cumulative average time learning curve that the company expects to experience in producing the units.

Cumulative Lots	×	Cumulative Average Time (Hours)	=	Cumulative Time (Total Hours)
1				
2				
4				
8				

2. Compute the standard amount allowed for direct labor cost to produce the first 8 lots.

3. Compute the standard amount allowed for direct labor cost to produce an order for 7 lots, assuming that 1 lot had already been produced.

CHAPTER 11
LABOR:
ACCOUNTING FOR LABOR-RELATED COSTS

REVIEW SUMMARY

1. According to a U.S. Chamber of Commerce study, American workers have enjoyed a spectacular growth in non-wage benefits. The study indicated that employee benefits as a percentage of payroll cost had risen from 18.7% to 36.6% over the last 30 years. Major components of employee benefits include employer FICA and unemployment insurance contributions, vacation pay and paid holidays, employer contributions to pension funds and supplemental unemployment pay funds, and recreation, health services, life insurance, and medical care. Many employers offer *cafeteria plans* that enable employees to specify what benefits they want with a fixed dollar amount of coverage.

2. The Federal Wage and Hour Law established a minimum wage per hour with time and a half for hours worked in excess of 40 in one week. To comply with this law, the records for each employee must indicate the hours worked each day and each workweek, the basis on which wages are paid, the total daily and weekly earnings at straight time, and the total wages paid during each pay period.

3. When work is randomly scheduled, the overtime premium pay should be included in factory overhead rather than charged to the jobs that happened to be worked on in the overtime period. In theory, bonus payments, vacation pay, and other direct-labor-related costs are additional labor costs that should be charged to Work in Process. In practice, however, these costs are generally included in the predetermined factory overhead rate.

4. *Guaranteed annual wage plans* guarantee a worker either a percentage of normal take-home pay during layoffs or that a worker's weekly paycheck will not fall below a minimum figure. In apprenticeship and training programs, the portion of the wages paid in excess of the standard paid for the productive output, plus the cost of instruction, is an indirect labor cost to be included in the factory overhead rate.

5. *Human resource accounting* is the process of developing financial assessments of people or groups of people within organizations and society and of monitoring these assessments over time. A human resource accounting system needs to identify incurred human resource costs. The quantification of human resources is the biggest stumbling block to the creation of human resource accounting. Proposals that have attempted to utilize human resource accounting include capitalizing salaries, capitalizing the cost of acquiring an employee, capitalizing startup costs, the behavioral variables approach, the opportunity cost approach, the economic value approach, the present value method, and the stochastic rewards valuation model.

6. A *pension plan* provides retirement benefits for all employees in recognition of their work contributed to a company. Pension costs are chargeable currently to factory overhead or to commercial expense, although it may be many years before pension benefits are actually paid. The Pension Reform Act of 1974 (ERISA) was enacted in order to make certain that promised pensions are actually paid at retirement. The law prohibits a plan from excluding an employee due to advanced age and lack of years of service. Also, a plan's minimal annual contribution must include the normal cost for the year plus amortization of past service costs and certain other costs, including interest.

7. Employers other than those in excluded classes of employment are required to pay FICA tax on wages paid and certain fringe benefits, equal to the amount paid by the employees. The employer is further required to collect the FICA tax from employees by deducting the current percentage from the wages paid each payday up to the current annual limit or base to which the tax applies. Federal income tax withheld and employee and employer FICA taxes must be deposited with either an authorized commercial bank depository or a Federal Reserve Bank on a periodic basis and a quarterly report must be filed.

8. Under the Federal Unemployment Tax Act, an employer in covered employment must pay an unemployment insurance tax to the federal government. While the federal act requires no employee contribution, some states levy an unemployment insurance tax on the employee. The federal portion of the unemployment tax is generally payable quarterly, and the related tax return is due annually on January 31. The various state unemployment compensation laws also require reports from employers to determine their liability to make contributions, the amount of taxes to be paid, and the amount of benefit to which each employee is entitled if unemployment occurs.

9. Workmen's compensation insurance laws provide insurance benefits for workers or their supervisors for losses caused by accidents or occupational diseases suffered in the course of employment. While the benefits, premium costs, and other details vary from state to state, the total insurance cost is borne by the employer.

10. Income taxes are withheld from each wage payment in accordance with the amount of the employee's earnings and withholding allowances claimed on the W-4 form. The

withholding statement (Form W-2) generally must be delivered to the employee on or before January 31 of the following year. A reconciliation of the quarterly reports (Form 941) filed by the employer with the duplicate copies of the W-2 forms furnished employees must be filed annually.

11. For each payroll, the total amount earned by workers is debited to Payroll with credits to Accured Payroll and to the withholding accounts. The cost of labor purchased is summarized and recorded as debits to Work in Process, Factory Overhead Control, Marketing Expenses Control, and Administrative Expenses Control, and as a credit to Payroll. Employer payroll taxes and other labor-related costs are recorded and, at appropriate times, payments are made to discharge payroll-related liabilities.

PART 1

Instructions: *Place a check mark in the appropriate column to indicate whether each of the following statements is **True** or **False**.*

	True	False
1. The Federal Wage and Hour Law established a minumum wage per hour with time and a half for hours worked in excess of 7½ in one day.	___	___
2. When a rush order is accepted with the knowledge that it will result in overtime being worked, the overtime premium pay that results should be charged to the specific job worked on in the overtime period.	___	___
3. In practice, bonus payments are generally charged to work in process.	___	___
4. Vacation pay is generally considered a cost of the period in which the absence occurs.	___	___
5. Guaranteed annual wage plans guarantee that a worker's weekly paycheck will not fall below a minimum figure.	___	___
6. In apprenticeship programs, the portion of the wages paid in excess of the standard paid for the productive output achieved is an indirect labor cost to be included in factory overhead.	___	___
7. Human resource accounting is more useful for external financial reporting than it is for management decision making.	___	___
8. A pension plan is probably the most important as well as the most complicated factor associated with labor and labor costs.	___	___
9. An employer's minimum annual pension plan contribution generally is the normal cost for the year plus a level funding, including interest, of past service costs and certain other costs.	___	___
10. "Vesting" means that benefits cannot be forfeited even in the event of dismissal or discontinuance of company operations.	___	___
11. An actuary is generally the chief financial officer of a corporation.	___	___
12. An employer is required to collect the FICA tax from an employee on the last day of the month following each calendar quarter.	___	___
13. While the Federal Unemployment Tax Act requires no employee contribution, a few states levy an unemployment insurance tax on the employee.	___	___
14. Before new employees begin work, they are required to fill out a withholding exemption certificate known as Form W-4.	___	___
15. The withholding statement showing the total wages earned and the amount of taxes withheld during a calendar year is known as Form W-2.	___	___

PART 2

Instructions: *In the blank space at the left of each of the following items, place the letter from the right-hand column that identifies the term that best matches the statement in the column on the left. No letter should be used more than once.*

_____ 1. Established a minimum wage per hour with time and a half for hours worked in excess of 40 in one week.

_____ 2. When production is randomly scheduled, the cost of this should be included in the predetermined factory overhead rate.

_____ 3. May be a fixed amount per employee, a percentage of profits, a fraction of one month's wages, or some other calculated amount.

_____ 4. Guarantees certain specified vested benefits for each participant or beneficiary.

_____ 5. Fringe benefit that assures that a worker's weekly paycheck will not fall below a pre-determined minimum figure.

_____ 6. When a new shift is activated, a case can be made for treating this cost as a starting load cost and deferring a portion of it over a period of time.

_____ 7. The process of developing financial assessments of people or groups of people within organizations and of monitoring these assessments over time.

_____ 8. A proposal for utilizing human resource accounting that suggests that investment center managers be encouraged to bid for any employee resource that they desire.

_____ 9. A proposal for utilizing human resource accounting that considers the synergistic components of cost and time required for members of a firm to establish effective cooperative working relationships.

_____ 10. Examples of these would include variation in leadership styles and proficiency levels.

_____ 11. Examples of these would include changes in subordinate attitudes, motivation, and behavior.

_____ 12. A proposal for utilizing human resource accounting that involves a process defined as a natural system that changes in time in accordance with the laws of probability.

_____ 13. A proposal for utilizing human resource accounting that involves determining wage payments over perhaps a five-year period, and then discounting these payments at the rate of return of owned assets in the economy for the most recent year.

_____ 14. An arrangement whereby a company provides retirement benefit payments for all employees in recognition of their work contribution to the company.

_____ 15. Enacted in order to make certain that promised pensions are actually paid at retirement.

_____ 16. Means that pension benefits cannot be forfeited even in the event of dismissal or discontinuance of company operations.

_____ 17. Provides a specified dollar amount for each employee to defray the cost of various available benefits.

_____ 18. An equal amount of this is contributed by both employer and the employee.

_____ 19. The entire amount of this is paid through employer contributions.

_____ 20. In most states, the employer pays the entire amount of this.

a. intervening variables
b. present value method
c. overtime premium pay
d. bonus payments
e. vesting
f. Pension Benefit Guaranty Corporation
g. FICA tax
h. FUTA tax
i. ERISA
j. training program
k. state unemployment tax
l. human resource accounting
m. capitalizing startup costs
n. cafeteria plan
o. pension plan
p. causal variables
q. guaranteed annual wage plan
r. stochastic rewards valuation model
s. Federal Wage and Hour Law
t. opportunity costs approach

PART 3

Instructions: *In the blank space at the left of each of the following items, place the letter of the choice that most correctly completes each item.*

_____ 1. In job order costing, payroll taxes paid by the employer for factory employees are preferably accounted for as:
    a. direct labor
    b. factory overhead
    c. indirect labor
    d. administrative costs
    e. none of the above
    (AICPA adapted)

_____ 2. When a rush order is received during the week and it must be completed during an overtime shift, the overtime premium is charged to:
    a. General and Administrative Expenses
    b. Accured Overtime Premium Receivable
    c. Factory Overhead Control
    d. the job worked on during the overtime period
    e. none of the above

_____ 3. An employee is paid a base rate of $600 per week for 52 weeks. The employee is entitled to a four-week vacation each year. Factory Overhead Control is debited each week for accrued vacation pay of:
    a. $0   **b.** $46.15   **c.** $12.50   **d.** $50   **e.** none of the above

_____ 4. A human resource accounting approach that is presently used in some professional sports is the:
    a. capitalization of acquisition approach
    b. capitalization of salaries
    c. behavioral variables approach
    d. present value method
    e. none of the above

_____ 5. A human resource accounting approach that reflects the realization that an individual's contribution to an organization changes in time according to laws of probability is the:
    a. behavioral variables approach
    b. opportunity cost method
    c. present value method
    d. stochastic rewards valuation method
    e. none of the above

_____ 6. A method for determining the costs of a pension plan that would *not* be acceptable under current pension reform laws is the:
    a. aggregate cost method
    b. attained-age normal cost method
    c. individual level premium cost method
    d. current funding cost method
    e. none of the above

_____ 7. Before employees begin work they are required to complete a withholding allowance certificate. This report is called a:
    a. Form 941
    b. Form 1040
    c. W-4 form
    d. W-2 form
    e. none of the above

_____ 8. To spread the cost of an annual bonus over production throughout the year, the weekly payroll entry would include a debit to which of the following accounts for the bonus portion of the entry?
    a. Work in Process
    b. Factory Overhead Control
    c. Payroll
    d. Liability for Bonus
    e. none of the above

_____ 9. Which of the following is not a factor that affects the ultimate cost of a company pension plan?
    a. The number of employees reaching retirement age each year
    b. Income from pension fund invenstments
    c. Management's decision as to when employees will be vested
    d. The average period over which the benefits will be paid
    e. None of the above

_____ 10. The annual earnings base of each employee's wages paid on which the employer pays unemployment insurance tax is:
    a. $42,000
    b. $21,000
    c. $7,000
    d. $84,000
    e. none of the above

NOTE: Unless otherwise directed, use the following rates in the remaining parts of this chapter: FICA tax, 7.5%; FUTA tax, .8%; state unemployment insurance tax, 5.4%.

PART 4

The information below, taken from the daily time tickets of a producing department, summarizes time and piecework for the week ended January 30.

Employee	Clock No.	Job No.	Hours Worked	Production Pieces	Hourly Rate	Piece Rate
Connolly, S.	37	347	40	780	–	$.50
Lueke, M.	38	–	40	–	$ 7.00	–
Maxie, R.	39	343	46	–	8.80	–
Maier, L....................	40	–	40	–	15.00	–

The company operates on a 40-hour week and pays time and a half for overtime. FICA tax deductions should be made for each employee. A 5% deduction is to be made from each employee's wage for health insurance. Lueke works as a forklift operator; Maier is the supervisor; the others work directly on the jobs. Use 15% in computing income tax withheld.

Instructions:

1. Using the form provided below, determine each employee's gross pay, deductions, and net pay.

	Connolly	Lueke	Maxie	Maier	Total
Hours worked					
Piecework					
Rate (hourly/piece)					
Direct labor					
Indirect labor					
Overtime premium					
Gross pay	$_____	$_____	$_____	$_____	$_____
Income tax (15%)	$	$	$	$	$
FICA tax (7.5%)					
Health insurance (5%)................					
Total deductions.....................					
Net pay	$_____	$_____	$_____	$_____	$_____

2. Prepare journal entries to (a) set up the accrued payroll and other liabilities, (b) pay the payroll, and (c) distribute the payroll and record the employer's payroll taxes.

Account	Subsidiary Record	Debit	Credit
(a)			
(b)			
(c)			

PART 5

An employee of the Finishing Department is paid $14 per hour for a regular work week of 40 hours. During the week ended July 15, the employee worked 50 hours and earned time and a half for overtime hours.

Instructions:

1. Prepare the entry to distribute the labor cost if the job worked on during overtime was a rush order, the contract price of which included the overtime premium.

Account	Debit	Credit

2. Prepare the entry to distribute the labor cost if the job worked on during overtime was the result of random scheduling.

PART 6

A production worker earns $3,300 per month and the company pays the worker a year-end bonus equal to one month's wages. The worker is also entitled to a one-month paid vacation per year. Bonus and vacation benefits are treated as indirect costs and accrued during the 11 months that the employee is at work.

Instructions: *Prepare the journal entry to record and distribute the labor cost of the production worker for a month. Assume that there are no deductions from gross wages.*

Account	Subsidiary Record	Debit	Credit

CHAPTER 12
COST BEHAVIOR ANALYSIS

REVIEW SUMMARY

1. A *fixed cost* remains the same in total as activity increases or decreases. However, *programmed fixed expenses* may change in the short run due to changes in operations. *Committed fixed expenses,* such as depreciation, commit management to the allocation of resources for a much longer period of time. *Variable costs* increase proportionately with an increase in activity and decrease proportionately with a decrease in activity. A measure of activity, such as direct labor hours or machine hours, must be selected as an independent variable for use in estimating the variable expense, the dependent variable, at specified levels of activity. *Semivariable costs* display both fixed and variable characteristics because items such as maintenance or power require a minimum of organization or quantity in order to maintain readiness to operate, and beyond this minimum, additional cost varies with volume. The relevant range is the range of activity over which the calculated amount of fixed expense and the variable expense rate remain unchanged.

2. The *high and low points method* of determining the fixed and variable elements of a semivariable cost selects data points that are the high and low periods as to activity level. In the *statistical scattergraph method* of analyzing semivariable costs, various costs (the dependent variable, e.g., electricity expense) are plotted on the *y* axis, and measurement figures (the independent variable, e.g., direct labor hours) are plotted on the *x* axis. For a more exact determination of cost behavior, the *method of least squares* determines mathematically a line of best fit or a linear regression line drawn through a set of plotted points, so that the sum of the squared deviations of each actual plotted point from the point directly above or below it on the regression line is at a minimum.

3. The *standard error of the estimate* is the standard deviation about the regression line and can be used to develop a confidence interval to decide whether a given level of expense requires management action. *Correlation* is the relationship between the values of two attributes, i.e., the independent variable and the dependent variable. The *coefficient of correlation (r)* is a measure of the extent to which two variables are related linearly. The *coefficient of determination (r^2),* obtained by squaring the coefficient of correlation, represents the percentage of explained variance in the independent variable.

4. After computing the fixed and variable components of cost using the method of least squares, it is useful to plot the regression line against the sample data so that the pattern of deviations of the actual observations from the corresponding estimates on the regression line can be inspected. If the distribution of observations around the regression line is uniform for all values of the independent variable, it is referred to as *homoscedastic*. If the variance differs at different points on the regression line (known as *heteroscedastic*) or the observations around the regression line appear to be correlated with one another (*serial correlation* or *autocorrelation*) the standard error of the estimate and the confidence intervals based on the standard error are unreliable measures.

5. If more than one independent variable is required to describe cost behavior, then multiple regression analysis should be used. An assumption is that the independent variables are not correlated with one another. The presence of *multicollinearity* (related independent variables) would not affect the estimate of cost unless one or more important independent variables were omitted. Omitting important independent variables from the multiple regression model is known as *specification error*. If the behavior of a group of costs is being observed, costs may be grouped and classified in sufficient detail so that costs in a particular group are all largely related to one independent variable, thus avoiding multiple regression analysis.

PART 1

Instructions: *Place a check mark in the appropriate column to indicate whether each of the following statements is **True** or **False**.*

	True	False
1. Examples of committed fixed expenses include advertising and training costs.		
2. In estimating expenses, an example of a dependent variable would be electricity cost, whereas an independent variable would be machine hours.		
3. The relevant range is the range of activity over which the amount of fixed expense and the rate of variability remain unchanged.		
4. In the high and low points method, if the periods having the highest and lowest activity levels are not the same as those having the highest or lowest expense being analyzed, the activity level should be used.		
5. The advantage of the high and low points method is that it uses two data points to determine cost behavior.		
6. There should generally be as many data points above as below the trend line on a statistical scattergraph.		
7. A more exact trend line than is possible by using the statistical scattergraph method may be computed by using simple regression analysis.		
8. If more than one independent variable is required to describe cost behavior, multiple regression analysis should be used.		
9. Levels of expenditures that are determined by management rather than being directly related to sales or production activity, such as for recruiting new employees, are known as committed fixed expenses.		
10. In reality, the relationship between a business activity and the related variable cost is usually perfectly linear over the entire range of activity.		
11. Examples of semivariable costs include utilities, maintenance, indirect labor, and travel and entertainment.		
12. The coefficient of correlation and the coefficient of determination establish a cause-and-effect relationship between the dependent variable and the independent variable.		
13. The standard error of the estimate is used by management in developing a confidence interval for deciding whether a given level of expense requires management action.		
14. In multiple regression analysis, the cost relationships are shown on a two-dimensional graph.		
15. When the degree of multicollinearity is high, the relationship between one or more of the independent variables and the dependent variable may be obscured.		

PART 2

Instructions: *In the blank space at the left of each of the following items, place the letter from the right-hand column that identifies the term that best matches the statement in the column on the left. No letter should be used more than once.*

_____ 1. When the observations around the regression line appear to be correlated with one another.

_____ 2. Term used to describe the situation where the variance differs at different points on the regression line.

_____ 3. Increases in total proportionately with an increase in activity and decreases proportionately with a decrease in activity.

_____ 4. The number of values that are free to vary after certain restrictions have been placed on the data.

_____ 5. Remains the same in total as activity increases or decreases within a relevant range.

_____ 6. When the distribution of observations around the regression line is uniform for all values of the independent variable.

_____ 7. Occurs when important variables are omitted from the multiple regression model.

_____ 8. May change because of changes in the volume of activity or for such reasons as changes in the number of salaries of the management group.

_____ 9. Examples include depreciation and long-term lease agreements.

_____ 10. Displays both fixed and variable characteristics.

_____ 11. Range of activity over which the amount of fixed expense and the rate of variability remain unchanged.

_____ 12. Because this method uses only two data points, it may not yield answers that are as accurate as those derived by other methods of estimating cost behavior.

_____ 13. Method of estimating cost behavior that determines mathematically a line of best fit drawn through a set of plotted points.

_____ 14. Defined as the standard deviation about the regression line.

_____ 15. A measure of the extent to which two variables are related linearly.

_____ 16. Computed by squaring the coefficient of correlation, and represents the percentage of explained variance in the dependent variable.

_____ 17. A further application of the method of least squares, permitting the consideration of more than one independent variable.

_____ 18. A measure of the covariation between any independent variable and a dependent variable.

_____ 19. Various costs are plotted on a vertical line and measurement figures are plotted along a horizontal line.

_____ 20. When the degree of this is high, the relationship between one or more of the independent variables and the dependent variable may be obscured.

a. programmed fixed expenses
b. variable cost
c. standard error of the estimate
d. fixed cost
e. correlation
f. statistical scattergraph
g. relevant range
h. multicollinearity
i. degrees of freedom
j. multiple regression analysis
k. coefficient of determination
l. committed fixed expenses
m. specification error
n. high and low points method
o. homoscedastic
p. coefficient of correlation
q. heteroscedastic
r. serial correlation
s. method of least squares
t. semivariable expense

PART 3

Instructions: *In the blank space at the left of each of the following items, place the letter of the choice that most correctly completes each item.*

_____ 1. The term "fixed costs" refers to:
   a. all costs that are associated with marketing, shipping, warehousing, and billing activities
   b. all costs that do not change in total for a given period and relevant range but become progressively smaller on a per-unit basis as volume increases
   c. all manufacturing costs incurred to produce units of output
   d. all costs that fluctuate in total in response to changes in the rate of utilization of capacity
   e. none of the above   (ICMA adapted)

_____ 2. A procedure that can be used to determine the fixed and variable elements of a semivariable expense is:
   a. the statistical scattergraph method   d. the Program Evaluation and Review Technique
   b. linear programming   e. all of the above
   c. input-output analysis   (AICPA adapted)

_____ 3. Within a relevant range, the amount of variable cost per unit:
   a. differs at each production level   d. decreases as production increases
   b. remains constant at each production level   e. none of the above
   c. increases as production increases   (AICPA adapted)

_____ 4. Simple regression analysis involves the use of:
   a. one variable   d. more than three variables
   b. two variables   e. none of the above
   c. three variables   (AICPA adapted)

_____ 5. A measure of the extent to which two variables are related linearly is referred to as:
   a. cause-effect ratio   d. input-output analysis
   b. coefficient of correlation   e. none of the above
   c. sensitivity analysis   (AICPA adapted)

_____ 6. Which of the following best describes a fixed cost?
   a. It may change in total when such change is un-   d. It may change in total when such change depends
      related to changes in production.   on production within the relevant range.
   b. It may change in total when such change is   e. none of the above.
      related to changes in production.
   c. It is constant per unit of change in production.   (AICPA adapted)

_____ 7. If the coefficient of correlation between two variables is negative, a scatter diagram of these variables would appear as:
   a. random points   d. a curvilinear function
   b. a least squares line that slopes up to the right e. none of the above
   c. a least squares line that slopes down to the right   (AICPA adapted)

_____ 8. Ray Corporation has developed the following flexible budget formula for annual indirect labor cost: $480 + $.50 per machine hour. The operating budget for the current month is based on 20,000 hours of planned machine time. Indirect labor cost included in this planning budget would be:
   a. $14,800   b. $10,000   c. $14,400   d. $10,400   e. none of the above   (AICPA adapted)

_____ 9. The term "committed fixed costs" refers to:
   a. fixed costs that management decides to incur in the current period to enable the company to achieve objectives other than the filling of customers' orders
   b. fixed costs likely to respond to the amount of attention devoted to them by a specified manager
   c. fixed costs that are governed mainly by past decisions that established the present levels of operating and organizational capacity and that change slowly only in response to changes in society
   d. fixed costs that fluctuate in total in response to small changes in the rate of capacity utilization
   e. none of the above   (ICMA adapted)

_____ **10.** Which of the following quantitative methods will separate a semivariable cost into its fixed and variable components with the highest degree of precision under all circumstances?

    a. High-low method   **d.** Scattergraph method

    b. Simplex method   **e.** None of the above

    c. Least squares method   (AICPA adapted)

PART 4

Semola Company developed the following relationships to indicate cost at various activity levels:

Direct labor	$25 per unit
Materials	$30 per unit
Supervision	$4,000 + $2 per unit
Power	$1,000 + $1 per unit + $2 per machine hour
Factory supplies	$1,750 + $.50 per unit
Depreciation—equipment	$7 per machine hour
Depreciation—building	$80,000

During the next period, the company anticipates production of 10,000 units and usage of 1,000 machine hours. The overhead application rate is $13 per unit.

Instructions:

1. Determine the production costs to be incurred during the next period.

    Production costs:

        Direct labor . . . . $

        Direct materials . . . .

    Overhead to be incurred:

        Supervision . . . . $

        Power . . . .

                . . . .

        Factory supplies . . . .

        Depreciation—equipment . . . .

        Depreciation—building . . . .   _____   _____

        Total production cost . . . . $_____

2. Compute the over- or (under)applied overhead, assuming that 10,000 units were produced.

                Overhead applied . . . . $

                Overhead to be incurred . . . .   _____

                _____ overhead . . . . $_____

PART 5

A controller is interested in an analysis of the fixed and variable costs of machine repairs and maintenance as related to machine hours. The following data have been accumulated:

Month	Repairs and Maintenance	Machine Hours
January	$1,548	297
February	1,667	350
March	1,405	241
April	1,534	280
May	1,600	274
June	1,600	266
July	1,613	285
August	1,635	301

Instructions:

1. Determine the amount of fixed overhead and the variable cost ratio, using:
   (a) The high and low points method.

	Repairs and Maintenance	Machine Hours
High	$	
Low		
Difference	$	
Variable rate		

	High	Low
Total repairs and maintenance cost	$	$
Variable cost		
Fixed cost	$	$

(b) A scattergraph with trend line fitted by inspection

Average cost .... $

Less fixed cost .... _____

Variable cost .... $_____

Variable cost per machine hour:

(c) The method of least squares.

Month	(1) Machine Hours	(2) Difference from Average Hours	(3) Factory Repair and Maintenance Cost	(4) Difference from Average of Repair and Maintenance Cost	(5) (2) Squared	(6) (2) × (4)	(7) (4) Squared
January			$	$		$	$
February							
March							
April							
May							
June							
July							
August							
Total			$	$		$	$

Average machine hours (x):

Average repairs and maintenance cost (y):

Variable rate (b):

Fixed cost per month:

2. Determine the standard error of the estimate.

Month	(1) Machine Hours	(2) Factory Repairs and Maintenance Cost	(3) Predicted Repairs and Maintenance Cost	(4) Prediction Error (2) – (3)	(5) Prediction Error Squared [(4) Squared]
January		$	$	$	$
February					
March					
April					
May					
June					
July					
August					
Total............		$	$	$	$

3. Determine the confidence interval at 95% (Table Factor 2.477) if the actual activity level for the period is 300 machine hours, resulting in budgeted repairs and maintenance cost of $1,600.

4. Determine the coefficient of correlation (r) and the coefficient of determination (r^2).

CHAPTER 13
FACTORY OVERHEAD:
PLANNED, ACTUAL, AND APPLIED; VARIANCE ANALYSIS

REVIEW SUMMARY

1. *Factory overhead* consists of indirect materials, indirect labor, and all other factory expenses that cannot conveniently be identified with or charged directly to specific jobs or products. A *predetermined factory overhead rate* is used to equitably allocate overhead because of the impossibility of tracing overhead costs to specific jobs or products. Its use is the only feasible method of computing product overhead costs promptly enough to serve management needs, identify inefficiencies, and smooth out uncontrollable month-to-month fluctuations in unit costs.

2. In applying factory overhead, the base selected should be closely related to functions represented by the overhead cost being applied. All other things being equal, the simplest base should be used in order to minimize clerical costs. The following bases are used for applying factory overhead: (a) The *physical output* base in which the factory overhead charge per unit is determined by dividing the estimated factory overhead for the period by the estimated units of production for the same period. This base is satisfactory when a company manufactures one product or closely related products whose difference is merely one of weight or volume. (b) The *direct materials cost* base, in which the percentage of estimated materials cost is multiplied by the materials cost for the job or product to obtain the factory overhead to be charged to the order. This base has limited usage, because in most instances there is no logical relationship between the direct materials cost of a product and the factory overhead used in its production. (c) The *direct labor cost* base, in which the percentage of the estimated factory overhead to estimated direct labor cost is multiplied by the direct labor cost for the job or product to obtain the factory overhead charge. Its use is particularly favored when (1) there is a direct relationship between direct labor cost and factory overhead and (2) the rates of pay per hour for similar work are comparable. (d) The *direct labor hour* base, in which the factory overhead rate is determined by dividing the estimated factory overhead by the estimated direct labor hours. This rate is then multiplied by the number of direct labor hours worked on a job or product to determine the overhead charge. As long as labor operations are the chief factor in production processes, the direct labor hour base is an equitable base for applying overhead. (e) The *machine hour* base, in which the factory overhead rate is determined by dividing the estimated factory overhead by the estimated machine hours. This rate is then multiplied by the number of machine hours used in completing a job or

product to determine the overhead charge. This base is considered an accurate method of applying overhead if it is composed predominantly of facility-related costs, such as depreciation, maintenance, and utilities. (f) The *transactions base approach*, in which each activity, such as setups or inspections, is viewed as a transaction, with costs assigned to products based on the number and complexity of the transactions. *Transactions* such as setups, inspections, and materials movements often are responsible for a large percentage of overhead costs, and the key to managing overhead is controlling the transactions that drive it. The transactions base approach gives particular attention to the fact that certain overhead costs are not volume-driven.

3. The *theoretical capacity* of a department is its ability to produce at full speed without interruption, and it is achieved only if the department is producing at 100% of its rated capacity. *Practical capacity* is theoretical capacity less allowances for such things as unavoidable interruptions, unsatisfactory materials, labor shortages, and model changes. The *normal capacity concept* advocates an overhead rate in which expenses and production are based on average utilization of the physical plant over a period long enough to level out production highs and lows. The *expected actual capacity concept* advocates a rate in which overhead and production are based on the expected actual output for the next production period. The argument for using normal capacity is that a job or product should not cost more to produce in any one accounting period just because production was lower and fixed expenses were spread over fewer units. *Idle capacity* results from the idleness of production workers and facilities due to a temporary lack of sales, whereas *excess capacity* results either from greater productive capacity than the company could ever hope to use or from an imbalance of equipment or machinery.

4. Under *full* or *absorption costing*, both fixed and variable expenses are included in overhead rates. Under *direct costing*, only variable expenses are included in overhead rates, and fixed expenses are charged against income in the period in which they are incurred.

5. *Variable expenses* change in total with production volume and remain constant on a per-unit basis. *Fixed expenses* remain the same in total, but the expense per unit is different for each production level. The factory overhead rate can be broken down into its fixed and variable components as follows:

Fixed factory overhead rate =

$$\frac{\text{Estimated factory overhead}}{\text{Estimated direct labor hours (or other base)}}$$

Variable factory overhead rate =

$$\frac{\text{Estimated factory overhead}}{\text{Estimated direct labor hours (or other base)}}$$

6. The principal source documents used for recording overhead are purchase vouchers, materials requisitions, labor time tickets, and general journal vouchers. Actual factory overhead expenses are summarized in a factory overhead control account in the general ledger. Individual factory overhead accounts are kept in a subsidiary ledger. Debits to the factory overhead control account are for actual expenses incurred during the period, while credits are for applied expenses. A debit balance in the factory overhead control account indicates that overhead has been underapplied; i.e., actual overhead charges for the period exceeded factory overhead applied. A credit balance in the factory overhead control account indicates that overhead has been overapplied; i.e., factory overhead applied to production exceeded actual factory overhead expense for the period.

7. The *spending variance* is the difference between the actual factory overhead incurred and the budget allowance estimated for the capacity utilized. The *idle capacity variance* is the difference between the budget allowance estimated for the capacity utilized and the applied factory overhead. The procedure most often used for disposing of over- or underapplied factory overhead, provided the amount involved is not significant, is to close it to Cost of Goods Sold or Income Summary, thus treating it as a period cost rather than a product cost.

PART 1

Instructions: *Place a check mark in the appropriate column to indicate whether each of the following statements is **True or False**.*

	True	False
1. Factory overhead includes all factory costs except costs of indirect materials and indirect labor.	___	___
2. Fixed costs are constant per unit, whereas variable costs per unit vary inversely with production volume.	___	___
3. Predetermined overhead rates are uniquely associated with job order costing, while actual overhead should be used with process costing.	___	___
4. Transactions base costing is becoming a more widely used base for applying overhead to production. .	___	___
5. Use of the normal capacity concept would, over a period of years, ideally result in favorable and unfavorable idle capacity variances that would counterbalance each other.	___	___
6. During a predicted and severe recession (and accompanying reduction in production and sales), use of expected actual capacity for costing would result in lower product unit costs than would use of normal capacity.	___	___
7. During a period of above average production, use of normal capacity would result in a favorable idle capacity variance.	___	___
8. If the machine hours base is used, the fixed overhead rate should be calculated by dividing estimated fixed overhead by actual machine hours.	___	___
9. Labor time tickets are used to record only direct labor charges.	___	___
10. Actual factory overhead is recorded as a debit on the books, while applied overhead is shown as a credit.	___	___
11. When direct labor dollars are used for the overhead base, the amount of overhead applied is calculated by multiplying the overhead rate by the number of direct labor dollars actually expended.	___	___
12. An unfavorable spending variance suggests that variable overhead costs were not adequately controlled.	___	___
13. The idle capacity variance is calculated by comparing actual overhead costs with what should have been spent for the actual activity of the period.	___	___
14. The Internal Revenue Service requires that inventories include an allocated portion of significant annual overhead variances.	___	___
15. The amount by which applied overhead is greater than actual overhead is known as overapplied overhead.	___	___

PART 2

Instructions: *In the blank space at the left of each of the following items, place the letter from the right-hand column that identifies the term that best matches the statement in the column on the left. No letter should be used more than once.*

_____ 1. Expected production volume for the coming year.

_____ 2. A method of measuring activity that assumes that a large part of overhead costs arise from machinery.

_____ 3. A method of product costing that results in high unit costs during recessions and low costs in prosperity.

_____ 4. Estimated factory overhead divided by estimated materials cost times 100.

_____ 5. The simplest overhead costing base in multiproduct plants.

_____ 6. Total overhead rate times direct labor hours worked or other base.

_____ 7. An appropriate overhead base for single product plants.

_____ 8. Indirect materials, indirect labor, and all other factory expenses that cannot conveniently be identified with or charged directly to specific jobs or products.

_____ 9. An equitable method for applying overhead, as long as labor operations are the chief factor in production processes.

_____ 10. The account to which actual factory costs are charged.

_____ 11. Actual overhead less applied overhead.

_____ 12. Total overhead rate less the fixed overhead rate.

_____ 13. A costing method that associates all production costs with product units.

_____ 14. Variance for which executive management has primary responsibility.

_____ 15. Account debited when Applied Factory Overhead is credited for actual production times the overhead rate.

_____ 16. Costing method that associates only variable production costs with product units.

_____ 17. Variance for which production supervisor has primary responsibility.

_____ 18. Achieved only if the department is producing at 100% of its rated capacity.

_____ 19. Approach to overhead costing that gives particular consideration to the fact that certain overhead costs may not be driven by volume of output.

_____ 20. Includes allowances for such things as unavoidable interruptions, unsatisfactory materials, labor shortages, and model changes.

a. direct costing
b. actual unit cost
c. applied overhead
d. practical capacity
e. direct labor cost
f. expected annual capacity
g. direct labor hour base
h. Factory Overhead Control
i. transactions base
j. absorption costing
k. idle capacity variance
l. machine hours base
m. direct materials cost base
n. factory overhead
o. theoretical capacity
p. over/underapplied overhead
q. spending variance
r. units of production
s. variable overhead rate
t. Work in Process

Instructions: *In the blank space at the left of each of the following items, place the letter of the choice that most correctly completes each item.*

_____ 1. Overapplied factory overhead will always result when a predetermined factory overhead rate is employed and:
  a. production is greater than defined capacity
  b. actual overhead costs are more than expected
  c. defined capacity is less than normal capacity
  d. overhead incurred is less than applied overhead
  e. none of the above
                                        (AICPA adapted)

_____ 2. The difference over a period of time between actual factory overhead and applied factory overhead will usually be minimal when the predetermined overhead rate is based on:
  a. normal capacity
  b. defined capacity
  c. direct labor hours
  d. machine hours
  e. none of the above

_____ 3. If a predetermined factory overhead rate is not used and the volume of production is decreased from the level planned, the cost per unit would be expected to:
  a. remain unchanged for fixed cost and increase for variable cost
  b. decrease for fixed cost and remain unchanged for variable cost
  c. increase for fixed cost and remain unchanged for variable cost
  d. decrease for fixed cost and decrease for variable cost
  e. none of the above
                                        (AICPA adapted)

_____ 4. A spending variance for factory overhead is the difference between actual factory overhead cost and factory overhead cost that should have been incurred for the actual hours worked and results from:
  a. price differences for factory overhead costs
  b. quantity differences for factory overhead costs
  c. price and quantity differences for factory overhead costs
  d. differences caused in production volume variation
  e. none of the above
                                        (AICPA adapted)

_____ 5. Factory overhead should be allocated on the basis of:
  a. an activity basis that relates to cost incurrence
  b. direct labor hours
  c. direct labor cost
  d. machine hours
  e. none of the above

_____ 6. Overapplied factory overhead costs are:
  a. fixed factory costs not allocated to units produced
  b. factory overhead costs not allocated to units produced
  c. excess variable factory overhead costs
  d. costs that cannot be controlled
  e. fixed factory costs that are overallocated to units produced

_____ 7. A company found that the differences in product costs resulting from the application of predetermined factory overhead rates rather than actual factory overhead rates were immaterial, even though actual production was substantially less than planned production. The most likely explanation is that:
  a. factory overhead was composed chiefly of variable costs
  b. several products were produced simultaneously
  c. fixed factory overhead was a significant cost
  d. costs of factory overhead items were substantially larger than anticipated
  e. none of the above
                                        (AICPA adapted)

_____ 8. When a manufacturing company has a labor-intensive manufacturing plant producing many different products, the most appropriate base for applying factory overhead to work in process is:
  a. direct labor hours
  b. direct labor dollars
  c. machine hours
  d. cost of materials used
  e. none of the above
                                        (AICPA adapted)

_____ 9. According to the Internal Revenue Service regulations, significant underpaid factory overhead resulting from unanticipated price increases should be disposed of by:
  a. decreasing cost of goods sold
  b. increasing cost of goods sold
  c. decreasing cost of goods sold, work in process inventory, and finished goods inventory
  d. increasing cost of goods sold, work in process inventory, and finished goods inventory
  e. none of the above

_____ 10. If a company uses a predetermined rate for applying factory overhead, the idle capacity variance is the:
  a. over- or underapplied fixed cost element of overhead
  b. over- or underapplied variable cost element of overhead
  c. difference in budgeted costs and actual cost of fixed overhead items
  d. difference in budgeted costs and actual cost of variable overhead items
  e. none of the above

PART 4

Mon Cheri Company budget data for March are shown below:

Estimated factory overhead............................ $500,000
Production scheduled .... 25,000 units
Direct labor hours scheduled .... 50,000 hours
Estimated direct labor cost.......................... $400,000
Machine hours scheduled .... 10,000 hours

Instructions:

1. Compute the overhead rate using the various bases given and complete the table below.

Activity Base	Total Overhead Rate
Physical output	_____
Direct labor hours.................................	_____
Direct labor cost	_____
Machine hours	_____

2. Assuming that the total overhead estimate is composed of a variable estimate of $200,000 and a fixed estimate of $300,000, complete the table below. (The machine hour base is used.)

Variable overhead rate	_____
Fixed overhead rate	_____
Total overhead rate	_____

3. Prepare a journal entry that would be required to charge the predetermined overhead of $500,000 to production.

_____

_____

4. Complete the following journal entry.

	550,000	
Stores (factory supplies)		120,000
Accumulated Depreciation—Machinery		150,000
Prepaid Insurance—Factory Building		60,000
Accrued Payroll (indirect labor)		161,000
Accounts Payable (repairs)		59,000

5. Assume that Mon Cheri Company uses direct labor hours for the overhead base, that 52,000 direct labor hours were worked in March, and that actual overhead was $500,000.

(a) Prepare the entry in the T-accounts below to charge predetermined overhead to production.

Work in Process	Factory Overhead Control

(b) Was the factory overhead over- or underapplied during March? _____

By how much? _____

(c) Complete the table below, using the data given in (1), (2), and (5) above for direct labor hours.

	Overhead Rate	March Overhead Applied
Variable cost	_____	_____
Fixed cost	_____	_____
Total overhead.......................................	_____	_____

PART 5

Instructions: *The format for an overhead budget is shown below. Calculate the amount that should be budgeted for each indicated level of activity by completing the schedule. (Round to two decimal places.)*

Factory Expense Category	Budget Rate	Level of Activity (Direct Labor Hours) 45,000	50,000	55,000	60,000
Variable costs (per direct labor hour):					
Indirect labor	$2.00	$	$	$	$
Indirect materials	.80				
Repairs	.60	___	___	___	___
Total variable cost	$3.40	$___	$___	$___	$___
Fixed costs (total):					
Depreciation—factory and machinery	$200,000	$	$	$	$
Insurance—factory and machinery	50,000	___	___	___	___
Total fixed cost	$250,000	$___	$___	$___	$___
Total overhead budget		$___	$___	$___	$___
Factory overhead rate per hour		$___	$___	$___	$___
Fixed overhead rate per hour		$___	$___	$___	$___

PART 6

Factory overhead for Fantasia Company has been estimated as follows:

Fixed factory overhead	$ 50,000
Variable factory overhead	100,000
Estimated direct labor hours	20,000

Production for the month reached 120% of the budget, and actual factory overhead totaled $200,000.

Instructions:

1. Determine the over- or underapplied factory overhead.

Actual factory overhead	$
Applied factory overhead	_____
Over- or underapplied factory overhead	$_____

2. Determine the spending and idle capacity variances.

Actual factory overhead		$
Overhead for capacity attained:		
Fixed factory overhead	$	
Variable factory overhead	_____	_____
Spending variance		$_____
Factory overhead for capacity attained		$
Factory overhead applied		_____
Idle capacity variance		$_____

CHAPTER 14
FACTORY OVERHEAD:
DEPARTMENTALIZATION

REVIEW SUMMARY

1. *Departmentalization* of factory overhead means dividing the plant into segments, called departments, cost centers, or cost pools, to which costs are charged. A job or product going through a department is charged with factory overhead for work done in that department, using the department's predetermined overhead rate. Responsible control of overhead costs is possible because departmentalization makes the incurrence of costs the responsibility of a specific supervisor or manager.

2. *Producing departments* engage in the actual manufacture of the product, whereas *service departments* render a service that contributes indirectly to the manufacture of the product. Examples of producing departments include Assembly, Machining, and Refining, while service departments include Production Control, Maintenance, and Personnel. The most common approach in establishing producing departments for the purpose of costing and controlling costs is to divide the factory along lines of functional activities, with each activity or group of activities constituting a department. Determination of the kinds and number of service departments to be established should consider the number of employees needed for each service function, the cost of providing the service, the importance of the service, and the assignment of supervisory responsibility.

3. *Direct departmental costs* are generally readily identified with the originating department and can be charged directly to that department. These costs include supervision, indirect labor, overtime, labor fringe benefits, indirect materials and factory supplies, repairs and maintenance, and equipment depreciation. *Indirect departmental costs* do not originate with any specific department, but rather are incurred for all departments and must, therefore, be prorated to the user departments. They include factory costs such as depreciation, property tax, and insurance. To charge each department with its fair share of an indirect departmental cost, a base using some factor common to all departments (such as square footage in prorating building depreciation) must be found.

4. The use of departmental overhead rates requires separate consideration of each producing department's overhead, which often results in the use of different bases for applying overhead for different departments. Sometimes different overhead bases and rates are used for cost pools within a single producing department. For example, there may be a pool of machine-related overhead costs and labor-related overhead costs all within the same work center. To establish departmental factory overhead rates, one must: (a) estimate or budget the total direct factory overhead of producing and service departments at the selected activity levels; (b) prepare a factory survey for the purpose of distributing indirect factory overhead and service department costs; (c) estimate or budget total indirect factory overhead at the selected activity levels and allocate these costs on a rational basis; (d) distribute service department costs to benefiting departments; and (e) calculate departmental factory overhead rates.

5. The costs of service departments must ultimately be transferred to producing departments to establish predetermined factory overhead rates and to analyze variances. Service department costs may be transferred only to producing departments, using the *direct method*, if there is no material difference in the final costs of a producing department when the costs of a service department are not prorated first to other service departments. Otherwise, service department costs should be transferred on the basis of producing and other service departments' use of the respective services, using the *step method*, with the costs of the service department rendering the greatest amount of services transferred first. Once costs for a service department are distributed, that department is usually considered closed and no further distributions are made to it. If greater precision is desired in overhead distribution so that service departments receive cost prorations from each other before distribution to producing departments, the *algebraic method* using simultaneous equations for overhead distribution may be used.

6. Departmentalization of factory overhead requires that each cost be charged to a department as well as to a specific expense account via *departmental expense analysis sheets*. When all overhead has been assembled in the producing departments at the end of the fiscal period, it is possible to compare actual with applied overhead and to determine the over- or underapplied factory overhead for each department. Each department over- or underapplied figure may be analyzed and separate spending and idle capacity variances determined for each department.

7. Nonmanufacturing businesses and not-for-profit organizations should also departmentalize for cost planning and control. Examples of entities that have done so include retail stores, financial institutions, insurance companies, and educational institutions.

PART 1

Instructions: *Place a check mark in the appropriate column to indicate whether each of the following statements is True or False.*

	True	False
1. Producing departments render a service that contributes indirectly to the manufacture of a product. ..	____	____
2. Examples of producing departments include Production Control, Maintenance, and Shipping.	____	____
3. A departmentalized factory is usually divided along lines of functional activities.	____	____
4. When relatively few employees are involved, service functions are generally combined for the sake of economy.	____	____
5. Indirect departmental expenses do not originate with any specific departments, but rather are incurred for all departments.	____	____
6. The overtime premium portion of overtime paid to direct labor employees should usually be charged to factory overhead.	____	____
7. Indirect departmental expenses include factory costs such as power, light, and rent.	____	____
8. Factory costs such as depreciation, property tax, and insurance would most appropriately be allocated by using the number of factory employees as a distribution base.	____	____
9. It is unusual to use different distribution bases for applying overhead to different departments.	____	____
10. Repairs and maintenance are usually classified as indirect departmental expenses because they frequently originate in a maintenance department before being charged to the department receiving service......	____	____
11. The costs of service departments must ultimately be transferred to producing departments to establish predetermined factory overhead rates.	____	____
12. Selecting appropriate bases for the distribution of indirect departmental expenses has, for the most part, been reduced to an exact science.	____	____
13. Usually, service department costs are transferred in the order of the amount of service rendered and received, with the costs of the department serving the greatest number of other departments and receiving service from the smallest number of other departments transferred first.	____	____
14. Once costs for a service department are distributed, that department is usually considered closed and no further distributions are made to it..	____	____
15. Sometimes different overhead rates are used for cost pools within the same department.	____	____

PART 2

Instructions: *In the blank space at the left of each of the following items, place the letter from the right-hand column that identifies the term that best matches the statement in the column on the left. No letter should be used more than once.*

_____ 1. The act of dividing the plant into segments to which costs are charged.

_____ 2. Engages in the actual manufacture of the product by changing the shape, form, or nature of the material worked upon.

_____ 3. Contributes indirectly to the manufacture of the product.

_____ 4. The specific service is not identified if service costs applicable to producing and service functions are accumulated in this.

_____ 5. Examples of these would include fringe benefits, small tools, and supplies.

_____ 6. The straight-time portion of overtime paid to assemblers would be charged to this expense.

_____ 7. States that, in allocating direct and indirect costs, a department should be homogeneous, and specifies that this criterion is met if each significant activity of which costs are included has the same or a similar beneficial or causal relationship as the other activities for which costs are included in the department.

_____ 8. The cost of a service if each department obtained it separately rather than centrally at a lower aggregate price.

_____ 9. Examples of these would include repairs and maintenance, setups, lubricants, and energy.

_____ 10. Prepared for the purpose of facilitating the distribution of indirect factory overhead and service department costs.

_____ 11. The usual procedure is to transfer service department costs step-wise in this order.

_____ 12. When the answer in Question 11 is not readily determinable, service department costs may be transferred in this order.

_____ 13. An approach to overhead distribution that results in the most precise proration of service department costs.

_____ 14. To use this procedure for allocating service department costs, a decision must be made as to the order in which service departments are closed, because no further distributions are made to a department once its costs have been distributed.

_____ 15. Method of distributing service department costs that can be justified if there is no material difference in the final costs of a producing department when the costs of a service department are not first prorated to other service departments.

_____ 16. Charges to a department for its share of factory overhead are recorded on this.

_____ 17. Variance determined by comparing actual overhead to the budget allowance for the level of production attained.

_____ 18. Variance determined by comparing the budget allowance for the activity level attained to the factory overhead applied.

_____ 19. Example of a nonmanufacturing business that has practiced departmentalization for many years.

_____ 20. An overhead grouping used in nonmanufacturing businesses that is equivalent to the general factory grouping in a manufacturing business.

a. factory survey
b. algebraic method
c. retail store
d. direct labor
e. spending variance
f. step method
g. CAS 418
h. occupancy
i. stand-alone cost
j. departmentalization
k. amount of service rendered
l. dollar amount of overhead
m. service department
n. idle capacity variance
o. general factory cost pool
p. direct method
q. labor-related overhead costs
r. departmental expense analysis sheet
s. producing department
t. machine-related overhead costs

Instructions: *In the blank space at the left of each of the following items, place the letter of the choice that most correctly completes each item.*

_____ 1. A segment of an organization is referred to as a producing department if it has:
  a. responsibility for developing markets for and selling of the organization's output
  b. responsibility for combining the raw materials, direct labor, and other production factors into a final output
  c. authority to make decisions affecting the major determinants of profit, including the power to choose its markets and sources of supply
  d. authority to provide specialized support to other units within the organization
  e. none of the above   (ICMA adapted)

_____ 2. A department that would be classified as a producing department is:
  a. Materials Handling   b. Finishing   c. Inspection   d. Storage   e. none of the above

_____ 3. A department that would be classified as a service department is:
  a. Plating   b. Knitting   c. Cutting   d. Materials Handling   e. none of the above

_____ 4. Gamma Company operates with two producing departments (P1 and P2) and two service departments (S1 and S2). Factory overhead before allocation of service department costs, together with the usage of services from the service departments, follows:

| | Overhead Before Allocation of Service | Services Provided | |
Department	Department Costs	S1	S2
P1	$400,000	40%	30%
P2	300,000	30	50
S1	52,640	–	20
S2	105,280	30	–
	$857,920	100%	100%

Assuming that the step allocation method is used, what is the total factory overhead (including service department costs) charged to Department P1?
  a. $400,000   b. $84,224   c. $473,696   d. $384,224   e. $10,000

_____ 5. The most reasonable base for allocating supervision is:
  a. number of employees   d. building depreciation
  b. materials used   e. none of the above
  c. square footage

_____ 6. The method for allocating service department costs that results in the least precision is the:
  a. step method   d. direct method
  b. simultaneous equation method   e. none of the above
  c. algebraic method

_____ 7. Spearfish Corp. has three producing departments, A, B, and C, with 35, 25, and 40 employees respectively in each department. Factory payroll costs other than direct labor are accumulated in a Payroll Department account and are assigned to producing departments on the basis of number of employees. The total payroll in each department was: A, $300,000; B, $275,000; C, $325,000; and Payroll, $10,000. Other costs accumulated in the Payroll Department amounted to $190,000. The amount of Payroll Department costs chargeable to Department B is:
  a. $50,000   b. $68,750   c. $200,000   d. $47,500   e. none of the above

_____ 8. Factors to be considered in deciding what kinds of departments required for establishing accurate departmental overhead rates with which to control costs include all of the following except:
  a. similarity of operations, processes, and machinery in each department
  b. location of operations, processes, and machinery
  c. the number of employees within each department
  d. number of departments and cost centers
  e. none of the above

_____ **9.** All of the following are generally direct departmental overhead costs except:
  a. depreciation, insurance, and property taxes on the factory building
  b. supervision, direct labor, and overtime
  c. labor fringe benefits
  d. equipment depreciation
  e. none of the above

_____ **10.** All of the following departmental expenses logically might use square footage as the distribution base except:
  a. factory rent
  b. building repairs
  c. telephone and telegraph
  d. heat
  e. none of the above

PART 4

The factory overhead work sheet shown below for Loch Ness Products Company had the indicated columnar totals after the actual direct charges and the indirect departmental expense allocations had been made. The company has three service departments, X, Y, and Z, and two producing departments, A, and B.

Instructions: *Complete the work sheet if the service department costs are allocated in the following order:*

Department X costs: 40% to Y; 30% to Z; 20% to A; 10% to B.
Department Y costs: 40% to Z; 35% to A; 25% to B.
Department Z costs: 70% to A; 30% to B.

(1) Using the step method of allocation:

	Service Departments			Producing Departments		Total
	X	**Y**	**Z**	**A**	**B**	
Total	$40,000	$30,000	$25,000	$100,000	$150,000	$345,000
Dept. X distribution	$_____	_____				
Dept. Y distribution		$_____	_____			
Dept. Z distribution			$_____	_____	_____	_____
Total				$_____	$_____	$_____

(2) Using the direct method of allocation:

	Service Departments			Producing Departments		Total
	X	**Y**	**Z**	**A**	**B**	
Total	$40,000	$30,000	$25,000	$100,000	$150,000	$345,000
Dept. X distribution	$_____	_____				
Dept. Y distribution		$_____	_____			
Dept. Z distribution			$_____	_____	_____	_____
Total				$_____	$_____	$_____

PART 5

Cuomo Candy Co. consists of three producing departments and four service departments. For the purpose of creating factory overhead rates, the accountant prepared the cost distribution sheet, shown below, containing operational data that were gathered.

For the distribution of expenses of the service departments, the following procedures had been decided upon:
- (a) Utilities: 70% on metered hours—power; 30% on floor square footage
- (b) Maintenance: Maintenance hours excluding utilities
- (c) Materials Handling: 45% to Preparation; 35% to Mixing; and 20% to Packaging; pounds handled—300,000 in Preparation; 500,000 in Mixing
- (d) Factory Office: Preparation, 40%; Mixing, 40%; Packaging, 20%

Instructions: *Complete the cost distribution sheet using the step method of cost allocation. No reciprocal charging should take place. Factory overhead rates should be based on pounds handled in Preparation and Mixing and on direct labor cost of $20,000 in Packaging. (Round off all amounts except overhead rates to the nearest dollar. Overhead rates should be rounded to four decimal places.)*

	Total	Producing Departments			Service Departments			
		Preparation	Mixing	Packaging	Utilities	Maintenance	Materials Handling	Factory Office
Operational data:								
Floor space—sq. ft.	53,000	18,000	13,000	12,000	3,000	2,000	1,000	4,000
Maintenance hours	7,000	3,000	1,500	600	1,000	–	600	300
Metered hours	5,000	1,500	1,800	700	–	500	300	200
Expenses:								
Indirect labor	$26,000	$4,500	$4,000	$3,500	$6,000	$3,500	$2,500	$2,000
Payroll taxes	2,500	450	400	350	500	350	250	200
Indirect materials	6,000	900	1,100	3,000	500	200	50	250
Depreciation	1,000	150	200	100	200	150	75	125
Total	$35,500	$6,000	$5,700	$6,950	$7,200	$4,200	$2,875	$2,575
Distribution of service departments:								
Utilities:								
70% metered hours								
30% sq. footage					$_____	$_____		
Maintenance						$_____		
							$_____	$_____
Materials Handling							$_____	
Factory Office								
	$_____	$_____	$_____	$_____				
Bases:								
Pounds handled								
Direct labor cost								
Rates								

PART 6

Hudak Mills, Inc. has two service departments that not only serve the two producing departments but also one another. The relationships between the four departments can be expressed as follows:

Service Departments	Percentage of Services Consumed by Departments				Service Costs To Be Distributed
	Milling Dept.	Planing Dept.	Utilities Dept.	Maintenance Dept.	
Utilities	50%	40%	–	10%	$25,000
Maintenance.....	40%	35%	25%	–	$40,000

Instructions:

1. Determine the amount of service costs applicable to each service department, using the algebraic method. (Round answers to the nearest whole dollar.)

2. Compute the total factory overhead in each producing department if primary overhead amounts to $90,000 in the Milling Department and $60,000 in the Planing Department. (Round to the nearest dollar.)

	Total	Milling	Planing	Utilities	Maintenance
Primary overhead .	$	$	$	$	$
Distribution of:					
Utilities					
Maintenance ...	_____	_____	_____	_____	_____
	$_____	$_____	$_____	$_____	$_____

CHAPTER 15
FACTORY OVERHEAD:
RESPONSIBILITY ACCOUNTING AND REPORTING

REVIEW SUMMARY

1. The following are prerequisites for a responsibility accounting system to be effective.
   a. The individual in charge of each responsibility classification should be accountable for the expenses of that activity.
   b. Each individual's budget should clearly identify the costs controllable by that person.
   c. Management should provide a complete clarification of the objectives and responsibilities of all levels of the organization.
   d. The lines of communication should be open between the accounting department, the responsible supervisors, and executive management.
   e. Any overhead charges shown on a responsibility report furnished to a supervisor should be limited to those expenses over which the supervisor has control

2. The distribution of service hours provided to a recipient department should be based on what is termed a *predetermined billing rate, sold-hour rate, charging rate,* or *transfer rate.* This rate is determined as follows:
   a. Estimate or budget costs of any service department according to their nature.
   b. Classify costs as fixed or variable.
   c. Determine a rate by dividing total estimated departmental cost by the number of use hours the service is expected to be needed.
   d. Compare actual service department costs incurred in the department with estimated or budgeted costs.

3. EDP services provide an example of the need for careful attention to the use of appropriate billing rates. The EDP department should develop a service charge that users can include in their departmental budgets. The price of a given system is a predetermined rate including fixed and variable costs or a fixed amount plus a variable amount per transaction, the volume of which would affect the total processing time. This type of one-rate allocation may be supplanted by the partitioning of the computer into cost centers, with major costs classified as direct costs to a cost center.

4. Maintenance cost is a good example of the problem associated with assigning cost responsibility. Maintenance supervisors believe that their department incurs no cost, because all costs are for the benefit of the user departments, whereas factory supervisors argue that they have no influence on either personnel or machinery costs of the maintenance department. The control is really twofold: factory supervisors control the amount of maintenance work, while maintenance supervisors control the quantity of people and materials required to serve the various departments.

5. In the direct materials and direct labor areas, many individuals may be assigned the responsibility for cost incurred, thus obscuring individual responsibility. The variances from a predetermined standard for direct materials result in materials price variances, materials quantity or mix and yield variances, and excessive defective work, rejects, or scrap costs. The deviations from a predetermined norm for direct labor result in pay rate variations, efficiency variations, and overtime costs.

6. All supervisors are responsible for costs incurred by their subordinates. Monthly reports that compare actual results with budget allowances should be issued to allow short-run comparisons of those costs for which operating management is responsible. Variable costs are generally controllable at the departmental level, while fixed costs are not. Certain variable costs, such as employee fringe benefits, are controllable only at a higher level, whereas certain *committed fixed costs*, such as equipment depreciation, and *programmed fixed costs*, such as the number of department heads, may be controlled by the department manager.

7. In responsibility accounting, the emphasis rests upon the comparison of actual departmental costs with budgeted costs exclusive of service department costs. Many accountants believe that only controllable costs for which the department head is responsible should be compared and not the total overhead. An idle capacity variance based entirely on departmental costs without any allocation of service department costs may also be calculated.

8. A service department's cost variances need a great deal of additional investigation. The manager of the service department is responsible for the variance between the actual cost and the cost based on the number of hours or service units charged out. The manager of the producing department receiving the services is responsible for the number of hours or service units consumed in the department.

9. *Responsibility-performance reports* are accountability reports intended to inform managers of their performance in responsible areas and to motivate managers to generate the direct action needed to improve performance. *Information reports* serve the broader purpose of providing managers with information relevant to their areas of interest. Responsibility-performance reports should:

a. Be addressed primarily to the individuals responsible for controlling the items covered in the reports.
b. Be consistent in form and content each time they are issued.
c. Be prompt and timely.
d. Be issued regularly.
e. Be easy to understand.
f. Convey sufficient but not excessive detail.
g. Include comparative figures of predetermined standards and actual results.
h. Analyze underlying data and reasons for poor performance.
i. Be stated in physical units as well as in dollars.
j. Highlight departmental efficiencies and inefficiencies.

PART 1

Instructions: *Place a check mark in the appropriate column to indicate whether each of the following statements is **True** or **False**.*

	True	False
1. A well-designed information system should provide a control mechanism encompassing responsibility accounting.	____	____
2. Responsibility accounting is based on the concept that the individual in charge of each responsibility classification should be accountable for the expenses of his or her activity.	____	____
3. Generally, costs charged directly to a department, with the exception of fixed costs, are controllable by the department's manager.	____	____
4. The distribution of service hours to the user department is based on what is called a billing rate.	____	____
5. A billing rate is determined by dividing the total estimated departmental cost by the number of hours the service is expected to be used.	____	____
6. The charge for the services of a data processing department is usually based on a fixed amount per transaction plus a variable amount.	____	____
7. Experience indicates that availability of hours of data processing time are often utilized at a rate less than 80%.	____	____
8. Maintenance engineers control the quantity of people and materials required to serve the various departments, while factory supervisors control the amount of maintenance work.	____	____
9. It is usually easy to pinpoint responsibility for direct materials and direct labor costs because few individuals are responsible for such costs.	____	____
10. In the materials area, variances from predetermined standards result in price variations, efficiency variations, and mix and yield variances.	____	____
11. Supervisors are responsible for costs incurred by their subordinates.	____	____
12. Lease payments would be an example of a programmed fixed expense.	____	____
13. Committed fixed expenses are those that can be changed in the short run.	____	____
14. In responsibility accounting, emphasis rests upon the comparison of actual departmental expenses with budgeted costs exclusive of service department costs.	____	____
15. Information reports serve a broader set of goals than responsibility performance reports.	____	____

PART 2

Instructions: *In the blank space at the left of each of the following items, place the letter from the right-hand column that identifies the term that best matches the statement in the column on the left. No letter should be used more than once.*

_____ 1. Include productivity.

_____ 2. Provides a control mechanism encompassing responsibility accounting and makes meaningful cost data available for making decisions.

_____ 3. Should be adapted to permit recording of controllable or accountable costs.

_____ 4. Based on a classification of managerial departments at every level in the organization for the purpose of establishing a budget for each.

_____ 5. The starting point for a responsibility accounting information system.

_____ 6. Especially effective in conveying qualitative information and analyzing and interpreting quantitative data.

_____ 7. Basis of distribution of service hours to the recipient center.

_____ 8. A basis of cost apportionment that has limitations because it fails to contribute to efficient use of an EDP facility.

_____ 9. Include planning ability, market share, and dealer opinion.

_____ 10. Especially effective in offering opportunities to convey information, raise questions, and voice opinions.

_____ 11. Control the amount of maintenance work performed.

_____ 12. Control the quantity of people and materials required to serve the maintenance needs of various departments.

_____ 13. Include reliability, cooperation, and flexibility.

_____ 14. Deviation from a predetermined standard for direct materials may result in these.

_____ 15. Fixed costs that can be readily changed in the short run.

_____ 16. Fixed costs such as equipment depreciation or lease payments.

_____ 17. Issued for the purpose of providing managers with information relevant to their areas of interest.

_____ 18. Issued to inform managers of their performance in responsible areas and to motivate them to generate the direct action needed to improve their performance.

_____ 19. The concept of management's consideration of only those items that vary materially from plans.

_____ 20. Of most relevance in deciding which costs should be assigned to a responsibility center.

a. organization chart
b. interdependency factors
c. responsibility-performance reports
d. degree of controllability
e. percentage of general utilization
f. billing rate
g. written reports
h. chart of accounts
i. committed fixed costs
j. mix and yield variations
k. oral reports
l. management by exception
m. factory supervisors
n. information reports
o. information system
p. programmed fixed costs
q. responsibility accounting
r. maintenance supervisors
s. internal factors
t. environmental factors

PART 3

Instructions: *In the blank space at the left of each of the following items, place the letter of the choice that most correctly completes each item.*

_____ 1. Which of the following should generally not appear on a monthly cost control report of a department manager?
   a. Departmental direct labor cost
   b. Departmental supplies cost
   c. Salary of department manager
   d. Cost of materials used in the department
   e. None of the above

(AICPA adapted)

_____ 2. Periodic internal performance reports based on a responsibility accounting system should not:
   a. distinguish between controllable and uncontrollable costs
   b. be related to the organization chart
   c. include allocated fixed overhead in determining performance variation
   d. include variances between actual and controllable costs
   e. all of the above

(AICPA adapted)

_____ 3. The concept of management by exception refers to management's:
   a. lack of a predetermined plan
   b. consideration of only rare events
   c. consideration of items selected at random
   d. consideration of only those items that vary materially from plans
   e. none of the above

(AICPA adapted)

_____ 4. Of most relevance in deciding how or which costs should be assigned to a responsibility center is the degree of:
   a. avoidability
   b. causality
   c. controllability
   d. variability
   e. none of the above

(AICPA adapted)

_____ 5. Of most relevance in deciding how indirect costs should be assigned to a product is the degree of:
   a. avoidability
   b. causality
   c. controllability
   d. variability
   e. none of the above

(AICPA adapted)

_____ 6. The most desirable measure for evaluating the performance of the departmental manager is departmental:
   a. revenue less controllable expenses
   b. net income
   c. contribution to indirect expenses
   d. revenue less departmental expenses
   e. none of the above

(AICPA adapted)

_____ 7. The term that identifies an accounting system in which the operations of the business are broken down into cost centers and the control function of the supervisor or the manager is emphasized is:
   a. responsibility accounting
   b. operations-research accounting
   c. control accounting
   d. budgetary accounting
   e. none of the above

(AICPA adapted)

_____ 8. A desirable characteristic of a factory overhead control report for a production manager is that:
   a. it is more important that the report be precise than timely
   b. the report should include information on all costs chargeable to the department, regardless of their origin or control
   c. the report should be stated in dollars rather than physical units, so that the department head knows the financial magnitude of any variances
   d. the report should specify those costs controllable by the department head
   e. all of the above

_____ 9. In general, costs incurred under a long-term lease for production equipment, when the lease calls for a level annual payment, are controllable by the:
   a. line supervisor
   b. production vice-president
   c. users of the equipment
   d. company treasurer
   e. none of the above

_____ **10.** The EDP Department provides service to producing departments at the exact level predicted for the current period. Variances in cost for this department are charged to:

    a. producing departments on the basis of usage

    b. producing departments on the basis of capacity provided

    c. miscellaneous overhead

    d. the EDP Department as a spending variance

    e. none of the above

PART 4

Hila Bend Products Inc. has two producing departments (Fabricating and Assembly) and one service department (Utilities). Allocation of fixed service costs is based on standby capacity available to each department. Variable service department costs are charged on the basis of actual consumption. These costs are distributed to departments at a predetermined rate based on variable costs at capacity. Data related to capacity and to the current month of July are as follows:

	Fabricating	Assembly	Utilities
Power consumption (July)	85,000 kwh	45,000 kwh	
Capacity available	100,000 kwh	50,000 kwh	
Fixed cost (July)			$25,000
Budgeted variable cost at capacity			48,000
Variable cost (July)			40,000

Instructions:

1. Compute the rate per kwh used to distribute variable costs.

2. Distribute the fixed and variable Utilities Department costs for the month to the Fabricating and Assembly Departments. (Round to the nearest dollar.)

	Fabricating	Assembly
Fixed cost distribution:	$	
		$
Variable cost distribution:		
Total cost distributed	$_____	$_____

3. Determine the over- or underestimated variable cost for July.

Total variable cost .... $

Cost distributed:

    Fabricating .... $

    Assembly ....   _____

                                                 $_____

PART 5

Breakstone Ball Bearings Inc. has two service departments that provide the following data:

Service Center	Monthly Budget	Service Hours Available	Actual Monthly Expense
General Maintenance	$100,000	10,000	$94,000
Machine Repairs	$ 40,000	2,000	45,000

The two service departments serve three producing departments that show the following budgeted and actual cost and service hours data:

Department	Estimated Services Required		Actual Services Used	
	General Maintenance	Machine Repairs	General Maintenance	Machine Repairs
Machining	5,500	1,200	4,600	1,300
Assembling	3,000	600	2,500	650
Finishing	2,000	200	1,600	250

Instructions:

1. Determine the billing-hour rates for the two service departments.

   General Maintenance:

   Machine Reparis:

2. Compute the amounts charged to the producing departments for services rendered.

	Department			
	Machining	Assembling	Finishing	Total
General Maintenance	$	$	$	$
Machine Repairs				
Total	$_____	$_____	$_____	$_____

3. Determine the spending variance for the two service departments, assuming that 75% of the budgeted expense is fixed in General Maintenance and 60% in Machine Repairs.

	Monthly Budget	Fixed Cost Percentage	Fixed Cost	Variable Cost	Variable Rate per Hour
General Maintenance	$	%	$	$	$
Machine Repairs	$	%	$	$	$

	General Maintenance	Machine Repairs
Actual overhead	$	$
Budget allowance:		
Fixed overhead	$	$
Variable overhead	_____	_____
Spending variance	$_____	$_____

4. Determine the idle capacity for the two service departments.

	General Maintenance	Machine Repairs
Budget allowance	$	$
Costs charged out	_____	_____
Idle capacity variance	$_____	$_____

CHAPTER 16
BUDGETING:
PROFITS, SALES, COSTS, AND EXPENSES

REVIEW SUMMARY

1. *Profit planning* is a well thought-out operational plan with its financial implications expressed in the form of long- and short-range income statements, balance sheets, and cash and working capital projections. Using the *a priori* method of setting profit objectives, management specifies a given rate of return that it seeks to realize in the long run by means of planning toward that end. Under the *a posteriori* method, the determination of profit objectives is subordinated to the planning, and the objectives emerge as the product of the planning itself. Using a target rate of profit derived from experience, expectations, or comparisons, management establishes a relative profit standard considered satisfactory for the company under the *pragmatic* method.

2. Market trends and economic factors, inflation, growth of population, personal consumption expenditures, and indexes of industrial production form the background for long-range planning. Quantitative and dollar sales estimates for a three- to five-year forecast may be developed from this information. Long-range plans with their future expectancy of profits and growth must be incorporated into a shorter-range budget for both planning and control of the contemplated course of action. Although one year is the usual planning period, the short-range budget may cover periods of three, six, or twelve months, depending on the nature of the business.

3. A company's organization chart and its chart of accounts form the basic framework on which to build a coordinated and efficient system of managerial planning and budgetary control. The budget process is usually directed by a budget committee that decides on general policies, reviews and suggests revisions in individual budget estimates, approves budgets, analyzes budget reports, and recommends action designed to improve efficiency. Budget development should include adherence to the following principles: (a) provide adequate guidance so that all management levels are working on the same assumptions, targeted objectives, and agenda; (b) encourage participation in the budgeting process at each level within the organization; (c) structure the climate of budget preparation to eliminate anxiety and defensiveness; (d) structure the preparation of the budget so that there is a reasonably high probability of successful attainment of objectives; and (e) evaluate numerous sets of assumptions in developing the budget through the use of computers and probability theory. Principles of budget implementation include establishing reward contingencies that will lead to achieving the organizational objectives, focusing on rewarding achievement rather than punishing failure, and providing rapid feedback on the performance of each work team or individual.

4. Cost accounting and budgeting play an important role in influencing individual and group behavior at these stages of the management process: (a) setting goals, (b) informing employees of the contributions expected of them, (c) motivating desired performance, (d) evaluating performance, and (e) suggesting corrective action. A manager's attitude toward the budget will depend greatly upon the relationship within the mangement group. Suggestions for motivating a company's personnel include (a) a compensation and promotion system that ties results to rewards, (b) a performance appraisal system that employees understand, (c) an open and honest communications system, (d) a counseling and career-planning system that considers employee skills and capacities, and (e) a system that emphasizes attainable standards.

5. One of the most important and most difficult-to-predict elements in a budgetary control system is a realistic sales forecast based on analysis of past sales and the present market. The preparation of sales estimates is usually the responsibility of the marketing manager, assisted by individual salespeople and market research personnel. In most large organizations, the forecasting procedure usually starts with known factors such as (a) the company's sales of past years broken down by product groups and profit margins, (b) industry or trade sales volumes and profits, and (c) unusual factors influencing sales in the past. In addition, a sound basis for determining future sales may be established by applying probability analysis techniques to the consideration of general business conditions, the industry's prospects, the company's potential share of the total industry market, and the plans of the competitors.

6. A sales budget should not only be placed on a monthly basis for each product, but should also be classified by territories or districts and by types of customers. A detailed sales budget can be a strong means for analyzing possible new trade outlets and for identifying and investigating reasons for a drop in sales. Prior to the final acceptance of a sales budget, the factory's capacity to produce the estimated quantities must be determined. If factory capacity is available, production should be planned at a level that will keep workers and equipment operating all year. A sales forecast follow-up should occur at intervals for pur-

poses of determining the (a) accuracy of past estimates, (b) location of major estimation errors, (c) best method by which to update estimates, and (d) steps needed for improving the making and monitoring of future estimates.

7. The *production budget* is stated in physical units and deals with the scheduling of operations, the determination of volume, and the establishment of maximum and minimum quantities of materials and finished goods inventories.

    With the forecast sales translated into physical units in the production budget, the estimated manufacturing costs essential to the sales and production program can be computed. The *direct materials budget* indicates the quantity and cost of materials required to produce the predetermined units of finished goods and is usually the first cost budget to be prepared. The *direct labor budget*, based upon specifications drawn up by production engineers, guides the personnel department in determining the number and types of workers needed. The *factory overhead budget* is usually prepared on a departmental basis, with expenses grouped according to natural classification. It is usually prepared as a report that enables executive management and individual department supervisors to make monthly comparisons of budgeted and actual expenses. Not only must inventory quantities be determined for materials, work in process, and finished goods, but the inventories must be costed in order to make available the necessary information leading to preparation of a budgeted cost of goods manufactured and sold statement.

8. The company's chart of accounts is also the basis for budgetary control of commercial expenses, which include both marketing and administrative expenses. To control commercial expenses effectively, it is necessary to group them by functional activities or operating units. The *mar-keting expenses budget* is prepared by the supervisors of functions connected with marketing activities, which include the costs of obtaining and filling an order. The *administrative expenses budget* includes costs such as professional fees and certain taxes that are peculiar to the administrative function, as well as costs such as purchasing and personnel that are shared with the production and marketing activities.

9. A *budgeted income statement* contains summaries of the sales, manufacturing, and expense budgets. It projects net income and it offers management the opportunity to judge the accuracy of the budget work and to investigate causes of variances. Percentages of sales figures are often included to aid in determining whether income statement components are in line with expectations.

10. A balance sheet for the beginning of the budget period, incorporating all changes in assets, liabilities, and capital in the budgets submitted by the various departments, is the starting point for the preparation of a *budgeted balance sheet* for the end of the budget period. The budgeted balance sheet discloses unfavorable ratios and serves as a check on the accuracy of all other budgets.

11. Recent years have seen increasing recognition of the importance of financial forecasts for external users, because investors and potential investors seek to enhance the process of predicting the future. The AICPA recommends that financial forecasts should (a) be presented in the same format as historical financial statements; (b) include a description of what management intends to present; (c) include a statement that the assumptions are based on information existing at the time the prospective information was prepared; (d) include a caveat that the prospective results may not be achieved; and (e) include a summary of significant assumptions.

PART 1

Instructions: *Place a check mark in the appropriate column to indicate whether each of the following statements is* ***True*** *or* ***False***.

	True	False
1. In most firms, budgeting is one of the most popular management activities.	___	___
2. Under the *pragmatic* method of setting profit objectives, management uses a target rate of profit derived from experience, expectations, or comparisons.	___	___
3. Accountants cannot ignore the behavioral sciences because the "information for decision making" function of accounting is essentially a behavioral function.	___	___
4. The rate of return on capital employed is an important statistic in long-range profit planning.	___	___
5. A complete motivational system for factory workers is unnecessary as long as you have an incentive pay system tied to productivity.	___	___
6. Continuous budgeting adds a month or quarter in the future as each current month or quarter is ended.	___	___
7. One of the advantages of profit planning is that sales forecasting can be reduced to an exact science.	___	___
8. A budgetary system has performed inadequately whenever it motivates an individual to take an action that is not in the best interests of the organization.	___	___
9. A company's organization chart and its chart of accounts form the basic framework on which to build a coordinated and efficient system of budgetary control.	___	___
10. Studies have usually shown that there is a low correlation between employees' acceptance of a budget and their general attitude towards the company's management.	___	___
11. The task of preparing the sales budget usually involves judging and evaluating both external and internal influences.	___	___
12. The sales variable is often the budget component that is the most difficult to predict with reasonable precision.	___	___
13. An advantage of a budgeted balance sheet is that it discloses unfavorable ratios that management may wish to change.	___	___
14. The AICPA is generally opposed to the inclusion of financial forecasts in annual reports.	___	___
15. A company's marketing activities can be divided into two broad categories: (a) obtaining an order and (b) filling an order.	___	___

PART 2

Instructions: *In the blank space at the left of each of the following items, place the letter from the right-hand column that identifies the term that best matches the statement in the column on the left. No letter should be used more than once.*

_____ 1. Represents the expected profit level or target to which management strives.

_____ 2. Using this method of setting profit objectives, the profit objectives take precedence over the planning process.

_____ 3. Method under which the determination of profit objectives is subordinated to the planning, and the objectives emerge as the product of the planning itself.

_____ 4. Method of setting profit objectives under which management, using a target rate of profit derived from experience, expectations, or comparisons, establishes a relative profit standard considered satisfactory for the company.

_____ 5. Provides the basic framework on which to build a coordinated and efficient system of managerial planning and budgetary control.

_____ 6. Directs the budgeting process and is usually composed of the sales manager, the production manager, the chief engineer, the treasurer, and the controller.

_____ 7. Level of revenue or cost that the organization predicts will occur.

_____ 8. Benefits of this include shortening of the planning cycle, time for reconsidering the planning assumptions, and ease of continuous budgeting.

_____ 9. The costs of obtaining an order and the costs of filling an order.

_____ 10. The general trend of industrial activity, governmental policies, purchasing power of the population, and changing buying habits.

_____ 11. Sales trends, factory capacities, seasonal products, and establishment of quotas for salespersons.

_____ 12. Incorporates all changes in assets, liabilities, and capital in the budgets submitted by the various departments.

_____ 13. A sound basis for determining future sales may be established by applying these to the consideration of general business conditions, the industry's prospects, and the plans of competitive companies.

_____ 14. Should not only be placed on a monthly basis for each product, but should also be classified by territories or districts and by types of customers.

_____ 15. Deals with the scheduling of operations, the determination of volume, and the establishment of maximum and minimum quantities of materials and finished goods inventories.

_____ 16. The estimated cost of materials, labor, and factory overhead, often based on standard costs, are summarized in this.

_____ 17. Indicates the quantity and cost of materials required to produce the predetermined units of finished goods and is usually the first cost budget to be prepared.

_____ 18. Based on specifications drawn up by product engineers, guides the personnel department in determining the number and type of workers needed.

_____ 19. Include both marketing and administrative expenses.

_____ 20. Using this, plans can be updated throughout the budget period, and in some cases, planning horizons can be extended beyond the current budget period.

a. *a posteriori* method
b. budget committee
c. budgeted cost of goods manufactured and sold statement
d. internal influences
e. probability analysis techniques
f. direct labor budget
g. continuous budgeting
h. sales budget
i. marketing expenses
j. production budget
k. pragmatic method
l. commercial expenses
m. *a priori* method
n. direct materials budget
o. organization chart
p. budgeted balance sheet
q. external influences
r. forecast
s. budget
t. computerized budgeting

Instructions: *In the blank space at the left of each of the following items, place the letter of the choice that most correctly completes each item.*

_____ 1. A continuous budget:
  a. drops the current month or quarter and adds a future month or quarter as the current month or quarter is completed
  b. presents the plan for only one activity level and does not adjust to activity level changes
  c. presents the plan for a range of activity so that the plan can be adjusted for activity level changes
  d. classifies budget requests by activity and estimates the benefits arising from each activity
  e. none of the above
             (ICMA adapted)

_____ 2. Probability (risk) analysis:
  a. ignores probability weights under 50%
  b. is only for situations in which there are three or fewer possible outcomes
  c. does not enhance the usefulness of sensitivity analysis data
  d. is an extension of sensitivity analysis
  e. none of the above
             (AICPA adapted)

_____ 3. When management sets profit objectives by specifying a given rate of return, which it then seeks to realize in the long run, the procedure is called the:
  a. *a priori* method
  b. ad hoc method
  c. pragmatic method
  d. *a posteriori* method
  e. none of the above

_____ 4. The development of an atmosphere of profit-mindedness and the encouragement of attitudes of cost-mindedness and maximum resource utilization is an advantage of:
  a. production analysis studies
  b. product costing
  c. sales objectives
  d. profit planning
  e. none of the above

_____ 5. Of the following items, the one used to form the background for long-range plans is:
  a. economic factors and market trends
  b. current inventory levels
  c. direct labor costs
  d. precise future product costs
  e. none of the above

_____ 6. A principal function of the budget committee is to:
  a. determine inventory values
  b. prepare the budget report
  c. suggest revisions to budget estimates
  d. prepare individual budget estimates
  e. all of the above

_____ 7. To point out possible unfavorable financial ratios at the end of a forecast period, managemet should prepare a:
  a. sales budget
  b. forecasted cash flow statement
  c. treasurer's budget
  d. budgeted balance sheet
  e. none of the above

_____ 8. Which of the following is a limitation of profit planning?
  a. Installation of a budgetary system takes time.
  b. The budget could focus management's attention on the wrong goals.
  c. Profit planning does not eliminate the role of administration.
  d. All of the above
  e. None of the above

_____ 9. The budget component that is usually the most difficult to predict with reasonable precision is:
  a. sales
  b. production
  c. factory overhead
  d. commercial expenses
  e. none of the above

_____ 10. If estimated sales and ending inventory in units are 60,000 and 12,000 respectively, and the amount of required production is 54,000 units, the beginning inventory in units would be:
  a. 6,000   b. -0-   c. 12,000   d. 3,000   e. none of the above

PART 4

Lin Qui Products prepares a budget forecast of its needs for the coming year. Last year's data are presented for the three models of video cassette recorders (VCRs) sold by the company. In addition, salespersons' estimates for the coming year are as follows:

VCR Model No.	Last Year Unit Price	Last Year Unit Sales	Last Year Units— Ending Inventory	This Year Salespersons' Unit Estimates
007	$500	500	40	1,000
2525	450	700	20	1,600
1984	400	1,200	110	2,600

Management notes that the salespersons are very optimistic and that their predictions of sales levels must be halved to be realistic. In addition, the company wants an ending inventory equal to 5% of sales.

Instructions:

1. Complete the schedule below, predicting unit sales for each VCR and the production required to provide for sales and inventory needs.

VCR Model No.	Predicted Unit Sales	Less: Beginning Inventory	Plus: Ending Inventory	Production Required
007	_____	_____	_____	_____
2525	_____	_____	_____	_____
1984	_____	_____	_____	_____

2. Determine the dollar revenues to be obtained for each VCR.

VCR Model No.	Unit Sales	Unit Price	Total Sales
007	_____	_____	_____
2525	_____	_____	_____
1984	_____	_____	_____
Total sales			$_____

3. Determine the working capital required if each VCR produced costs 60% of the selling price and if the company requires working capital equal to 20% of total production costs.

VCR Model No.	Units Produced	Production Cost
007	_____	_____
2525	_____	_____
1984	_____	_____
Total production cost		$_____

Working capital required:

PART 5

The Fiorelli Noodle Company prepared the following figures as a basis for its 19B budget:

Product	Expected Sales	Estimated Per-Unit Sales Price	Required Materials per Unit Pasta	Salsa
Napoli	40,000 units	$5	4 lbs.	2 lbs.
Roma	20,000	8	5 lbs.	–
Venezia............	50,000	3	–	3 lbs.

Estimated inventories at the beginning and desired quantities at the end of 19B are:

Material	Beginning	Ending	Purchase Price per Pound
Pasta.............	5,000 lbs.	6,000 lbs.	$ .50
Salsa	6,000	7,500	1.00

Product	Beginning	Ending	Direct Labor Hours per 1,000 units
Napoli	2,500 units	3,000 units	200
Roma	2,000	1,000	400
Venezia............	5,000	4,000	50

The direct labor cost is budgeted at $20 per hour and variable factory overhead at $10 per hour of direct labor. Fixed factory overhead, estimated to be $100,000, is a joint cost and is not allocated to specific products in developing the master budget for internal management use.

Instructions:

1. Prepare the production budget.

	Napoli	Roma	Venezia
Units required to meet sales budget			
Add desired ending inventories			
Total units required			
Less estimated beginning inventories			
Planned production			

2. Determine the budgeted quantities and dollar amounts of purchase requirements for each material.

	Pasta	Salsa
Napoli..		
Roma		
Venezia		
Add desired ending inventories....................		
Less estimated beginning inventories		
Budgeted quantities of materials purchases............		
Budgeted price per pound........................	$	$
Budgeted dollar amounts of materials purchased	$	$

3. Prepare the manufacturing budgets by product and in total.

	Napoli	Roma	Venezia	Total
Materials:				
Pasta:	$			$
		$		
Salsa:				
	_____	_____	$_____	_____
	$_____	$_____	$_____	
Direct labor:				
	$			$
		$		
	_____	_____	$_____	_____
	$_____	$_____	$_____	$_____
Factory overhead—variable:				
	$			$
		$		
	_____	_____	$_____	_____
	$_____	$_____	$_____	$_____
Total variable manufacturing cost..................	$_____	$_____	$_____	$
Fixed manufacturing cost				_____
Total manufacturing cost				$_____

PART 6

The following financial information relates to the operations of B.J. Hastings Company for the year ending December 31, 19C:

Materials:		
Beginning inventory	$	87,500
Purchases		568,663
Ending inventory		107,125
Direct labor		2,161,680
Factory overhead		226,503
Finished goods:		
Beginning inventory		84,745
Ending inventory		60,895
Sales		3,650,000
Commercial expenses:		
Marketing expenses		300,000
Administrative expenses		200,000
Other income		90,000
Other expenses		65,000
Income tax rate		30%

Instructions:

1. Prepare a budgeted cost of goods manufactured and sold statement.

B.J. Hastings Company
Budgeted Cost of Goods Manufactured and Sold Statement
For the Year Ending December 31, 19C

Materials:

Beginning inventory . . . . $

Add purchases . . . . _____

Total goods available for use . . . . $

Less ending inventory . . . . _____

Cost of materials used . . . . $

Direct labor . . . .

Factory overhead . . . . _____

Total manufacturing cost . . . . $

Add beginning inventory of finished goods . . . . _____

Cost of goods available for sale . . . . $

Less ending inventory of finished goods . . . . _____

Cost of goods sold . . . . $_____

2. Prepare a budgeted income statement, including percentage of sales figures.

B.J. Hastings Company
Budgeted Income Statement
For the Year Ending December 31, 19C

	Amount	% of Sales
Sales	$	
Cost of goods sold	_____	_____
Gross profit	$	
Commercial expenses:		
Marketing expenses		
Administrative expenses	_____	_____
Income from operations	$	
Other (income) expense	_____	_____
Income before income tax	$	
Less provision for income tax	_____	_____
Net income	$_____	_____

(Round dollar amounts to the nearest whole dollar and percentages to the nearest tenth of a percent.)

PART 7

The 19D forecast for Lozado Corporation appears below in the form of a projected trial balance as of December 31, 19D (000s omitted):

Cash	2,400	
Accounts Receivable	120,000	
Inventory (1/1/19D, 50,000 units)	60,000	
Plant and Equipment	480,000	
Accumulated Depreciation		82,000
Accounts Payable		65,000
Accrued Payables		40,000
Notes Payable (due in 1 year)		75,000
Common Stock		95,000
Retained Earnings		197,900
Sales		900,000
Other Income		15,000
Manufacturing costs:		
Materials	225,000	
Direct Labor	270,000	
Variable Factory Overhead	140,000	
Depreciation	15,000	
Other Fixed Factory Overhead	9,000	
Marketing:		
Salaries	21,000	
Commissions	25,000	
Promotion and Advertising	55,000	
General and administrative:		
Salaries	25,000	
Travel	4,000	
Office Costs	11,000	
Income Tax	?	
Dividends	7,500	
	$1,469,900	$1,469,900

Adjustments for the change in inventory and for income tax have not been made. The scheduled production for 19D is 500,000 units, while the sales volume will reach 475,000 units. A full cost, first-in, first-out inventory system is used. The company is subject to a 30% income tax rate.

Instructions:
1. Prepare a projected statement of income and retained earnings for the year 19D, including the computation of the cost of the ending inventory. (Use the forms provided on the following two pages. Round unit costs to four decimal places and dollar totals to the nearest dollar.)

Lozado Corporation
Projected Statement of Income and Retained Earnings
For the Year Ending December 31, 19D
(000s omitted)

Revenue:

  Sales ....

  Other income ....   _____

Costs of goods manufactured and sold:

  Materials ....

  Direct labor ....

  Variable factory overhead ....

  Fixed factory overhead .... _____

  Beginning inventory .... _____

  Ending inventory .... _____

Marketing:

  Salaries ....

  Commissions ....

  Promotion and advertising .... _____

General and administrative:

  Salaries ....

  Travel ....

  Office costs .... _____ _____ _____

Income before tax ....

Income tax .... _____

Net income ....

Beginning retained earnings .... _____

  Subtotal ....

  Less Dividends .... _____

Ending retained earnings .... ═══════════

Inventory

  Units:

   Beginning inventory . . . .

   Added to inventory . . . .   _____

   Ending inventory . . . .   _____

  Cost:

   19D Manufacturing costs . . . .   _____

   Units manufactured . . . .   _____

   Cost per unit . . . .

   Ending units . . . .   _____

   Cost of ending inventory . . . .   _____

2. Prepare a budgeted balance sheet for 19D.

Lozado Corporation
Budgeted Balance Sheet
December 31, 19D
(000s omitted)

Assets

Current assets:

 Cash . . . . $

 Accounts receivable . . . .

 Inventory . . . .   _____ $

Plant and equipment . . . . $

 Less accumulated depreciation . . . .   _____   _____

  Total assets . . . . $_____

Liabilities and Shareholders' Equity

Current liabilities:

 Accounts payable . . . . $

 Accrued payables . . . .

 Income tax payable . . . .

 Notes payable . . . .   _____ $

Shareholders' equity:

 Common stock . . . . $

 Retained earnings . . . .   _____   _____

 Total liabilities and shareholders' equity . . . . $_____

CHAPTER 17
BUDGETING: CAPITAL EXPENDITURES, RESEARCH AND DEVELOPMENT EXPENDITURES, AND CASH; PERT/COST; THE FLEXIBLE BUDGET

REVIEW SUMMARY

1. *Capital expenditures* are long-term commitments of resources to realize future benefits. Managerial control of capital expenditures requires facts regarding engineering estimates, expected sales volumes, production costs, and marketing costs. Management is interested in making certain that a project will contribute to the earnings position of the company.

2. The *research and development (R&D) budget* involves identifying program components and estimating their costs. It is considered the best tool for (a) balancing the R&D program, (b) coordinating the program with the company's other projects, and (c) checking certain phases of nonfinancial planning. The overall R&D program should be supported by a specific budget request that indicates the jobs or steps within each project, the necessary labor hours, the service department time required, and required direct departmental funds. R&D costs generally should be expensed in the period incurred, due to the uncertainty of the length of future benefit to the company.

3. A *cash budget* involves detailed estimates of anticipated cash receipts and disbursements for the budget period. It (a) indicates cash requirements for current operations, (b) focuses on cash usage priorities, currently unavoidable and required versus postponable or permanently avoidable, (c) indicates the effect on cash position of such factors as seasonal requirements and speed in collecting receivables, (d) indicates the availability of cash for taking discounts, (e) indicates the cash requirements for plant expansion, (f) assists in planning the financial requirements of bond retirements, income taxes, and pension funds, (g) shows the availability of excess funds for investment, (h) shows the need for additional funds from sources such as bank loans, and (i) serves as a basis for evaluating the actual cash management performance of individuals. A long-range cash management projection may cover periods ranging from three to five years and is useful in planning business growth, investments in projects, and introduction of new products. A yearly cash budget should usually be prepared by months, with changes made at the end of each month to incorporate deviations from the previous forecast and to add a month to replace the month just past. A short-range cash budget depicts the daily availability of cash for current operations and indicates needs for short-term financing.

4. In cash budget preparation, all anticipated cash receipts are carefully estimated, based on the sales budget and the company's experience in collecting accounts receivable. Similarly, cash requirements for items such as payroll, which is based on the labor budget, must be determined. After all the cash receipts and cash disbursements have been estimated for each month of the budget year, the year-end cash balance for inclusion in the budgeted balance sheet can be determined.

5. *Electronic cash management* involves cash concentration by means of nationwide electronic transfers that accelerate the collection of deposits from local banks into a central account on a same-day basis. For whatever number of bank accounts a firm may have, electronic balance reporting affords a valuable aid to cash management. *Electronic funds transfer systems* are designed to reduce the number of paper documents and to increase the use of electronic data in carrying out banking cash transfer functions, thus reducing bank transaction costs and expediting cash transfers.

6. The merchandise budget of a retail store shows predetermined sales and profits, generally on a six-month basis following the two merchandising seasons. It also includes purchases, expenses, capital expenditures, cash, and annual statements. Other nonmanufacturing businesses, such as banks and insurance companies, should also create long-range profit plans coordinating long-term goals and objectives. In spite of the many decades in which governmental budgeting has been practiced, the general public is increasingly critical of services received for money spent. The difficulty of planning and budgeting in governments and nonprofit organizations is measuring the benefits or outputs of programs.

7. *Zero-base budgeting* is a budget-planning procedure for the reevaluation of an organization's program and expenditures. It requires each manager to justify the entire budget request in detail and places the burden of proof on the manager to justify why authorization to spend any money at all should be granted.

8. Many companies have been using *PERT* or *CPM* in planning, scheduling, and costing such diverse projects as constructing buildings, installing equipment, and research and development. PERT is a probabilistic diagram of the interrelationships of a complex series of activities. The major use of PERT is in the determination of the longest time duration for the completion of an entire project.

9. The fact that costs and expenses are affected by fluctuations in volume limits the use of the fixed budget and leads

to the use of a flexible budget. The preparation of a flexible budget results from the development of formulas indicating the fixed amount or variable rate for each department and for each account within a department. The application of the formulas to the level of activity actually experienced produces the allowable expenditures for the volume of activity attained. These budget figures are compared with actual costs in order to measure the performance of each department.

10. The application of data-processing techniques to the determination of the fixed and variable elements in each departmental expense provides the necessary tools for budgetary control and responsibility reporting. A *step chart* may be used to enhance the development of monthly departmental budgets by subexpense classifications. Flexible budgets for service departments permit the establishment of a fairer sold-hour rate by charging operating departments with fixed expenses regardless of activity and with a variable cost based on departmental activity. In contrast to the factory overhead budget, which bases its expense levels in most cases on direct labor hours, machine hours, or direct labor dollars, the budget for marketing and administrative expenses is most often based on net sales.

PART 1

Instructions: *Place a check mark in the appropriate column to indicate whether each of the following statements is **True or False**.*

	True	False
1. Capital expenditures are long-term commitments of resources to realize future benefits.	____	____
2. The flexible budget is a useful planning device because it provides cost behavior information that can be used to evaluate the effects of different volumes of activity and profit.	____	____
3. Research and development projects compete with other projects for available financial resources.	____	____
4. Research and development costs generally should be capitalized and written off over the periods of anticipated benefit.	____	____
5. Even of a company does not prepare extensive budgets for sales and production, it should set up a budget of cash receipts and disbursements as an aid to cash management.	____	____
6. In contrast to the budget for commercial expenses, which bases its expense levels on direct labor hours, machine hours, or direct labor dollars, the factory overhead budget is often based on net sales.	____	____
7. Electronic funds transfer systems are designed to reduce the number of paper documents and to increase the use of electronic data in carrying out banking transactions.	____	____
8. A probabilistic budget is developed based on one set of assumptions as to the most likely performance in the forthcoming period.	____	____
9. Manufacturing expenses are prepared on a flexible budget basis whereas marketing and administrative expenses are prepared on a fixed budget basis.	____	____
10. Nonmanufacturing businesses generally do a better job of planning and budgeting than do manufacturing businesses.	____	____
11. The difficulty of planning and budgeting in governments and nonprofit organizations is measuring the benefits or outputs of programs.	____	____
12. In zero-base budgeting, what a manager is already spending is acceptable as a starting point for budget negotiations.	____	____
13. The major task of PERT is the determination of the longest time duration for the completion of an entire project.	____	____
14. If available slack time is not exceeded, noncritical activities can be delayed without delaying a project's completion date.	____	____
15. The PERT/cost system assigns cost to time and activities, thereby providing total financial planning and control by functional responsibility.	____	____

PART 2

Instructions: *In the blank space at the left of each of the following items, place the letter from the right-hand column that identifies the term that best matches the statement in the column on the left. No letter should be used more than once.*

_____ 1. Long-term commitments of resources to realize future benefits.

_____ 2. Provision must be made in the current budget for these.

_____ 3. Will not be implemented in the current budget period and need only be stated in general terms.

_____ 4. A budget adjusted to actual volume.

_____ 5. The translation of research findings or other knowledge into a plan for a new product or for a significant improvement to an existing product.

_____ 6. Type of account to generally charge research and development costs to because of the uncertainty of the extent or length of future benefit to the company.

_____ 7. Type of account that public utilities charge research and development to because of the rate-regulated aspects of the industry.

_____ 8. Involves detailed estimates of anticipated cash receipts and disbursements for the budget period.

_____ 9. The inclusion of these in external financial statements should be provided when they will enhance the reliability of users' predictions.

_____ 10. Designed to reduce the number of paper documents and to increase the use of electronic data in carrying out banking transactions.

_____ 11. Involves cash concentration by means of nationwide electronic transfers that accelerate the collection of deposits from local banks into a central account on a same-day basis.

_____ 12. Use of cash during the time that it takes a check to be cleared back to a central account.

_____ 13. In zero-base budgeting, identifies an activity in a definite manner for evaluation and comparison with other activities.

_____ 14. In a PERT network, shortening of the total time to complete a task can only be accomplished by shortening this.

_____ 15. Using statistical estimation to spread a forecast of the total monthly minor cash flow components over the days of the month in order to reflect the known intramonth cash flow.

_____ 16. A tool to assist management in the analysis of alternatives as the basis for rational decision making.

_____ 17. A budget planning procedure for the reevaluation of an organization's program and expenditures.

_____ 18. A probabilistic diagram of the interrelationships of a complex series of activities.

_____ 19. The construction of a cash forecast from information-system-based data, such as disbursement data from invoices and purchase authorizations.

_____ 20. An integrated management information system designed to furnish management with timely information for planning and controlling schedules and costs of projects.

a. flexible budget
b. cash budget
c. float
d. long-range projects
e. PERT
f. PERT/cost
g. scheduling
h. distribution
i. capital expenditures
j. PPBS
k. expense
l. development
m. critical path
n. financial forecasts
o. zero-base budgeting
p. asset
q. short-range projects
r. electronic funds transfer systems
s. electronic cash management
t. decision package

PART 3

Instructions: *In the blank space at the left of each of the following items, place the letter of the choice that most correctly completes the item.*

_____ 1. A budget system referred to as PPBS:
  a. drops the current month or quarter and adds a future month or quarter as the current month or quarter is completed
  b. consolidates the plans of separate departments into an overall plan
  c. classifies budget requests by activity and estimates the benefits arising from each activity
  d. presents the plan for a range of activity so that the plan can be adjusted for changes in activity levels
  e. all of the above   (ICMA adapted)

_____ 2. The critical path is the:
  a. amount of time an activity may be delayed without delaying the total project beyond its target time
  b. earliest starting time that an activity for a project can begin
  c. shortest time path from the first event to the last event for a project
  d. longest time path from the first event to the last event for a project
  e. none of the above   (ICMA adapted)

_____ 3. In preparing a cash budget, which of the following is usually the starting point for projecting cash requirements?
  a. Fixed assets   d. Inventories
  b. Sales   e. None of the above
  c. Accounts receivables   (CIA adapted)

_____ 4. Zero-based budgeting:
  a. involves the review of changes made to an organization's original budget
  b. does not provide a projection of annual expenditures
  c. is a method peculiar to budgeting by program
  d. involves the review of each cost component from a cost/benefit perspective
  e. emphasizes the relationship of effort to projected annual revenues   (CIA adapted)

_____ 5. A company is controlling a complex project by determining the activities that must take place and the relationship between these activities. Attention then is focused upon those activities that have the greatest influence on the project's estimated completion date. The quantitative technique most relevant to this situation is:
  a. cost-volume-profit analysis   d. queuing analysis
  b. parametric programming   e. none of the above
  c. Program Evaluation and Review Technique (PERT)   (AICPA adapted)

_____ 6. Ginger Company has budgeted its activity for April. Selected data are as follows:

Net income	$120,000
Increases in gross amount of trade accounts receivable during month	35,000
Decrease in accounts payable during month	25,000
Depreciation expense	65,000
Provision for income tax..	80,000
Provision for doubtful accounts receivable	45,000

On the basis of the above data, Ginger had budgeted a cash increase for the month in the amount of:
  a. $90,000   b. $195,000   c. $250,000   d. $300,000   e. none of the above   (AICPA adapted)

_____ **7.** Forty-Niner Inc. is preparing its cash budget for November. The following information is available concerning its inventories:

Estimated inventories at beginning of November	$180,000
Estimated cost of goods sold for November	900,000
Estimated inventories at end of November	160,000
Estimated payments in November for purchases prior to November	210,000
Estimated percentage of payments in November for purchases in November	80%

The estimated cash disbursements for inventories in November are:
a. $720,000   **b.** $930,000   **c.** $914,000   **d.** $1,042,000   **e.** none of the above   (AICPA adapted)

_____ **8.** Plainview Inc. is considering a three-phase research project. The time estimates for completion of Phase 1 of the project are:

	Months
Optimistic	4
Most likely	8
Pessimistic	18

Using the Program Evaluation and Review Technique (PERT), the expected time for completion of Phase 1 should be:
a. 8 months   **d.** 18 months
b. 10 months   **e.** none of the above
c. 9 months   (AICPA adapted)

_____ **9.** Carter Corporation had the following transactions in 19A, its first year of operations:

Sales (90% collected in 19A)	$1,500,000
Receivables write-offs	60,000
Disbursements for costs and expenses	1,200,000
Disbursements for income taxes	90,000
Payments for plant assets	400,000
Depreciation on plant assets	80,000
Proceeds from issuance of common stock	500,000
Proceeds from short-term borrowings..	100,000
Payments on short-term borrowings	50,000

The cash balance at December 31, 19A is:
a. $150,000   **b.** $170,000   **c.** $260,000   **d.** $280,000   **e.** none of the above   (AICPA adapted)

_____ **10.** A flexible budget is:
a. not appropriate when costs and expenses are affected by fluctuations in volume limits
b. appropriate for any relevant level of activity
c. appropriate for control of factory overhead but not for control of direct materials and direct labor
d. appropriate for control of direct materials and direct labor but not for control of factory overhead
e. none of the above   (AICPA adapted)

PART 4

Knutson Nut Co. prepared cash estimates for the next four months. The following estimates were developed for certain items:

Item	March	April	May	June
Cash sales	$20,000	$12,000	$16,000	$22,000
Credit sales	10,000	4,000	12,000	18,000
Payroll	4,000	3,000	5,000	6,000
Purchases	6,000	5,200	5,600	8,000
Other expenses	5,000	4,800	5,200	5,600

In February, credit sales totaled $18,000, and purchases totaled $10,000. January credit sales were $24,000. Accounts receivables collections amount to 60% in the month after the sale and 35% in the second month after the sale; 5% of the receivables are never collected. Payroll and other expenses are paid in the month incurred, as are 50% of the purchases. The remainder of the purchases are paid in the following month. The cash balance was $5,000 on March 1. A $35,000 tax payment is due on June 15.

Instructions: *Prepare a cash budget for the four-month period (March through June), using the form provided below.*

Knutson Nut Co.
Cash Budget
For March–June, 19X

Receipts from:	March	April	May	June
Cash sales	$	$	$	$
January credit sales...........................				
February credit sales..........................				
March credit sales				
April credit sales				
May credit sales				
Total receipts	$_____	$_____	$_____	$_____
Disbursements for:				
Payroll	$	$	$	$
Other expenses				
February purchases				
March purchases.............................				
April purchases..............................				
May purchases				
June purchases				
Tax payment				
Total disbursements	$_____	$_____	$_____	$_____
Net increase (decrease) in cash:				
Receipts less disbursements	$	$	$	$
Cash balances:				
Beginning				
Ending	$_____	$_____	$_____	$_____

PART 5

A budget prepared the following time estimates for a contemplated project with 72 days as the target date:

Event	Activity	t_o	t_m	t_p
B	A-B	4	6	8
C	A-C	16	18	20
D	A-D	6	9	12
E	B-E	6	10	14
F	C-F	5	9	19
F	D-F	3	5	7
H	E-H	10	16	22
E	F-E	3	7	11
G	F-G	4	6	14
H	G-H	7	11	15

Instructions:

1. Prepare a calculation for t_e (expected time) for each activity.

Activity	t_e
A-B	
A-C	
A-D	
B-E	
C-F	
D-F	
E-H	
F-E	
F-G	
G-H	

2. Design the PERT network for the data in 1.

3. Determine the total t_e for each path and identify the critical path for the project.

Path	t_e
1	
2	
3	
4	
5	

PART 6

Tuscon Tortilla Inc. employs 30 production workers who work 8 hours per day, 20 days per month, and normal capacity is 500,000 units per month. The direct labor wage rate is $12 per hour; direct materials are budgeted at $4 per unit produced. Fixed factory overhead is $2,500; supplies average $.50 per direct labor hour; indirect labor is 1/4 of direct labor cost, and other manufacturing charges are $1 per direct labor hour.

Instructions: *Prepare a monthly flexible budget at 60%, 80%, and 100% of normal capacity, showing itemized manufacturing costs, total manufacturing costs, manufacturing cost per unit, and factory overhead rate per direct labor hour, rounded to the nearest cent.*

Tuscon Tortilla Inc.
Monthly Flexible Budget

	60% of Normal Capacity	80% of Normal Capacity	100% of Normal Capacity
Units..			
Direct labor hours			
Direct materials	$	$	$
Direct labor			
Variable factory overhead:			
Supplies			
Indirect labor			
Other charges			
Fixed factory overhead...................................			
Total manufacturing cost	$_____	$_____	$_____
Manufacturing cost per unit.............................	$_____	$_____	$_____
Factory overhead rate per direct labor hour..................	$_____	$_____	$_____

CHAPTER 18
STANDARD COSTING:
SETTING STANDARDS AND ANALYZING VARIANCES

REVIEW SUMMARY

1. A *standard cost* is the predetermined cost of manufacturing a single unit or a number of units during a specific period in the immediate future. The use of standard costs for accounting purposes simplifies costing procedures through the reduction of clerical expense. A complete standard cost file by parts and operations simplifies assigning costs to materials, work in process, and finished goods inventories.

2. When manufacturing budgets are based on standards for materials, labor, and factory overhead, a strong team is created for possible control and reduction of costs. Both budgets and standard costs make it possible to prepare reports that compare actual costs and predetermined costs for management. With the use of standard costs, the preparation of budgets for any volume and mixture of products is more reliably and speedily accomplished.

3. A *basic standard* is a yardstick against which both expected and actual performances are compared. *Current standards* are of three types: (1) the *expected actual standard* is a standard set for an expected level of operation and efficiency; (2) the *normal standard* is a standard set for a normal level of operation and efficiency; and (3) the *theoretical* standard is a standard set for an ideal or maximum level of operation and efficiency. Standards are usually computed for a six- or twelve-month period. The success of a standard cost system depends on the reliability, accuracy, and acceptance of the standards. Standards must be set, and the system implemented, in an atmosphere that gives full consideration to behavior characteristics of managers and workers.

4. Materials price standards should reflect current market prices and are generally used throughout the forthcoming fiscal period. The *materials purchase price variance* is computed as: Actual quantity purchased × (Actual unit cost – Standard unit cost). Materials quantity standards should be set after the most economical size, shape, and quantity of the product and the results expected from the use of various kinds and grades of materials have been analyzed. The *materials quantity variance* is computed as follows: Standard unit cost × (Actual quantity used – Standard quantity allowed).

5. Labor rate standards are based on rates established in collective bargaining agreements or as determined by agreement between the employee and the personnel department at the time of hiring. The *labor rate variance* is computed as follows: Actual hours worked × (Actual rate – Standard rate). Labor efficiency standards are based on the actual performance of a worker or group of workers possessing average skill and using average effort while performing manual operations or working on machines operating under normal conditions. The *labor efficiency variance* is computed as follows: Standard rate × (Actual hours worked – Standard hours allowed).

6. Variable overhead variances result from a comparison of actual variable costs with the flexible budget (applied) variable factory overhead. Fixed overhead variances result from a difference between budgeted fixed expenses and absorbed fixed overhead. The *standard factory overhead rate* is a predetermined rate that is based on an activity measure such as machine hours or direct labor hours at normal capacity, and it may be computed as follows:

   Total factory hours ÷ Direct labor hours, machine hours, etc.

   The overall factory overhead variance is computed as follows:

   Actual overhead – (Standard hours allowed × Standard overhead rate)

7. In the *two-variance method* of analyzing the overall overhead variance, the two variables are the (a) controllable variance and (b) volume variance. The *controllable variance* is the difference between the actual expenses incurred and the budget allowance based on standard hours allowed for the work performed. The *volume variance* is the difference between the budget allowance and the standard expenses charged to work in process, and it represents the cost of capacity available but not used.

8. In the *three-variance method*, the three variances are the (a) spending variance, (b) idle capacity variance, and (c) efficiency variance. They are computed as follows:

   Spending variance = Actual factory overhead – Budget allowance based on actual hours worked.
   Idle capacity variance = (Normal capacity hours – Actual hours worked) × Fixed expense rate
   Efficiency variance = (Actual hours worked – Standard hours allowed) × Standard overhead rate

9. In the *four variance method*, the four variables are the (a) spending variance, (b) variable efficiency variance, (c) fixed efficiency variance, and (d) idle capacity variance.

The spending variance and the idle capacity variance are identical with those of the three-variance method, and the others are computed as follows:

Variable efficiency variance = (Actual hours worked – Standard hours allowed) × Variable expense rate

Fixed efficiency variance = (Actual hours worked – Standard hours allowed) × Fixed overhead rate

10. A *mix variance* is the result of mixing basic materials in a ratio different from standard materials specifications.

The *yield variance* is the result of obtaining an amount of prime product manufactured from a given amount of materials that is different from what is expected on the basis of input. Because the final product cost contains not only materials but also labor and factory overhead, a yield variance for labor and factory overhead should be determined when the product is finished. A labor yield variance is the result of the quality or quantity of the materials handled, while the factory overhead yield variance is due to the greater or smaller number of hours worked.

PART 1

Instructions: *Place a check mark in the appropriate column to indicate whether each of the following statements is **True or False**.*

	True	False
1. The use of standard costs for accounting purposes decreases the clerical labor required for costing procedures.	___	___
2. The standard cost system is more often used in job order cost accounting because of the greater practicality of setting standards for heterogeneous production.	___	___
3. A budget emphasizes the volume of business and the cost level that should be maintained if the firm is to operate as desired.	___	___
4. If standards are too tight, they are likely to reduce the worker's motivation to achieve the designated level of activity or productivity.	___	___
5. Standards are usually computed for a six- or twelve-month period, although a longer period is sometimes used.	___	___
6. A materials purchase price variance is unfavorable when the actual price paid for the materials is less than the standard price.	___	___
7. Any difference between standard and actual labor hours results in a labor efficiency variance.	___	___
8. Labor efficiency standards are usually established by industrial engineers, using time and motion studies.	___	___
9. The purchasing department carries the primary responsibility for the materials price variance.	___	___
10. The volume variance indicates the cost of capacity available but not used and is considered the responsibility of executive management.	___	___
11. The idle capacity variance consists of fixed expense only, and it indicates the amount of overhead that is either under- or overabsorbed.	___	___
12. The controllable variance of the two-variance method consists of the fixed efficiency variance and the idle capacity variance of the four-variance method.	___	___
13. Although all methods of factory overhead variance analysis are commonly used, the two-variance method seems to be most popular.	___	___
14. A blend variance is the result of mixing basic materials in a ratio different from standard materials specifications.	___	___
15. Of the two labor variances, the labor efficiency variance is the more controllable by production department managers.	___	___

PART 2

Instructions: *In the blank space at the left of each of the following items, place the letter from the right-hand column that identifies the term that best matches the statement in the column on the left. No letter should be used more than once.*

_____ 1. The predetermined cost of manufacturing a single unit or a number of product units during a specific period in the immediate future.

_____ 2. The difference between the actual factory overhead incurred and the budget allowance based on the actual number of units of the allocation base used in actual production.

_____ 3. Emphasizes the volume of business and cost level that should be maintained if the firm is to operate as desired.

_____ 4. The difference between the budget allowance based on the actual number of units of the allocation base used in actual production and the amount of factory overhead chargeable to production in the absence of a standard cost system.

_____ 5. A standard set for an anticipated level of operation and efficiency.

_____ 6. Standard intended to represent challenging yet attainable results.

_____ 7. A standard set for an ideal or maximum level of operation and efficiency.

_____ 8. Should be given due consideration when implimenting a standard cost system.

_____ 9. Requires the computation of the spending variance, the idle capacity variance, and the efficiency variance.

_____ 10. Should reflect current market prices and is generally used throughout the forthcoming fiscal period.

_____ 11. Computed by multiplying the actual quantity of materials used by the difference between the actual cost per unit and the standard cost per unit.

_____ 12. Determined by comparing the actual amount of materials used with the standard amount allowed, both priced at standard cost.

_____ 13. Determined by multiplying the actual hours worked by the difference between the actual hourly pay and the standard hourly pay.

_____ 14. Time factors for acceptable levels of fatigue and personal needs are included in these standards.

_____ 15. Computed at the end of any reporting period by comparing actual hours worked with standard hours allowed, but at the standard labor rate.

_____ 16. Requires the computation of the spending variance, the variable efficiency variance, the fixed efficiency variance, and the idle capacity variance.

_____ 17. The difference between normal factory overhead expenses incurred and the standard number of units of the allocation base allowed for actual production.

_____ 18. Indicates the cost of capacity available but not used and is generally considered the responsibility of executive management.

_____ 19. The result of blending basic materials in a ratio different from standard materials specifications.

_____ 20. The result of obtaining output different from that expected on the basis of input.

a. expected actual standard
b. behavioral consequences
c. standard cost
d. materials price standard
e. budget
f. theoretical standard
g. spending variance
h. normal standard
i. idle capacity variance
j. three-variance method
k. four-variance method
l. labor efficiency method
m. yield variance
n. materials quantity variance
o. mix variance
p. labor efficiency standards
q. volume variance
r. labor rate variance
s. controllable variance
t. materials price usage variance

PART 3

Instructions: *In the blank space at the left of each of the following items, place the letter of the choice that most correctly completes each item.*

_____ 1. The best basis upon which cost standards should be set to measure controllable production efficiencies is:

a. theoretical standards

b. expected actual standards

c. normal standards

d. practical capacity

e. none of the above

(ICMA adapted)

_____ 2. An unfavorable factory overhead volume variance is most often caused by:

a. actual fixed overhead incurred exceeding budgeted fixed overhead

b. an overapplication of fixed overhead to production

c. production levels exceeding sales levels

d. normal capacity exceeding actual production levels

e. none of the above

(ICMA adapted)

_____ 3. PEI Company uses the two-variance method for analysis of factory overhead in its standard costing system. Selected data for February follow:

Standard machine hours	32,000
Actual machine hours	33,000
Budgeted fixed factory overhead	$ 66,000
Actual factory overhead incurred	$220,000
Variable factory overhead rate per machine hour	$5

The controllable variance is:

a. $11,000 favorable

b. $11,000 unfavorable

c. $6,000 favorable

d. $6,000 unfavorable

e. none of the above

(AICPA adapted)

_____ 4. The labor rate variance is computed as:

a. the difference between the standard and actual rate multiplied by actual hours

b. the difference between the standard and actual rate multiplied by standard hours

c. the difference between the standard and actual hours multiplied by the actual rate

d. the difference between the standard and actual hours multiplied by the difference between the standard and actual rate

e. none of the above

(AICPA adapted)

_____ 5. Slyde Company manufactures tables with vinyl tops. The standard material cost for the vinyl used per Type R table is $7.80, based on six square feet of vinyl at a cost of $1.30 per square foot. A production run of 1,000 tables in January resulted in usage of 5,800 square feet of vinyl at a cost of $1.20 per square foot, for a total cost of $6,960. The materials quantity variance resulting from this production run was:

a. $240 favorable

b. $240 unfavorable

c. $260 unfavorable

d. $640 unfavorable

e. none of the above

(AICPA adapted)

_____ 6. Information on Franco Company's factory overhead costs follows:

Standard applied to factory overhead	$80,000
Budgeted factory overhead based on standard direct labor hours allowed.	84,000
Budgeted factory overhead based on actual direct hours,	83,000
Actual factory overhead.	$86,000

The total factory overhead variance is:

a. $2,000 favorable

b. $6,000 unfavorable

c. $4,000 unfavorable

d. $6,000 unfavorable

e. none of the above

(AICPA adapted)

_____ 7. Actual units of direct materials used were 20,000, at an actual cost of $44,000. Standard unit cost is $2.10. The materials price usage variance is:
   a. $1,000 favorable
   b. $1,000 unfavorable
   c. $2,000 favorable
   d. $2,000 unfavorable
   e. none of the above

_____ 8. If the actual number of liters of materials used exceeds standard liters allowed but actual cost is less than standard cost, the materials price and usage variances, respectively, are:
   a. unfavorable, favorable
   b. favorable, favorable
   c. favorable, unfavorable
   d. unfavorable, unfavorable
   e. none of the above
                                                                                          (AICPA adapted)

_____ 9. If a company computes a materials price usage variance, the variance is isolated:
   a. when materials are issued
   b. when materials are purchased
   c. when materials are converted in the production process
   d. when materials are priced
   e. none of the above
                                                                                          (AICPA adapted)

_____ 10. Of the following, the most probable reason a company would experience an unfavorable labor rate variance and a favorable labor efficiency variance is that:
   a. the mix of workers assigned to the particular job was heavily weighted towards the use of higher paid, experienced individuals
   b. the mix of workers assigned to the particular job was heavily weighted towards the use of new, relatively low paid, unskilled workers
   c. because of the production schedule, workers from other production areas were assigned to assist this particular process
   d. defective materials caused more labor to be used in order to produce a standard unit
   e. none of the above
                                                                                          (AICPA adapted)

PART 4

Haradon Company has a budgeted normal monthly capacity of 20,000 labor hours, with a standard production of 10,000 units at this capacity. Standard costs are:

Materials	3 lbs.@ $1	3.00/unit
Labor	$15 per hour	30.00/unit
Factory overhead at normal capacity:		
Fixed	$20,000	2.00/unit
Variable	$5 per labor hour	10/unit

During March, actual factory overhead totaled $118,000, and 19,500 labor hours cost $282,750. During the month, 9,500 units were produced using 29,200 lbs. of material at a cost of $1.10 per lb.

Instructions:

1. Compute the materials cost variances.

	Pounds	Unit Cost		Amount
Actual quantity used		$	Actual	$
Actual quantity used		_____	Standard	_____
Materials price usage variance		$_____		$_____
Actual quantity used		$	Standard	$
Standard quantity allowed	_____		Standard	_____
Materials quantity variance	======		Standard	$_____

2. Compute the labor cost variances.

	Time	Rate		Amount
Actual hours worked		$	Actual	$
Actual hours worked		_____	Standard	_____
Labor rate variance		$_____		$_____
Actual hours worked		$	Standard	$
Standard hours allowed	_____		Standard	_____
Labor time variance	_____		Standard	$_____

3. Compute the factory overhead variances—two-variance method.

Actual factory overhead		$
Budget allowance based on standard hours allowed:		
Fixed overhead budgeted..	$	
Variable overhead	_____	_____
Controllable variance		$_____
Budget allowance based on standard hours allowed		$
Overhead charged to production.....................................		_____
Volume variance	$_____	

4. Compute the factory overhead variances—three-variance method.

Actual factory overhead		$
Budget allowance based on actual hours worked:		
Fixed overhead budgeted..	$	
Variable overhead	_____	_____
Spending variance		$_____
Budget allowance based on actual hours worked		$
Actual hours × standard overhead rate		_____
Idle capacity variance		$_____
Actual hours × standard overhead rate		$
Overhead charged to production.....................................		_____
Efficiency variance	$_____	

5. Compute the factory overhead variances—four-variance method.

Actual factory overhead		$
Budget allowance based on actual hours worked		_____
Spending variance		$_____
Budget allowance based on actual hours worked		$
Budget allowance based on standard hours allowed		_____
Variable efficiency variance...		$_____
Actual hours × fixed overhead rate		$
Standard hours allowed × fixed overhead rate...........................		_____
Fixed efficiency variance..		$_____
Normal capacity hours × fixed overhead rate		$
Actual hours worked × fixed overhead rate		_____
Idle capacity variance		$_____

PART 5

Yang Industries uses a standard cost card system. The standard cost card for one of its products shows the following materials standards:

Materials	Pounds	×	Standard Price Per Pound	=	Amount
X	20		$1.75		$35.00
Y	5		.85		4.25
Z	15		3.25		48.75
					$88.00

The standard 40 lb. mix cost per lb. is $2.40 ($88 ÷ 40 lbs.). The standard mix should produce 32 lbs. of finished product, and the standard cost of finished product per lb. is $2.75 (88 ÷ 32 lbs.).

450,000 of materials were used as follows:

Material X . . . .   220,000 lbs. @ $2.00
Material Y . . . .   60,000 lbs. @ 1.00
Material Z . . . .   170,000 lbs. @ 3.00

The output of finished product was 375,000 lbs.

Instructions:

1. Compute the materials price usage variance.

Material	Pounds	Actual Cost Per Pound	Amount
X		$	$
Y			
Z			$

Material	Pounds	Standard Cost Per Pound	Amount
X		$	$
Y			
Z			
Materials price usage variance			$

2. Compute the materials mix variance.

Actual quantities at standard . . . . $

Actual quantities at standard materials cost . . . .

Materials mix variance . . . . $

3. Compute the materials yield variance.

Actual input quantities at standard materials cost . . . . $

Actual output quantity at standard materials cost . . . .

Materials yield variance . . . . $

CHAPTER 19
STANDARD COSTING:
INCORPORATING STANDARDS INTO THE ACCOUNTING RECORDS

REVIEW SUMMARY

1. Standard costs should be viewed as costs that pass through the data-processing system into financial statements. In the *partial plan* of standard cost accounting, the Work in Process account is debited for the actual cost of materials, labor, and factory overhead and is credited at standard cost when goods are completed and transferred to finished goods inventory. Under the *single plan* of standard costing, debits and credits are made to the Work in Process account at standard costs only, and variances are recorded in separate variance accounts.

2. The recording of materials purchased may be handled by three different methods: (a) the price variance may be recorded when materials are received and placed in the storeroom, (b) the materials may be recorded at actual cost when received, and the price variance determined when the materials are requisitioned for production, and (c) the price variance may be calculated when the materials are received, but not charged to production until the materials are actually placed in process. For control purposes, the price difference should be determined when the materials are received.

3. In a standard cost system, the clock cards, job tickets, and other labor time information provide the data for the computation of the labor variances. The journal entry to distribute the payroll and set up the variance accounts should be:
   Work in Process
   Labor Rate Variance (assume unfavorable)
       Labor Efficiency Variance (assume favorable)
       Payroll

4. Journal entries for factory overhead, assuming the use of the two-variance method, are as follows:
   (a) To record actual factory overhead:
       Factory Overhead Control
           Various Credits
   (b) To apply overhead to work in process:
       Work in Process
           Applied Factory Overhead
   (c) To close applied factory overhead at end of period:
       Applied Factory Overhead
           Factory Overhead Control
   (d) To close the factory overhead control account using the two-variance method, assume that both controllable variance and volume variance are unfavorable:
       Factory Overhead Controllable Variance
       Factory Overhead Volume Variance
           Factory Overhead Control

(e) To close the factory overhead control account using the three-variance method A, and assuming that all variances are favorable:
   Factory Overhead Control
       Factory Overhead Spending Variance
       Factory Overhead Idle Capacity Variance
       Factory Overhead Efficiency Variance
(f) To close the factory overhead control account, using the three-variance method B, and assuming that all variances are unfavorable:
   Factory Overhead Control
       Factory Overhead Spending Variance
       Factory Overhead Variable Efficiency Variance
       Factory Overhead Volume Variance
(g) To close the factory overhead control account using the four-variance method, and assuming that the favorable spending variance exceeds the other three unfavorable variances:
   Factory Overhead Control
   Factory Overhead Idle Capacity Variance
   Factory Overhead Variable Efficiency Variance
   Factory Overhead Fixed Efficiency Variance
       Factory Overhead Spending Variance

5. Journal entries for mix and yield variances are:
   (a) To charge materials into production, assuming an unfavorable mix variance and a favorable yield variance:
   Work in Process
   Materials Mix Variance
       Materials Yield Variance
       Materials
   (b) To charge work in process with direct labor, assuming a favorable rate variance and unfavorable yield and efficiency variances:
   Work in Process
   Labor Efficiency Variance
       Labor Rate Variance
       Payroll
   (c) To close factory overhead control and record the variances using the two-variance method, assuming a favorable yield variance and unfavorable controllable and volume variances:
   Factory Overhead Controllable Variance
   Factory Overhead Volume Variance
       Factory Overhead Yield Variance
       Factory Overhead Control

6. Variances may be disposed of either by (a) closing them to Income Summary or (b) treating them as adjustments

to Cost of Goods Sold and to inventories. If method (a) is used, unfavorable manufacturing cost variances are deducted from the gross profit at standard cost and favorable manufacturing cost variances are added to the gross profit at standard cost. Proponents of this method believe that variances should not be treated as increases or decreases in manufacturing costs, but as deviations in contemplated costs that should be charged against income in the period incurred. Proponents of method (b) above advocate that the variances should be prorated to Work in Process, Finished Goods, and Cost of Goods Sold. Cost Accounting Standards Board regulations require that significant standard cost variances be included in inventories. Current Internal Revenue Service regulations also require the inclusion of a portion of significant variances in inventories.

7. Standards should be changed only when underlying conditions change or when the standards no longer reflect the original concept. Events, rather than time, should determine whether standard costs are to be revised. When standard costs are changed, any adjustment to inventory should be made with care so that inventories are not written up or down arbitrarily.

PART 1

Instructions: *Place a check mark in the appropriate column to indicate whether each of the following statements is **True or False**.*

	True	False
1. Under the single plan of standard costing, debits and credits are made to the Work in Process account at standard costs only, and variances are recorded in separate variance accounts.	___	___
2. Under the partial plan of standard costing, the Work in Process account is debited for the actual cost of materials, labor, and factory overhead and is credited at standard cost when goods are completed and transferred to finished goods inventory.	___	___
3. For control purposes, the materials price variance should be determined when materials are used.	___	___
4. Under standard costing, the finished goods ledger card will show quantities only, because the standard cost of the units generally remains the same during a period.	___	___
5. In journalizing the yield variance, Work in Process is debited for the standard production that should be attained from the input into the system.	___	___
6. In a standard cost system, cost is transferred from the Work in Process account of one department to the Work in Process account of the next department at standard cost.	___	___
7. To avoid short-run fluctuations, variances should generally not be reported more often than every three months.	___	___
8. In journalizing variances, favorable variances are credited and unfavorable variances are debited.	___	___
9. If the entry to close the factory overhead control account includes credits to both Factory Overhead Controllable Variance and Factory Overhead Volume Variance, applied factory overhead was less than actual factory overhead.	___	___
10. The materials mix variance results from combining materials in a ratio different from the standard materials specifications	___	___
11. The three types of labor variances are the rate variance, efficiency variance, and yield variance.	___	___
12. When variances are closed to Cost of Goods Sold, favorable variances are added to the gross profit computed at standard cost.	___	___
13. Cost Accounting Standards Board regulations require that significant standard cost variances be included in inventories.	___	___
14. Standard costs should be changed at least once a year so that managers "keep on their toes."	___	___
15. Standard costing is most applicable to manufacturing situations and does not really work well in the nonprofit organization sector.	___	___

PART 2

Instructions: *In the blank space at the left of each of the following items, place the letter from the right-hand column that identifies the term that best matches the statement in the column on the left. No letter should be used more than once.*

_____ 1. Viewed as passing through the data-processing system into financial statements.

_____ 2. Approach in which the Work in Process account is debited at actual cost and is credited at standard cost.

_____ 3. Approach under which debits and credits to the Work in Process account are recorded at standard cost only, and variances are recorded in separate variance accounts.

_____ 4. Variance that, for control purposes, should be determined when materials are received.

_____ 5. Approach under which the amount of over- or underapplied factory overhead is divided into the spending, idle capacity, variable efficiency, and fixed efficiency variances.

_____ 6. Approach under which the amount of over- or underapplied factory overhead can be analyzed as spending, idle capacity, and efficiency variances.

_____ 7. Variance that appears on the books after the materials are issued and then only for the quantity issued.

_____ 8. Will show quantities only, because the standard cost of the units remains the same during a period unless severe cost changes occur.

_____ 9. Variance that would be recorded when materials are charged to production.

_____ 10. Variance that would be recorded when materials costs are transferred to finished goods.

_____ 11. Variance that appears on the books if the difference between the actual materials cost and the standard materials cost is recorded at the time the materials are purchased.

_____ 12. Approach under which the procedure for handling cost variances is to consider them as profit or loss items.

_____ 13. Approach that the Cost Accounting Standards Board requires be used if there are significant standard cost variances.

_____ 14. Requires the inclusion of a portion of significant variances in inventory.

_____ 15. Requires that unplanned price or volume variances should be reported at the end of an interim period, following the same procedures used as at the end of a fiscal year.

a. four-variance method
b. partial plan
c. materials price usage variance
d. finished goods ledger card
e. materials yield variance
f. materials price variance
g. materials mix variance
h. standard costs
i. three-variance method
j. single plan
k. closing variances to income summary
l. Internal Revenue Service
m. AICPA
n. allocating variances to cost of goods sold and inventories
o. materials purchase price variance

PART 3

Instructions: *In the blank space at the left of each of the following items, place the letter of the choice that most correctly completes the item.*

_____ 1. A credit balance in the labor-efficiency variance account indicates that:
   a. standard hours exceed actual hours
   b. actual hours exceed standard hours
   c. standard rate and standard hours exceed actual rate and actual hours
   d. actual rate and actual hours exceed standard rate and standard hours
   e. standard rate exceeds actual rate
   (AICPA adapted)

_____ 2. If a company follows a practice of isolating variances at the earliest point in time, what would be the appropriate time to isolate and recognize a direct materials price variance?
   a. When materials are issued
   b. When materials are purchased
   c. When materials are used in production
   d. When a purchase order is originated
   e. When materials leave the factory storeroom
   (AICPA adapted)

_____ 3. How should a usage variance that is significant in amount be treated at the end of an accounting period?
   a. Reported as deferred charge or credit
   b. Allocated among work in process inventory, finished goods inventory, and cost of goods sold
   c. Charged or credited to cost of goods manufactured
   d. Allocated among cost of goods manufactured, finished goods inventory, and cost of goods sold
   e. None of the above
   (AICPA adapted)

_____ 4. What is the normal year-end treatment of immaterial variances recognized in a cost accounting system utilizing standards?
   a. Reclassified to deferred charges until all related production is sold
   b. Allocated among cost of goods manufactured and ending work in process inventory
   c. Closed to Cost of Goods Sold in the period in which they arose
   d. Capitalized as a cost of ending finished goods inventory
   e. None of the above
   (AICPA adapted)

_____ 5. What does a credit balance in a direct labor efficiency variance amount indicate?
   a. The average wage rate paid to direct labor employees was less than the standard rate.
   b. The standard hours allowed for the units produced were greater than actual direct labor hours used.
   c. Actual total direct labor costs incurred were less than standard direct labor costs allowed for the units produced.
   d. The number of units produced was less than the number of units budgeted for the period.
   e. All of the above
   (AICPA adapted)

_____ 6. According to IRS regulations, at the end of an accounting period a usage variance that is significant in amount should be:
   a. reported as a deferred charge or credit
   b. allocated among work in process, finished goods, and cost of goods sold
   c. charged or credited to cost of goods manufactured
   d. allocated among cost of goods manufactured, finished goods, and cost of goods sold
   e. none of the above
   (AICPA adapted)

_____ 7. Information on Barber Company's direct labor costs for the month of January is as follows:

Actual direct labor hours	34,500
Standard direct labor hours	35,000
Total direct labor payroll	$241,500
Direct labor efficiency variance–favorable	$3,200

What is Barber's direct labor rate variance?
   a. $17,250 unfavorable
   b. $20,700 unfavorable
   c. $21,000 unfavorable
   d. $21,000 favorable
   e. none of the above
   (AICPA adapted)

_____ **8.** The following journal entry has been recorded:

Work in Process	7,560	
Factory Overhead Efficiency Variance	950	
Factory Overhead Control		8,510

This entry indicates that the:
a. two-variance method is in use and the variance is unfavorable
b. three-variance method is in use and the variance is favorable
c. four-variance method is in use and the variance is unfavorable
d. three-variance method is in use and the variance is unfavorable
e. none of the above

_____ **9.** The following journal entry has been recorded:

Work in Process	84,000	
Materials Mix Variance		2,000
Materials		79,000
Materials Price Usage Variance		3,000

This entry indicates that the materials:
a. mix variance was unfavorable
b. price usage variance was recorded at the time of purchase
c. yield will be greater than standard
d. mix variance was favorable
e. none of the above

_____ **10.** If standard costs represent conditions that are expected to prevail in the coming period but that have not affected costs in the past period, then ending inventories are costed at:
a. the new standard   d. the old standard
b. actual cost   e. fifo
c. the contra amount carried in cost of sales

PART 4

Hurwitz Corp. determines that the following variances arose in production during June:

Variance	Amount
Materials purchase price	$ 900 fav.
Materials price usage	750 fav.
Labor efficiency	1,000 fav.
Labor rate	600 fav.
Efficiency	750 fav.
Idle capacity	1,500 unfav.
Spending	500 fav.

Materials purchases totaled $90,000 at standard cost. Labor payroll totaled $80,000, while actual overhead incurred was $60,000.

Instructions: *Prepare the journal entries to record the above variances.*

Account	Debit	Credit

PART 5

Wales-Scott Company makes a product for which the following standards have been set:

Materials: 3 square yards @ $4.95		$ 14.85
Direct labor: 2 hours @ $8		16.00
Variable factory overhead: 2 hours @ $1.50		3.00
Fixed factory overhead: 2 hours @ $2		4.00
		$ 37.85
Normal output		5,000 units

Actual data for March:

Production (no work in process inventories)	4,000 units
Sales at $50 per unit	3,000 units
Materials purchased (inventoried at standard cost), actual cost, $5.20 per square yard	15,000 square yards
Materials used	12,500 square yards
Direct labor @ $8.25 per hour	8,500 hours
Factory overhead	$ 32,100

It was decided that all variances—two variances each for materials and direct labor, four variances for factory overhead—should be closed to Cost of Goods Sold.

Work in Process is charged with standard costs for actual production.

Instructions:

1. Complete the schedules below.

	Square Yards	Unit Cost		Amount
Actual quantity purchased		$	Standard	$
Actual quantity purchased		_____	Actual	_____
Materials purchase price variance		$_____		$_____
Actual quantity used		$	Standard	$
Standard quantity allowed	_____		Standard	_____
Materials quantity variance	_____			_____

	Time	Rate		Amount
Actual hours worked		$	Actual	$
Actual hours worked		_____	Standard	_____
Labor rate variance		$_____		$_____
Actual hours worked		$	Standard	$
Standard hours allowed	_____		Standard	_____
Labor efficiency variance	_____			$_____
Actual factory overhead				$

Budget allowance based on actual hours worked:

Fixed overhead budgeted	$	
Variable overhead	_____	_____
Spending variance		$_____

Budget allowance based on actual hours worked . . . . $

Budget allowance based on standard hours allowed:

   Fixed overhead budgeted . . . . $

   Variable overhead . . . .   _____   _____

Variable efficiency variance . . . . $_____

Actual hours × fixed overhead rate . . . . $

Standard hours allowed × fixed overhead rate . . . .   _____

Fixed efficiency variance . . . . $_____

Budget allowance based on actual hours worked . . . . $

Actual hours worked × factory overhead rate . . . .   _____

Idle capacity variance . . . . $_____

2. Prepare the appropriate journal entries.

Account	Debit	Credit

PART 6

S. Freud Co. employs a standard cost system and blends input products—Id and Ego—to produce Super according to the following standards:

Materials	Standard Quantity and Price	Standard Materials Cost per Unit
Id	60 lbs. @ $3	$180
Ego	180 lbs. @ $1.50	270
		$450

The standard weight per unit of finished goods is 200 pounds. During May, 2,100 pounds of Super were produced. Materials were purchased and consumed as follows:

Materials	Purchased	Consumed
Id	900 lbs. @ $3.20	800 lbs
Ego	2,000 lbs. @ $1.35	1,300 lbs.

There were no beginning inventories of materials.

Instructions: *Prepare the journal entries to record (1) the inventory purchased and (2) the mix and yield variances for materials. (Use the following page for computations.)*

Account	Debit	Credit

Computations

PART 7

The management of Riordan Products Inc. was presented with the following distribution of materials, labor, and overhead costs in inventories and cost of goods sold:

	Materials Costs	Direct Labor Costs	Overhead Costs
Materials—ending inventory	$ 25,000	–	–
Work in Process—ending inventory	40,000	$ 35,000	$ 62,000
Finished Goods—ending inventory	35,000	35,000	88,000
Cost of Goods Sold	300,000	680,000	450,000
Total	$450,000	$750,000	$600,000

During the year, the following variances were noted:

Materials purchase price variance	$ (7,000)	fav.
Materials price usage variance	9,240	unfav.
Labor rate variance	(12,160)	fav.
Labor efficiency variance	6,340	unfav.
Overhead variances	9,790	unfav.

Instructions:

1. Allocate the variances to inventories and cost of goods sold, using the following schedule.

Materials purchase price variance to:

Materials . . . . $

Work in Process . . . .

Finished Goods . . . .

Cost of Goods Sold . . . .   _____

    Total . . . . $_____

Materials price usage variance to:

Work in Process . . . . $

Finished Goods . . . .

Cost of Goods Sold . . . .   _____

    Total . . . . $_____

Labor rate variance to:

Work in Process .... $

Finished Goods..

Cost of Goods Sold ....   _____

Total .... $_____

Labor efficiency variance to:

Work in Process .... $

Finished Goods..

Cost of Goods Sold ....   _____

Total .... $_____

Overhead variances to:

Work in Process .... $

Finished Goods..

Cost of Goods Sold ....   _____

Total .... $_____

2. Compute the cost of goods sold after the variance allocation.

Standard:

Materials .... $

Labor ....

Overhead ....   _____

$

Add unfavorable variances:

_____ $

_____

_____   _____   _____

$

Less favorable variances:

_____ $

_____   _____   _____

Cost of Goods Sold .... $_____

CHAPTER 20
DIRECT COSTING AND COST-VOLUME-PROFIT ANALYSIS

REVIEW SUMMARY

1. Absorption costing assigns direct materials and direct labor costs and a share of both fixed and variable factory overhead to units of production. In *direct costing*, also referred to as *variable costing* or *marginal costing*, only direct materials, direct labor, and variable factory overhead are charged to the product and are referred to as *product costs*, while fixed manufacturing costs are totally expensed in the period incurred and are called *period costs*.

2. Executive management generally has praised the planning, control, and analytical potentialities of direct costing. With its separation of variable and fixed costs and the calculation of the *contribution margin* or *marginal income*, direct costing facilitates analysis of cost-volume-profit relationships. A knowledge of variable costs, fixed costs, and the contribution margin provides guidelines for the selection of the most profitable products, customers, and territories.

3. Direct costing can serve as a guide in making pricing decisions, because the direct cost segment of unit cost consists of those cost elements that are comparable among firms in the same industry. Direct costing also provides a basis for the study of contemplated changes in production levels or proposed actions concerning new markets, plant expansion, or special promotional activities. Reports constructed on the direct costing basis become valuable control tools by reminding management of the profit objective for the period.

4. Proponents of direct costing for external reporting purposes believe that the separation of fixed and variable expenses, and the accounting for each under some direct costing plan, simplifies both the understanding of the income statement and the assignment of costs to inventories. To keep fixed overhead out of reported product costs, variable and fixed expenses should be recorded in separate accounts.

5. If the number of units produced differs from the number sold, reported net income under absorption costing will differ from reported net income under direct costing. The difference is caused by the elimination of fixed manufacturing expenses from inventories in direct costing. In direct costing, fixed factory overhead is charged to period expense and does not become a part of the product's cost. Generally, when production exceeds sales, absorption costing shows a higher profit than does direct costing, and when sales exceed production, the reverse occurs. The difference in operating income under the two methods can be reconciled as follows:

(Units Produced – Units Sold) × Fixed Factory Overhead Rate for Absorption Costing

Managers prefer income statements prepared on a direct costing basis because the variable cost of goods sold varies directly with sales volume, and the influence of production on profit is eliminated.

6. The use of direct costing for financial reporting is not accepted by the accounting profession, the Internal Revenue Service, or the Securities and Exchange Commission. The position of these groups is generally based on their opposition to excluding fixed costs from inventories. Companies using direct costing internally adjust to absorption costing when preparing income tax returns and reporting externally.

7. *Break-even analysis* indicates the point at which the company neither makes a profit nor suffers a loss. A *break-even chart* is a graphic analysis of the relationship of costs and sales to profit. *Cost-volume-profit analysis* is concerned with determining the optimal level and mix of output to be produced with available resources.

8. Break-even analysis may be based on historical data, past operations, or future sales and costs. The data in a flexible budget can be used directly and without refinement for break-even analysis or it can be converted into a break-even chart. The *contribution margin ratio* is determined by dividing the contribution margin (sales minus variable costs) by sales revenue. The *contribution margin per unit* is the difference between the sales price per unit and the variable costs per unit. Formulas for break-even computations are as follows:

$$\text{Break-even sales volume in dollars} = \frac{\text{Fixed cost}}{1 - \dfrac{\text{Variable cost}}{\text{Sales}}}$$

$$\text{Break-even sales volume in units} = \frac{\text{Fixed cost}}{\text{Contribution margin per unit}}$$

9. In the conventional break-even chart, the fixed cost line is parallel to the x axis and the variable cost is plotted above the fixed cost. Many analysts prefer an alternative chart in which the variable cost is drawn first and the fixed cost is plotted above the variable cost line. A break-even chart can be constructed in even greater detail by breaking down fixed and variable costs into subclassifications.

10. The break-even chart is fundamentally a static analysis. The amount of fixed and variable costs, as well as the slope of the sales line, is meaningful only in a defined

range of activity and must be redefined for activity outside the relative range. In using break-even analysis, management should understand that (a) a change in per-unit variable cost or in sales price changes the contribution margin ratio and the break-even point, (b) a change in fixed cost changes the break-even point but not the contribution margin figure, and (c) a combined change in fixed and variable costs in the same direction causes an extremely sharp change in the break-even point.

11. When firms produce more than one product, the variable costs per dollar of sales revenue may be different for different products; thus, the contribution margin ratio, the break-even point, and the level of sales required to achieve targeted profit levels also would be different. Computations of the above items in the multiple-product case are essentially the same as those in the single-product case, except that the results are valid only for one specific sales mix. Rather than performing multiple-product analysis, a separate break-even analysis may be prepared for each product. However, if arbitrarily allocated common or joint costs are included, the results are of limited value.

12. Dollar sales and expense figures can be translated into a profit-per-unit graph in order to show more vividly the influence of fixed costs on the product unit cost. Analyses illustrated in the unit profit graph together with break-even analysis are important tools in determining which unit costs should be used in setting selling prices.

13. The *margin of safety* indicates how much sales may decrease from a selected sales figure before the company will incur a loss. The margin of safety expressed as a percentage of sales is called the *margin of safety ratio* and is computed as follows:

$$M/S = \frac{\text{Selected sales figure} - \text{Break-even sales}}{\text{Selected sales figure}}$$

14. In most cases, a price reduction must be accompanied not only by increased volume but also by a reduction in the cost of the product in order to achieve a profit that is greater than what existed prior to the price change. The results, of course, will vary depending on the elasticity of demand for the product. A *profit-volume analysis graph* may be prepared to illustrate the effect of possible price changes on profit.

15. It is desirable to investigate cost-volume-profit relationships for individual products or product lines. To determine a better product cost for purposes of planning and control, many firms have departmentalized their factory output, so that the contribution of each product or product group to the total contribution margin can be gauged more effectively.

PART 1

Instructions: *Place a check mark in the appropriate column to indicate whether each of the following statements is **True** or **False**.*

	True	False
1. Absorption costing assigns direct materials, direct labor costs, and a share of both fixed and variable factory overhead to units of production.	_____	_____
2. Direct costing charges variable cost to the product and expenses fixed manufacturing costs in the period in which they are incurred.	_____	_____
3. Marginal income is the result of subtracting all variable costs from sales revenue.	_____	_____
4. A profit plan covers all phases of future operations to attain a stated profit goal.	_____	_____
5. Absorption costing is quite useful in planning for short periods, in pricing special orders, or in making current operating decisions.	_____	_____
6. In direct costing, there are no variances in fixed expenses, because all fixed costs are charged currently against revenue.	_____	_____
7. Generally, when sales exceed production, absorption costing shows a higher profit than direct costing.	_____	_____
8. Gross contribution margin is sales less variable cost of goods sold.	_____	_____
9. The major objection of the accounting profession to direct costing is its exclusion of variable costs from inventory.	_____	_____
10. In filing reports with the SEC, a firm that uses direct costing must adjust its inventories and reported net income to what they would have been had absorption costing been used.	_____	_____
11. The purpose of break-even analysis is to determine the optimal level and mix of output to be produced with available resources.	_____	_____
12. Break-even analysis is generally accomplished with the aid of a break-even chart because it is a compact, readable reporting device.	_____	_____
13. Data for break-even analysis can be taken directly from the conventional or full-cost income statement.	_____	_____
14. The contribution margin ratio is determined by dividing sales minus variable costs by sales revenue.	_____	_____
15. Break-even sales volume in dollars is computed by dividing fixed costs by the contribution margin ratio.	_____	_____
16. The break-even chart is fundamentally a static analysis, in that the amount of fixed and variable costs, as well as the slope of the sales line, are only meaningful for a certain range of activity.	_____	_____
17. In using break-even analysis, management should understand that a change in variable cost changes the break-even point, but not the contribution margin figure.	_____	_____
18. One problem in a multiproduct firm is that it is not possible to prepare a separate break-even analysis for each product or product line.	_____	_____
19. A unit profit graph illustrates that as unit volume increases, the fixed cost per unit decreases.	_____	_____
20. If the contribution margin ratio and the profit percentage are known, the margin of safety ratio can be computed.	_____	_____

PART 2

Instructions: *In the blank space at the left of each of the following items, place the letter from the right-hand column that identifies the term that best matches the statement in the column on the left. No letter should be used more than once.*

_____ 1. The costing method that assigns a portion of both fixed and variable factory overhead to production.

_____ 2. The costing method that charges units of product with only those manufacturing costs that vary directly with volume.

_____ 3. These are more closely associated with the passage of time than with production activity.

_____ 4. These are more closely associated with production activity than with the passage of time.

_____ 5. The difference between sales revenue and variable cost.

_____ 6. The point at which the company neither makes a profit nor suffers a loss.

_____ 7. Concerned with determining the optimal level and mix of output to be produced with available resources.

_____ 8. A graphic analysis of the relationship of costs and sales to profit.

_____ 9. Result of dividing the contribution margin by sales revenue.

_____ 10. Result of dividing fixed costs by the contribution margin ratio.

_____ 11. Result of dividing fixed costs by the contribution margin per unit.

_____ 12. The amount of fixed and variable costs, as well as the slope of the sales line, is meaningful only within this.

_____ 13. When a shift in this occurs, a change in profit can also be expected unless the same contribution margin ratio is realized on all products.

_____ 14. A chart showing the influence of fixed and variable costs on unit cost.

_____ 15. Result of multiplying the margin of safety ratio times the contribution margin ratio.

_____ 16. The margin of safety expressed as a percentage of sales.

_____ 17. Products make a favorable contribution as long as the sales revenue exceeds this.

_____ 18. When these are arbitrarily allocated in break-even analysis, the results are of limited value.

_____ 19. Indicates how much sales may decrease before the company will break even.

_____ 20. The effects of price changes on profits are more clearly indicated by the use of these.

a. direct costing
b. product costing
c. absorption costing
d. contribution margin
e. period costs
f. relevant range
g. unit profit graph
h. cost-volume-profit analysis
i. related variable cost
j. break-even chart
k. break-even analysis
l. margin of safety ratio
m. profit ratio
n. contribution margin ratio
o. sales mix
p. break-even point in dollars
q. break-even point in units
r. profit-volume graph
s. margin of safety
t. common costs

PART 3

Instructions: *In the blank space at the left of each of the following items, place the letter of the choice that most correctly completes each item.*

_____ 1. Direct costing is not in accordance with generally accepted accounting principles because:
a. it assumes fixed manufacturing costs to be period costs
b. its procedures are not well known in industry
c. net earnings are always overstated when using it
d. it ignores the concept of lower of cost or market when valuing inventory
e. none of the above

(AICPA adapted)

_____ 2. A tenet of direct costing is that period costs should be expensed currently. The rationale behind this procedure is that:
a. period costs are uncontrollable and should not be charged to a specific product
b. period costs are generally immaterial in amount and the cost of assigning the amounts to specific products would outweigh the benefits
c. allocation of period costs is arbitrary at best and could lead to erroneous decisions by management
d. period costs will occur whether or not production occurs and so it is improper to allocate these costs to production and thus defer a current cost of doing business
e. none of the above

(AICPA adapted)

_____ 3. Operating income computed using absorption costing and operating income computed using direct costing, related to manufacturing costs, differ because:
a. absorption costing considers all costs in the determination of operating income, whereas direct costing considers only direct costs
b. absorption costing inventories all direct costs, but direct costing considers direct costs to be period costs
c. absorption costing inventories all fixed costs for the period in ending finished goods inventory, but direct costing expenses all fixed costs
d. absorption costing allocates fixed costs between cost of goods sold and inventories, while direct costing considers all fixed costs to be period costs
e. none of the above

(AICPA adapted)

_____ 4. Gracie, Inc. manufactured 700 units of Product A, a new product, in 19A. Product A's variable and fixed manufacturing costs per unit were $6 and $2, respectively. There was no inventory of Product A on January 1, 19A. The inventory on December 31, 19A, consisted of 400 units. The difference between the dollar amount of inventory on December 31, 19A, using the direct costing method and the dollar amount using the absorption costing method would be:
a. $1,600 decrease
b. $400 decrease
c. $1,200 decrease
d. $400 increase
e. none of the above

(AICPA adapted)

_____ 5. A company has operating income of $50,000 using direct costing for a given period. Beginning and ending inventories for that period were 18,000 units and 13,000 units, respectively. If the fixed factory overhead application rate is $4 per unit, the operating income using absorption costing is:
a. $40,000
b. $60,000
c. $50,000
d. $30,000
e. not determinable from the information given

(AICPA adapted)

_____ 6. Knight Company, a lamp manufacturer, made available to its customers a new line called "Twilight." The break-even point for sales of Twilight is $400,000, with a contribution margin of 40%. If the operating income for the Twilight line for 19A amounted to $200,000, total sales for 19A were:
a. $600,000
b. $900,000
c. $840,000
d. $950,000
e. none of the above

(AICPA adapted)

_____ 7. The Ship Company is planning to produce two products, Alt and Tude. Ship is planning to sell 100,000 units of Alt at $4 a unit and 200,000 units of Tude at $3 a unit. Variable costs are 70% of sales for Alt and 80% of sales for Tude. In order to realize a total profit of $160,000, what must the total fixed costs be?

    a. $80,000   **d.** $600,000

    b. $90,000   **e.** None of the above

    c. $240,000   (AICPA adapted)

_____ 8. The following data pertain to two types of products manufactured by Korn Corp.:

	Per Unit	
	Sales Price	Variable Costs
Product Y...............................	$120	$ 70
Product Z...............................	500	200

Fixed costs total $300,000 annually. The expected mix in units is 60% for product Y and 40% for product Z. How much is Korn's break-even sales in units?

    a. 857   **d.** 2,459

    b. 1,111   **e.** None of the above

    c. 2,000

_____ 9. If the fixed cost for a product increases and the variable cost (as a percentage of sales dollars) increases, what will be the effect on the contribution margin ratio and the break-even point, respectively?

	Contribution Margin Ratio	Break-Even Point
a.	Decreased	Increased
b.	Increased	Decreased
c.	Decreased	Decreased
d.	Increased	Increased

                                                              (AICPA adapted)

_____ 10. To obtain the break-even point stated in units, the total fixed cost is divided by:

    a. variable cost per unit

    b. (sales price per unit − variable cost per unit) ÷ sales price per unit

    c. fixed cost per unit

    d. sales price per unit − variable cost per unit

    e. none of the above   (AICPA adapted)

PART 4

The following information is available for Tysun Corporation's new product line:

Sales price per unit	$ 30
Variable manufacturing cost per unit of production	15
Total annual fixed manufacturing cost	60,000
Variable general and administrative cost per unit of production	5
Total annual fixed marketing and administrative expenses	25,000

There was no inventory at the beginning of the year. During the year, 30,000 units were produced and 25,000 units were sold.

Instructions:

1. Determine the ending inventory, using direct costing.

2. Determine the ending inventory, using absorption costing.

3. Using direct costing, determine the total variable cost charged to expense for the year.

4. Using absorption costing, determine the total fixed cost charged to expense for the year.

5. Using direct costing, determine the total fixed cost charged to expense for the year.

PART 5

Sergio Corporation produced 50,000 units (normal capacity) of product during the second quarter of the year; 40,000 units were sold at $25 per unit. The costs of this production were:

Materials	$100,000
Direct labor	250,000
Factory overhead	
Variable cost..	125,000
Fixed cost..	150,000

Marketing and administrative expenses for the quarter total $350,000; all are fixed expenses.

Instructions:

1. Prepare an income statement using absorption costing.

Sergio Corporation
Income Statement—Absorption Costing
For Quarter Ended June 30, 19–

2. Prepare an income statement using direct costing.

Sergio Corporation
Income Statement—Direct Costing
For Quarter Ended June 30, 19–

PART 6

Radcliffe Toothbrush Co. manufactures one style of deluxe toothbrush. The following information was received by management, covering the past three months:

	Oct.	Nov.	Dec.
Sales (at $10 per unit)	$5,000	$2,000	$20,000
Beginning inventory	-0-	$2,500	$ 6,500
Cost of goods manufactured in month	$5,000	5,000	5,000
Cost of goods available for sale	$5,000	$7,500	$11,500
Ending inventory	2,500	6,500	1,500
Cost of goods sold	$2,500	$1,000	$10,000
Gross profit	$2,500	$1,000	$10,000

Supplementary information:

Sales price per unit: $10
Units manufactured per month: 1,000
Standard cost per unit at normal volume: $5
Total manufacturing cost at normal volume:
Variable $3,000
Fixed 2,000

The Cost Department believes that a direct standard costing system may be more helpful for management purposes than the standard absorption system presently in use.

Instructions:

1. Prepare income statements for each of the three months on the direct standard cost basis.

Radcliffe Toothbrush Co.
Comparative Income Statements for October, November, and December
Direct Costing Method

	Oct.	Nov.	Dec.
Sales	$_____	$_____	$_____
Beginning inventory	$	$	$
Variable cost of goods manufactured (variable costs)	_____	_____	_____
Variable cost of goods available for sale	$	$	$
Ending inventory	_____	_____	_____
Variable cost of goods sold	$_____	$_____	$_____
Gross contribution margin	$	$	$
Less fixed factory overhead	_____	_____	_____
Gross profit (loss)	$_____	$_____	$_____

2. Show computations explaining the differences in gross profit for each month.

	Oct.	Nov.	Dec.
Gross profit—absorption costing	$	$	$
Gross profit—direct costing	_____	_____	_____
Difference	$_____	$_____	$_____
Inventory change—absorption costing	$	$	$
Less inventory change—direct costing	_____	_____	_____
Difference	$_____	$_____	$_____

PART 7

The following data of ZZ Co. are given for March:

Plant capacity	1,600 units for the month
Fixed cost	$80,000 per month
Variable cost	$90 per unit
Sales price	$150 per unit

Instructions:

1. Determine the break-even point in dollars.

2. Determine the break-even point in units.

3. Prepare a conventional break-even chart, using the accompanying form. Label and identify each element of the chart.

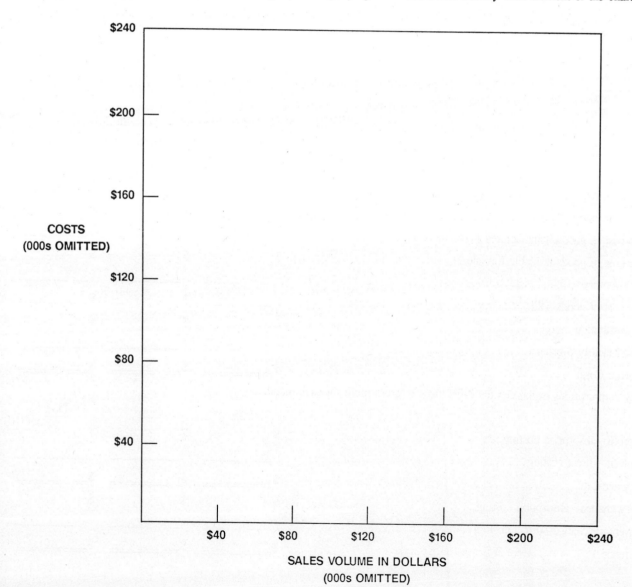

COSTS
(000s OMITTED)

SALES VOLUME IN DOLLARS
(000s OMITTED)

PART 8

Navajo Jewelry Company provides the following data:

Normal plant capacity .... 3,000 units
Fixed cost $600,000
Variable cost .... $140 per unit
Sales price .... $400 per unit

Instructions: *Determine each of the following items, rounding all dollar amounts to the nearest whole dollar and rounding all percentages to two decimal places.*

1. Compute the break-even point in:
   (a) Dollars

   (b) Number of units

   (c) Percent of capacity

2. When operating at normal capacity, compute the:
   (a) Margin of safety in dollars

   (b) Margin of safety ratio

3. Determine the new break-even point in dollars if the sales price is reduced to $350 and other data remain the same.

4. Determine the volume in dollars required to yield a profit of $100,000 if the calculation is based on:
   (a) The data in (1)

   (b) The data in (3)

5. Determine the expected profit if budgeted sales of $1,200,000 are realized, and costs and selling price are the same as at the beginning of the problem.

PART 9

Hi Fi Company presents the following per-unit data for two of its products:

	Woofers	Tweeters
Selling price	$20	$15
Variable cost	6	1
Fixed cost	3	1
Units per hour	50	70

Instructions: *Determine the following.*

1. The amount of profit per unit for each product

2. The percentage of profit to selling price for each product

3. The amount of contribution per unit towards fixed cost and profit for each product

4. The contribution margin ratio for each product

5. The contribution margin per hour toward fixed cost and profit for each product

6. The more profitable product for the company if there is a long-run commitment to the present level of fixed cost, and all units produced of either product can be sold

PART 10

Moore Memorial Hospital records provide the following patient mix data for the year:

Method of Payment	Patient Mix	Average Daily Reimbursement Rate	Average Daily Variable Cost
Self-pay	20%	$100	$80
Private insurance	25	200	80
Medicare	30	150	80
Medicaid	25	125	80

The annual fixed cost is $2,500,000.

Instructions: *Determine each of the following items.*

1. The weighted daily reimbursement rate (rounded to the nearest whole dollar)

Method of Payment	Patient Mix	Average Daily Reimbursement Rate	Weighted Daily Reimbursement Rate

2. The composite break-even point in dollars (rounded to the nearest whole dollar)

3. The composite break-even point in in-patient days (rounded to the nearest whole day)

CHAPTER 21
DIFFERENTIAL COST ANALYSIS

REVIEW SUMMARY

1. *Differential cost,* often referred to as *marginal* or *incremental cost,* is the difference in the cost of alternative choices. Differential cost studies deal with the determination of incremental revenues, costs, and margins with regard to alternative uses of fixed facilities or available capacity. Variable costs usually represent the differential costs, although additional fixed costs may be incurred. To enable management to have useful and meaningful cost data with which to maximize long-run profits, several other cost terms, concepts, and classifications, in addition to differential cost, must be incorporated in the decision-making process. *Opportunity costs* are the measurable value of an opportunity by-passed by rejecting an alternative use of resources. *Imputed costs* are hypothetical costs representing the cost or value of a resource measured by its use value. *Out-of-pocket costs* are the costs relevant to any decision when the total product cost are not pertinent. *Sunk costs* are past costs that are irrelevant to a future decision.

2. If available capacity is not fully used, a differential cost analysis might indicate the possibility of selling additional output at a figure lower than the existing average unit cost. The new or additional business can be accepted as long as the variable cost is recovered, because any contribution to the recovery of fixed costs and profit is desirable. Whenever a differential cost analysis leads management to accept a special order at or above the differential cost, it is assumed that the order is not going to disturb the market for the other products being offered. The firm must also be careful not to violate the Robinson-Patman Act and other governmental pricing restrictions.

3. The problem of whether to make or buy an item arises particularly in connection with the use of idle equipment, idle space, or idle labor. The accountant should prepare a statement presenting the differential costs of making the item, including a share of existing fixed expense and a profit figure that places the total cost of make versus buy on a comparable basis. A cost study with only the differential costs and with no allocation of existing fixed expenses or profit may indicate possible cost savings in the short run, but in the long run, the full cost must be covered and a reasonable profit achieved.

4. In the short run, a firm is better off operating than shutting down facilities, as long as the products or services sold re-cover the variable cost and make a contribution to the recovery of fixed costs that continue during periods of inactivity. Decisions to discontinue individual products require careful analysis of relevant differential cost and revenue data through a structured and continuous product evaluation program. Studies have shown that, mainly due to the lack of relevant data, firms do a poor job of identifying products that are in difficulty and that should be eliminated.

5. Differential cost studies must often determine the profitability of the short-run use of available capacity. *Linear programming* allows the accountant to determine the optimum course of action when the resource allocation problem is complex and its solution is neither obvious nor feasible by trial and error.

6. Linear programming may be used to solve contribution margin maximization problems. For example, assume that management is trying to decide how much of each of two products to produce, given different contribution margins and hours required for production of each product. To maximize the total contribution margin, management must decide on (a) the allocation of available production capacity to each product and (b) the number of units of each product to produce. This type of problem may be solved by either of two basic linear programming techniques—the *graphic method* or the *simplex method.* These methods may also be used to solve cost minimization problems.

7. When a linear programming problem involves only two variables, a two-dimensional graph can be used to determine the optimal solution. In the example mentioned above, the maximum number of units of each product that can be produced would be determined by dividing the hours of productive capacity available in each department by the number of departmental hours required to complete each product unit. To determine the combination of production levels in order to maximize the contribution margin, all the constraints would be plotted on a graph. The best feasible solution, according to mathematics, is at one of the four corner points on the graph. Consequently, all four corner point variables must be examined to find the combination that maximixes the contribution margin.

PART 1

Instructions: *Place a check mark in the appropriate column to indicate whether each of the following statements is True or False.*

	True	False
1. Historical costs drawn from accounting records generally give management the differential cost information needed to evaluate alternatives.	———	———
2. The term "marginal cost" is widely used by economists.	———	———
3. In differential cost studies, fixed costs are significant, because they usually represent the differential cost.	———	———
4. If one alternative in a differential cost study requires the addition of new equipment, the related fixed costs are differential costs.	———	———
5. If available capacity is not fully used, new or additional business can be accepted as long as all variable costs are recovered.	———	———
6. Whenever a differential cost analysis leads management to accept an additional order at above the differential cost, the Robinson-Patman Act and other government pricing restrictions may be applicable.	———	———
7. A shutdown of facilities eliminates all fixed costs in the short run.	———	———
8. In decisions to discontinue a product, management must consider not only the profitability of the product but also the extent to which sales of other products will be adversely affected when the product is removed.	———	———
9. Studies have shown that the lack of timely, relevant data is a major reason why firms do a poor job of identifying products that are in difficulty.	———	———
10. Linear programming is used when the resource allocation problem is simple and its solution is fairly obvious.	———	———
11. The undepreciated book value of an old asset is a sunk cost and is, therefore, irrelevant to a decision as to whether to keep or replace the asset.	———	———
12. Linear programming is a valuable aid to management because it provides a systematic and efficient procedure that can be used as a guide in decision making.	———	———
13. When the total contribution margin is maximized, management's profit objective should be satisfied.	———	———
14. When a linear programming problem involves more than two variables, the graphic method must be used to determine the optimal solution.	———	———
15. Using the simplex method of linear programming, the best feasible solution must fall within the area bounded by the four corner points.	———	———

PART 2

Instructions: *In the blank space at the left of each of the following items, place the letter from the right-hand column that identifies the term that best matches the statement in the column on the left. No letter should be used more than once.*

_____ 1. The difference in the cost of alternative choices.

_____ 2. A synonym for differential cost that is widely used by economists.

_____ 3. A term used by engineers to describe the added cost incurred when a project is extended beyond its originally intended goal.

_____ 4. Arises particularly in connection with the possible use of idle equipment, idle space, and even idle labor.

_____ 5. Departmental flexible budgets that state the amount for each class of expense at each production level.

_____ 6. Allows the accountant to determine the optimum course of action when the resource allocation problem is complex and its solution is not obvious by trial and error.

_____ 7. Based on quantifying the likelihood of the occurrence of possible events.

_____ 8. The measureable value of sacrifices associated with alternatives.

_____ 9. Hypothetical costs representing the cost or value of a resource measured by its use value.

_____ 10. Past costs that are irrelevant to future decisions.

_____ 11. When this is maximized, management's profit objective should be satisfied.

_____ 12. When a linear programming problem involves only two variables, this may be used to determine the optimal solution.

_____ 13. The best feasible solution when using the graphic method of linear programming is at one of these.

_____ 14. An iterative, stepwise process that approaches an optimum solution in order to reach an objective function of maximization or minimalization.

_____ 15. Evaluates the effect on the optimal solution to a problem of changes to the relevant variables.

a. marginal cost
b. probability
c. incremental cost
d. linear programming
e. differential cost
f. cost analysis budgets
g. make-or-buy decision
h. opportunity costs
i. sunk costs
j. imputed costs
k. two-dimensional graph
l. linear programming
m. simplex method
n. corner point
o. contribution margin

PART 3

Instructions: *In the blank space at the left of each of the following items, place the letter of the choice that most correctly completes each item.*

_____ 1. The opportunity cost of making a component part in a factory with excess capacity for which there is no alternative use is:

a. the variable manufacturing cost of the component   d. the fixed manufacturing cost of the component

b. the total manufacturing cost of the component   e. zero

c. the total variable cost of the component   (ICMA adapted)

_____ 2. A sunk cost is a cost that:

a. may be saved by adopting an alternative

b. may be shifted to the future with little or no effect on current operations

c. cannot be avoided because it has already been incurred

d. does not entail any dollar outlay but is relevant to the decision-making process

e. none of the above   (ICMA adapted

_____ 3. An imputed cost is:

a. the difference in total costs that results from selecting one alternative instead of another

b. a cost that may be shifted to the future with little or no effect on current operations

c. a cost that cannot be avoided because it has already been incurred

d. a cost that does not entail any dollar outlay but is relevant to the decision-making process

e. none of the above   (ICMA adapted)

_____ 4. In considering a special order situation that will enable a company to make use of present idle capacity, a cost that would be irrelevant is:

a. direct materials   d. variable factory overhead

b. depreciation   e. none of the above

c. direct labor   (AICPA adapted)

_____ 5. Jordan Company budgeted sales of 400,000 calculators at $40 per unit for the year. Variable manufacturing costs were budgeted at $16 per unit and fixed manufacturing costs at $10 per-unit. In March Jordan received a special order offering to buy 40,000 calculators for $18 each. Jordan has sufficient plant capacity to manufacture the additional quantity; however, the production would have to be done on an overtime basis at an estimated additional cost of $3 per calculator. Acceptance of the special order would not affect Jordan's normal sales and no selling expenses would be incurred. What would be the effect on operating profit if the special order were accepted?

a. $120,000 decrease   d. $80,000 increase

b. $40,000 decrease   e. None of the above

c. $140,000 decrease   (AICPA adapted)

_____ 6. Spencer Company's regular selling price for its product is $10 per unit. Variable costs are $6 per unit. Fixed costs total $1 per unit based on 100,000 units and remained unchanged within the relevant range of 50,000 units to total capacity of 200,000 units. After sales of 80,000 units were projected for the year, a special order was received for an additional 10,000 units. To increase its operating income by $10,000, what price per unit should Spencer charge for this special order?

a. $7   b. $8   c. $10   d. $11   e. None of the above   (AICPA adapted)

_____ 7. Nugget Inc. has been manufacturing 5,000 units of Part 10541, which is used in the manufacture of one of its products. At this level of production, the cost per unit of manufacturing Part 10541 is as follows:

Direct materials	$ 2
Direct labor	8
Variable overhead	4
Applied fixed overhead	6
Total	$20

Wynn Company has offered to sell Nugget 5,000 units of Part 10541 for $19 a unit. Nugget has determined that it could use the facilities presently used to manufacture Part 10541 to manufacture product RAC and generate an operating profit of $4,000. Nugget has also determined that two thirds of the applied fixed overhead will continue even if Part 10541 is purchased from Wynn. To determine whether to accept Wynn's offer, the net relevant cost to Wynn is:

a. $70,000   d. $95,000
b. $80,000   e. none of the above
c. $90,000
                                                                                                (AICPA adapted)

_____ 8. As part of the data presented in support of a proposal to increase the production of video games, the sales manager of Tojo Products reported the total additional cost required for the proposed increased production level. The increase in total cost is known as:

a. controllable cost   d. out-of-pocket cost
b. differential cost   e. none of the above
c. opportunity cost
                                                                                                (AICPA adapted)

_____ 9. Letter Company manufactures two products, q and p, in a small building with limited capactiy. The sales price, cost data, and production time are given below:

	Product q	Product p
Sales price per unit	$20	$17
Variable cost of producing and selling a unit	$13	$12
Hours to produce a unit	3	1

Based on this information, the contribution margin maximization objective function for a linear programming solution may be stated as:

a. 20q + 17p   d. 4⅓q + 12p
b. 13q + 12p   e. 7q + 5p
c. 3q + 1p
                                                                                                (AICPA adapted)

_____ 10. Maybury Company plans to expand its sales force by opening as many as ten new branch offices and has set $5,200,000 as the capital available for this purpose. Maybury will open only two types of branches: ten-person branches (type a), initial outlay of $650,000 each; and five-person branches (type b), initial outlay of $335,000 each. Expected annual after-tax cash inflow for types a and b is $46,000 and $18,000 respectively. No more than 100 employees will be hired for the new branch offices. In a system of inequalities for a linear programming model, the one not representing a constraint is:

a. a + b $\leq$ 10   d. $650,000a + $335,000b $\leq$ $5,200,000
b. 10a + 5b $\leq$ 100   e. all of the above
c. $46,000a + $18,000b $\leq$ $64,000
                                                                                                (AICPA adapted)

PART 4

Although Kermit Company has the capacity to producte 10,000 units per month, current plans call for monthly production sales of only 8,000 units at $15 each. Costs per unit at the 8,000 unit level are as follows:

Direct materials...	$4.00
Direct labor..	2.50
Variable factory overhead	2.00
Fixed factory overhead	1.75
Variable marketing expense.............................	.50
Fixed administrative expense...........................	1.25
	$12.00

Instructions:

1. Determine whether the company should accept a special order for 1,000 units @ $9.50.

2. Determine the maximum unit price that the company should be willing to pay an outside supplier to manufacture 10,000 units of this product, assuming that $2,500 of fixed factory overhead would not be incurred if the product were made outside.

PART 5

Studley Company manufactures Nerds for use in its assembly operation. Costs per unit for 1,000 units of Nerds are:

Direct materials..	$ 5
Direct labor...	17
Variable factory overhead	10
Fixed factory overhead	12
Total unit cost	$ 44

Collins Company has offered to sell Studley 1,000 units of Nerds for $45 each. If Studley accepts, some of the facilities presently used to manufacture Nerds could be used to help with the manufacture of Woolies, thus saving $10,000 in relevant cost in the manufacture of Woolies and eliminating two thirds of the fixed factory overhead incurred in making Nerds.

Instructions: *Prepare a make-or-buy decision analysis.*

PART 6

From a particular joint process, Greek Company produces three products—Chi, Phi, and Kappa. Each product may be sold at the point of split-off or processed further. Additional processing requires no special facilities, and production costs of further processing are entirely variable and traceable to the products involved. During the past year, these products were processed beyond split-off. The joint production cost for the year was $100,000. Sales value and costs needed to evaluate Greek's current production policy follow:

Product	Units Produced	Sales Value at Split-Off	If Processed Further Sales Value	If Processed Further Added Cost
Chi	10,000	$75,000	$90,000	$15,000
Phi	8,000	60,000	72,000	20,000
Kappa	5,000	43,000	58,000	10,000

The joint cost is allocated to the products in proportion to the relative physical volume of output.

Instructions:

1. Determine the unit production cost most relevant to a sell-or-process further decision for units of Chi.

2. Complete the following schedule for purposes of determining the products that the company should process further in order to maximize profits.

	Chi	Phi	Kappa
Sales value if processed further	$	$	$
Sales value at split-off			
Added sales value	$	$	$
Added cost			
Difference in favor (against) processing further	$	$	$

PART 7

N.A. Glick Company sells two products with the following characteristics:

	Micro	Macro
Quantity sold	50,000 units	25,000 units
Standard cost per unit:		
Fixed	$ 5	$ 10
Variable	12	18
	$17	$28
Sales price per unit	$25	$26

Instructions:

1. Compute the profit per unit and in total, assuming that the firm operates at normal capacity and that the standard cost and the actual cost are the same.

2. Recommend whether the firm should continue its sales of both products, assuming that the fixed cost will remain the same in total whether either or both are produced.

3. Decide whether it would be more profitable to drom Macro and add Macro Plus, assuming that the same facilities can be used for the production of either and that Macro Plus cost data are:

Quantity sold	12,500 units
Standard cost per unit:	
Fixed	$20
Variable	12
	$32
Sales price per unit	$50

4. Compute the opportunity cost for Macro.

PART 8

Aerospace Company produces two products, Apollos and Lunars, in two departments, Mixing and Molding. The mixing machines can be operated 80 hours per week, and the molding machines 60 hours per week. Each Apollo requires twice as much mixing time as a Lunar but requires only one half as much molding time. Each Lunar requires one hour of work in each process. The contribution margin on each Apollo is $100,000, and on each Lunar is $80,000.

Instructions:

1. Complete the schedule below and draw the graph on the form provided to determine the product mix that the Aerospace Company should maintain to maximize the total contribution margin. (Round answers to the nearest whole unit.)

Department	Hours Available	Hours Required Per Apollo	Hours Required Per Lunar	Maximum Units Apollo	Maximum Units Lunar
Mixing					
Molding					

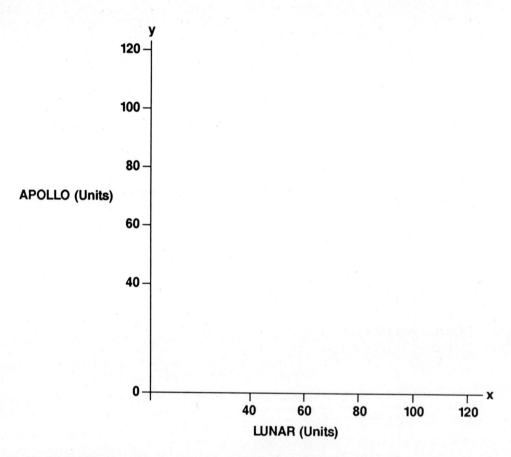

2. Determine the maximum weekly contribution margin figure. (Round all computations to the nearest whole number.)

PART 9

Arturo Enterprises Inc. manufactures two products, ravioli and ziti. Each product must be processed in each of three departments: Mixing, Stuffing, and Cooking. The minutes needed to produce one bag of ravioli and one bag of ziti per department and the maximum possible minutes per department are:

Department	Production Minutes per Ravioli	Ziti	Maximum Capacity in Minutes
Mixing	3	4	48,000
Stuffing	4	3	45,000
Cooking	3	2	34,500

Other restrictions:

Ravioli $\geq$ 2,400 packages

Ziti $\geq$ 2,400 packages

The objective function is to maximize the contribution margin where CM = $1 ravioli + $.50 ziti package.

Instructions: *From the following answers, determine the feasible solution that will maximize the contribution margin:*

6,000 ravioli and 6,000 ziti packages

Mixing ....

Stuffing ....

Cooking ....

7,200 ravioli and 4,800 ziti packages

Mixing ....

Stuffing ....

Cooking ....

8,400 ravioli and 3,600 ziti packages

Mixing ....

Stuffing ....

Cooking ....

9,600 ravioli and 2,400 ziti packages

Mixing ....

Stuffing ....

Cooking ....

Conclusion

CHAPTER 22
CAPITAL EXPENDITURES:
PLANNING, EVALUATING, AND CONTROLLING

REVIEW SUMMARY

1. *Capital budgeting* is the process of planning the continuing investment of an organization's resources and the monitoring of that investment. *Capital expenditures* involve long-term commitments of resources to realize future benefits. Planning for capital expenditures consists of relating plans to objectives, structuring the framework, searching for proposals, budgeting the expenditures, and requesting authority for the expenditures. The management accountant has an ethical responsibility to make sure that the company's policies and procedures are not circumvented and to make sure that the data used in the evaluation of capital projects are reliable and realistic. Evaluating capital expenditures refers to the basic theory, techniques, and procedures for the appraisal and reappraisal of projects throughout the course of their development.

2. Capital expenditure projects can be classified as (a) equipment-replacement expenditures, (b) expansion investments, and (c) improvements of existing products or additions of new products. The *cost of capital* represents the expected return that investors demand for a given level of risk. If a company obtains funds by some combination of bonds, preferred and common stock, retained earnings, and bank loans to achieve or maintain a particular capital structure, then the cost of capital is the weighted average cost of each money source.

3. In order for cash flow to be on an equivalent basis with the weighted average cost of capital, cash flow estimates must include an allowance for the effect of anticipated inflation. Another effect of inflation is that it increases discount rates and biases the decision-making process in favor of short-term projects, because as rates increase, cash flows in more distant years become less significant. Depreciation allowed for income tax purposes is also an important consideration in planning and evaluating capital expenditures because depreciation reduces taxable income and, consequently, tax liability, which is a cash flow.

4. The following four capital expenditure evaluation techniques are in current usage: (a) the payback (payout) period method, (b) the average annual return on investment method, (c) the present value method, and (d) the discounted cash flow method. The *payback period method* measures the length of time required by a project to recover its initial outlay. The calculated payback period is then compared to the payback period acceptable to management for that particular type of project. Under the *average annual return on investment method*, an investment

proposal is evaluated by comparing the estimated average annual rate of return on the investment with a target rate of return. The average annual return on original investment is computed as follows:

$$\frac{\text{Net income}}{\text{Economic life}} \div \text{Original investment}$$

Another approach is to divide the average annual net income by the average investment rather than the original investment.

5. Using the *present value method*, the estimated results of an investment proposal can be stated at its cash equivalent at the present time. It is preferable to discount all proposals at a constant rate, the cost of capital. If the true rate of return is greater than the cost of capital discount rate, then the net present value will be positive and the project should be accepted. In the *discounted cash flow* method, the discount rate is not known but is defined as the rate at which the sum of positive present values equals the sum of negative present values. The discounted rate of return can be determined by trial and error—by computing net present value at various percentages to find the rate at which the net present value is zero. The discounted cash flow method permits management to maximize corporate profits by selecting proposals with the highest rates of return as long as the rates are higher than the company's own cost of capital.

6. A project whose estimated desirability is near a cut-off point for the type of project being evaluated affords little cushion for errors. A higher degree of sophistication in evaluating a project, at a higher cost of obtaining the data, may be necessary to add confidence when the evaluation is close to a cutoff point or when two or more project alternatives yield about the same "best" answer. When a project or a series of projects has been approved, methods, techniques, and procedures must be set in motion to permit the control and review of all project elements until completion. PERT/cost uses the network scheme to show the relationships of the multiple activities required to complete the average to large-scale project. A follow-up or post-completion audit involves comparing and reporting results as related to the outcome predicted when the investment project was evaluated and approved. It affords a test of the existing planning and control procedure and allows for the possibility of reinforcing successful projects, salvaging or terminating failing projects, and improving upon future investment proposals and decisions.

PART 1

Instructions: *Place a check mark in the appropriate column to indicate whether each of the following statements is **True** or **False**.*

	True	False
1. Capital expenditures have a significant long-term effect on the economic well-being of the firm.	_____	_____
2. The higher the level at which a capital expenditure decision is authorized, the greater the need for guidelines extending to detailed procedures and standards.	_____	_____
3. The capital expenditures budget is typically prepared for a one-year period.	_____	_____
4. Authority to commit funds to a capital project should come by means of a DCF.	_____	_____
5. Accelerated depreciation increases the impact of inflation by slowing the recovery of capital expenditures.	_____	_____
6. In equipment-replacement decisions, the original cost of the present facility is a cost that is relevant to the decision.	_____	_____
7. The degree of uncertainty in an equipment-replacement decision is much smaller than in a decision to enlarge an existing plant.	_____	_____
8. The cost of capital for bonds is the after-tax rate of interest.	_____	_____
9. A disadvantage of the payback period method is that it excludes cash flows that may occur beyond the payback period.	_____	_____
10. A disadvantage of the average annual return on investment method is that it ignores the time value of money.	_____	_____
11. An advantage of the present value method is that it allows for different discount rates over the life of the project.	_____	_____
12. A disadvantage of the discounted cash flow method is that the percentage figures computed do not lend themselves to a generally sound, uniform ranking of projects.	_____	_____
13. Discounting using the present value method implies that cash inflows can be reinvested to earn the rate earned by the investment being evaluated.	_____	_____
14. When one alternative is clearly superior to others, there is a smaller error cushion than when two or more of the best alternatives indicate approximately the same expected results.	_____	_____
15. The use of PERT/cost is appropriate for evaluating capital expenditures where more than one estimate is needed due to risk and uncertainty.	_____	_____

PART 2

Instructions: *In the blank space at the left of each of the following items, place the letter from the right-hand column that identifies the term that best matches the statement in the column on the left. No letter should be used more than once.*

_____ 1. The process of planning the continuing investment of an organization's resources and the monitoring of that investment.

_____ 2. Involve long-term commitments of resources to realize future benefits.

_____ 3. Computes an average annual return on a project by dividing annual net income by the original investment.

_____ 4. Typically prepared for a one-year period.

_____ 5. In effect, a second look at budgeted projects based on an up-to-date set of documents justifying and describing the expenditure.

_____ 6. Originally enacted in 1962 for the stated purpose of stimulating the economy and generating additional employment.

_____ 7. Uses the network scheme to show the relationships of the multiple activities required to complete the average to large-scale project.

_____ 8. Represents the expected return investors demand for a given level of risk.

_____ 9. Computed on the basis of proportions and rates for bonds, preferred stock, common stock, and retained earnings.

_____ 10. Prescribes the capitalization of interest costs incurred in acquiring assets that require a period of time to be made ready for their intended use.

_____ 11. Presence indicates that the true rate of return is greater than the cost of capital discount rate.

_____ 12. When this method of evaluating capital expenditures is used, the discount rate is not known but is defined as the rate at which the sum of positive present values equals the sum of negative present values.

_____ 13. Virtually nonexistent when a project's estimated desirability is near a cut-off point for that particular type of project.

_____ 14. Involves comparing and reporting results as related to the outcome predicted when the investment was evaluated and approved.

_____ 15. Enables management to determine the minimum life for a project necessary to recover the original investment and earn a desired rate of return on the investment.

a. weighted average cost of capital
b. capital expenditures
c. positive net present value
d. error cushion
e. present value payback method
f. accounting rate of return method
g. post-completion audit
h. capital budgeting
i. DCF method
j. investment tax credit
k. capital expenditures budget
l. SFAS No. 34
m. cost of capital
n. PERT/cost
o. AFE procedure

PART 3

Instructions: *In the blank space at the left of each of the following items, place the letter of the choice that most correctly completes each item.*

_____ 1. In selecting the purchase of one of two machines to replace an old machine, the managemetn of Niles Company should consider as relevant:
  a. historical costs associated with the old machine
  b. future costs that will be classified as variable rather than fixed
  c. future costs that will be different under the two alternatives
  d. future costs that will be classified as fixed rather than variable
  e. none of the above   (AICPA adapted)

_____ 2. For a project such as a plant investment, the return that investors demand for investing in a firm is known as:
  a. DCF rate of return   **d.** cost of capital
  b. net present value   **e.** accounting rate of return
  c. payback   (AICPA adapted)

_____ 3. Manning Company is planning to purchase a new machine. The payback period is estimated to be six years. After-tax cash flow is estimated to be $2,000 yearly for the first three years and $3,000 yearly for the next three years of the payback period. Annual depreciation of $1,500 will be charged to income for each of the six years of the payback period. The machine will cost:
  a. $15,000   **b.** $12,000   **c.** $9,000   **d.** $6,000   **e.** none of the above   (AICPA adapted)

_____ 4. An advantage of using the payback method is that the method is:
  a. precise in estimates of profitability   **d.** sensitive to the life of the project being evaluated
  b. used to select investments yielding a quick return   **e.** all of the above
     of cash
  c. based on discounted cash-flow data   (AICPA adapted)

_____ 5. The present value and discounted cash flow rate of return methods of evaluating capital expenditure proposals are superior to the payback method in that they:
  a. are easier to implement   **d.** reflect the effects of depreciation and income tax
  b. consider cash flow over the entire life of the project   **e.** all of the above
  c. require less input   (AICPA adapted)

_____ 6. A planned factory expansion project has an estimated initial cost of $800,000. Using a 20% discount rate, the present value of future cost savings from the expansion is $843,000. To yield exactly a 20% time-adjusted rate of return, the actual investment cost cannot exceed the $800,000 estimate by more than:
  a. $160,000   **b.** $20,000   **c.** $43,000   **d.** $1,075   **e.** $0   (AICPA adapted)

_____ 7. On January 1, a company invested in an asset with a useful life of three years. The company's expected rate of return is 10%. The cash flow and present and future value factors for the three years are as follows:

Year	Cash Inflow from the Asset	Present Value of $1 at 10%	Future Value of $1 at 10%
1	$ 8,000	.91	1.10
2	$ 9,000	.83	1.21
3	$10,000	.75	1.33

All cash inflows are assumed to occur at year-end. If the asset generates a positive net present value of $2,000, what was the amount of the original investment?
  a. $20,250   **b.** $22,250   **c.** $30,991   **d.** $33,991   **e.** none of the above

_____ **8.** The effectiveness of the present value method has been appropriately questioned as a capital expenditure evaluation technique because:

   a. predicting future cash flows is often difficult and clouded with uncertainties

   b. the average return on investment method is usually more accurate and useful

   c. the payback method is theoretically more reliable

   d. the computation involves some difficult mathematical applications that most accountants cannot perform

   e. all of the above   (AICPA adapted)

_____ **9.** Basknight Inc., a calendar year company, purchased a new machine for $28,000 on January 1. The machine has an estimated useful life of eight years with no salvage value and is being depreciated on the straight-line basis. The accounting rate of return is expected to be 15% on the initial investment. On the assumption of a uniform cash inflow, this investment is expected to provide annual cash flow from operations, net of income taxes, of:

   a. $3,500   **b.** $4,025   **c.** $4,200   **d.** $7,700   **e.** none of the above   (AICPA adapted)

_____ **10.** Two projects have an initial outlay of $497 and each has an income stream lasting three years. Project A returns $200 per year for the three years. Project B returns $200 for the first two years and $248 for the third year.

		Present Value—Amount		
n	8%	10%	12%	14%
1	.9259	.9091	.8929	.8772
2	.8575	.8264	.7972	.7695
3	.7938	.7513	.7118	.6750

The appropriate internal rate of return valuation for Project B is:

   a. 200(.8772) + 200(.7695) + 248(.6750) = 496.74

   b. 200(.8929) + 200(.7972) + 248(.7118) = 514.41

   c. 200(.9091) + 200(.8264) + 248(.7513) = 533.42

   d. 200(.9259) + 200(.8573) + 248(.7938) = 553.50

PART 4

Rex Company wishes to compute a weighted average cost of capital for use in evaluating capital expenditure proposals. Earnings, capital structure, and current market prices of the company's securities are:

Earnings:

Earnings before interest and tax	$ 300,000
Interest expense on bonds	75,000
Pre-tax earnings	$ 225,000
Income tax (assume 30% tax rate)	67,500
After-tax earnings	$ 157,500
Preferred stock dividends	36,000
Earnings available to common stockholders	$ 121,500
Common stock dividends	25,000
Retained earnings	$ 96,500

Capital structure:

Mortgage bonds, 15%, 20 years	$ 500,000
Preferred stock, 12%, $100 par	250,000
Common stock, no par, 50,000 shares	300,000
Retained earnings (equity of common stockholders)	450,000
	$1,500,000

Market price of the company's securities:

Preferred stock	$96
Common stock	15

Instructions: *Determine the company's cost of capital. (Round all computations to four decimal places.)*

Funds	Proportion of Funds	After-Tax Cost	Weighted Cost
Bonds			
Preferred stock			
Common stock and retained earnings	_____		_____
	==========		==========

Computations

PART 5

Pidgeon Forge Amusement Park is considering the purchase of a new ride costing $100,000. The ride is to be depreciated using the MACRS recovery percentages for five-year property. The salvage value is zero. Assume a 30% tax rate, a cost of capital of 12%, and an economic life of six years. The estimated cash benefit before taxes is given in the table below.

Instructions:

1. Complete the table.

Year	Pre-tax Cash Benefit	Annual Depreciation	Taxable Income	Federal Income Tax	Net After-Tax Cash Inflow
1	$45,000	$	$	$	$
2	50,000				
3	44,000				
4	38,000				
5	34,000				
6	10,000				_____
					$_____

2. Determine the following:
   (a) The payback period. (Round to the nearest tenth of a year.)

Year	Cash Flow	Needed	Balance	Payback Years Required
1	$	$	$	
2				
3				
4				
5				
6				_____
Total payback period in years				======

   (b) The average annual return on original investment. (Round to the nearest tenth of a percent.)

(c) The average annual return on average investment. (Round to the nearest tenth of a percent.)

(d) The net present value. (Use the present value tables on pages 191 and 192, and round all computations to the nearest dollar.)

Year	Cash (Outflow) Inflow	Present Value of $1, 12%	Net Present Value of Cash Flow
0	$		$
1			
2			
3			
4			
5			
6			_____
Net present value...			$_____

(e) The discounted cash flow rate of return. (Round to the nearest tenth of a percent. Use the present value tables on pages 191 and 192, and round all computations to the nearest dollar.)

Year	Cash (Outflow) Inflow	Present Value of $1	Net Present Value of Cash Flow	Present Value of $1	Net Present Value of Cash Flow
0	$		$		$
1					
2					
3					
4					
5					
6			_____		_____
			$_____		$_____

Discounted cash flow rate of return

PART 6

Multombo Enterprises plans to operate a sightseeing boat in Montego Bay. In negotiating the purchase of a new boat from Nautico Inc., Multombo learned that Nautico would lease the boat to them as an alternative to selling it outright. Through such an arrangement, Multombo would not pay the $300,000 purchase price but would lease it for $70,000 annually. Multombo expects the boat to last for ten years, after which its value would be $30,000.

The annual net cash flow, excluding any consideration of lease payments and income tax, is expected to be $100,000. The company's income tax rate is 40% and its cost of capital is 12%. The straight-line depreciation method is to be used and salvage value may be ignored for tax purposes.

Instructions:

1. Use the present value method to evaluate each alternative.

(a) Purchase

(b) Lease

2. Give your decision.

PRESENT VALUE OF $1

Future Years	1%	2%	4%	6%	8%	10%	12%	14%	15%	16%	18%	20%	22%	24%	25%	26%	28%	30%	35%	40%	45%	50%
1	.990	.980	.962	.943	.926	.909	.893	.877	.870	.862	.847	.833	.820	.806	.800	.794	.781	.769	.741	.714	.690	.667
2	.980	.961	.925	.890	.857	.826	.797	.769	.756	.743	.718	.694	.672	.650	.640	.630	.610	.592	.549	.510	.476	.444
3	.971	.942	.889	.840	.794	.751	.712	.675	.658	.641	.609	.579	.551	.524	.512	.500	.477	.455	.406	.364	.328	.296
4	.961	.924	.855	.792	.735	.683	.636	.592	.572	.552	.516	.482	.451	.423	.410	.397	.373	.350	.301	.260	.226	.198
5	.951	.906	.822	.747	.681	.621	.567	.519	.497	.476	.437	.402	.370	.341	.328	.315	.291	.269	.223	.186	.156	.132
6	.942	.888	.790	.705	.630	.564	.507	.456	.432	.410	.370	.335	.303	.275	.262	.250	.227	.207	.165	.133	.108	.088
7	.933	.871	.760	.665	.583	.513	.452	.400	.376	.354	.314	.279	.249	.222	.210	.198	.178	.159	.122	.095	.074	.059
8	.923	.853	.731	.627	.540	.467	.404	.351	.327	.305	.266	.233	.204	.179	.168	.157	.139	.123	.091	.068	.051	.039
9	.914	.837	.703	.592	.500	.424	.361	.308	.284	.263	.225	.194	.167	.144	.134	.125	.108	.094	.067	.048	.035	.026
10	.905	.820	.676	.558	.463	.386	.322	.270	.247	.227	.191	.162	.137	.116	.107	.099	.085	.073	.050	.035	.024	.017
11	.896	.804	.650	.527	.429	.350	.287	.237	.215	.195	.162	.135	.112	.094	.086	.079	.066	.056	.037	.025	.017	.012
12	.887	.788	.625	.497	.397	.319	.257	.208	.187	.168	.137	.112	.092	.076	.069	.062	.052	.043	.027	.018	.012	.008
13	.879	.773	.601	.469	.368	.290	.229	.182	.163	.145	.116	.093	.075	.061	.055	.050	.040	.033	.020	.013	.008	.005
14	.870	.758	.577	.442	.340	.263	.205	.160	.141	.125	.099	.078	.062	.049	.044	.039	.032	.025	.015	.009	.006	.003
15	.861	.743	.555	.417	.315	.239	.183	.140	.123	.108	.084	.065	.051	.040	.035	.031	.025	.020	.011	.006	.004	.002
16	.853	.728	.534	.394	.292	.218	.163	.123	.107	.093	.071	.054	.042	.032	.028	.025	.019	.015	.008	.005	.003	.002
17	.844	.714	.513	.371	.270	.198	.146	.108	.093	.080	.060	.045	.034	.026	.023	.020	.015	.012	.006	.003	.002	.001
18	.836	.700	.494	.350	.250	.180	.130	.095	.081	.069	.051	.038	.028	.021	.018	.016	.012	.009	.005	.002	.001	.001
19	.828	.686	.475	.331	.232	.164	.116	.083	.070	.060	.043	.031	.023	.017	.014	.012	.009	.007	.003	.002	.001	.001
20	.820	.673	.456	.312	.215	.149	.104	.073	.061	.051	.037	.026	.019	.014	.012	.010	.007	.005	.002	.001		
21	.811	.660	.439	.294	.199	.135	.093	.064	.053	.044	.031	.022	.015	.011	.009	.008	.006	.004	.002	.001		
22	.803	.647	.422	.278	.184	.123	.083	.056	.046	.038	.026	.018	.013	.009	.007	.006	.004	.003	.001	.001		
23	.795	.634	.406	.262	.170	.112	.074	.049	.040	.033	.022	.015	.010	.007	.006	.005	.003	.002	.001			
24	.788	.622	.390	.247	.158	.102	.066	.043	.035	.028	.019	.013	.008	.006	.005	.004	.003	.002	.001			
25	.780	.610	.375	.233	.146	.092	.059	.038	.030	.024	.016	.010	.007	.005	.004	.003	.002	.001	.001			
26	.772	.598	.361	.220	.135	.084	.053	.033	.026	.021	.014	.009	.006	.004	.003	.002	.002	.001				
27	.764	.586	.347	.207	.125	.076	.047	.029	.023	.018	.011	.007	.005	.003	.002	.002	.001	.001				
28	.757	.574	.333	.196	.116	.069	.042	.026	.020	.016	.010	.006	.004	.002	.002	.002	.001	.001				
29	.749	.563	.321	.185	.107	.063	.037	.022	.017	.014	.008	.005	.003	.002	.002	.001	.001	.001				
30	.742	.552	.308	.174	.099	.057	.033	.020	.015	.012	.007	.004	.003	.002	.001	.001	.001					
40	.672	.453	.208	.097	.046	.022	.011	.005	.004	.003	.001	.001										
50	.608	.372	.141	.054	.021	.009	.003	.001	.001	.001												

PRESENT VALUE OF $1 RECEIVED OR PAID ANNUALLY FOR EACH OF THE NEXT N YEARS

Future Years	1%	2%	4%	6%	8%	10%	12%	14%	15%	16%	18%	20%	22%	24%	25%	26%	28%	30%	35%	40%	45%	50%
1	.990	.980	.962	.943	.926	.909	.893	.877	.870	.862	.847	.833	.820	.806	.800	.794	.781	.769	.741	.714	.690	.667
2	1.970	1.942	1.886	1.833	1.783	1.736	1.690	1.647	1.626	1.605	1.566	1.528	1.492	1.457	1.440	1.424	1.392	1.361	1.289	1.224	1.165	1.111
3	2.941	2.884	2.775	2.673	2.577	2.487	2.402	2.322	2.283	2.246	2.174	2.106	2.042	1.981	1.952	1.923	1.868	1.816	1.696	1.589	1.493	1.407
4	3.902	3.808	3.630	3.465	3.312	3.170	3.037	2.914	2.855	2.798	2.690	2.589	2.494	2.404	2.362	2.320	2.241	2.166	1.997	1.849	1.720	1.605
5	4.853	4.713	4.452	4.212	3.993	3.791	3.605	3.433	3.352	3.274	3.127	2.991	2.864	2.745	2.689	2.635	2.532	2.436	2.220	2.035	1.876	1.737
6	5.795	5.601	5.242	4.917	4.623	4.355	4.111	3.889	3.784	3.685	3.498	3.326	3.167	3.020	2.951	2.885	2.759	2.643	2.385	2.168	1.983	1.824
7	6.728	6.472	6.002	5.582	5.206	4.868	4.564	4.288	4.160	4.039	3.812	3.605	3.416	3.242	3.161	3.083	2.937	2.802	2.508	2.263	2.057	1.883
8	7.652	7.325	6.733	6.210	5.747	5.335	4.968	4.639	4.487	4.344	4.078	3.837	3.619	3.421	3.329	3.241	3.076	2.925	2.598	2.331	2.108	1.922
9	8.566	8.163	7.435	6.802	6.247	5.759	5.328	4.946	4.772	4.607	4.303	4.031	3.786	3.566	3.463	3.366	3.184	3.019	2.665	2.379	2.144	1.948
10	9.471	8.983	8.111	7.360	6.710	6.145	5.650	5.216	5.019	4.833	4.494	4.192	3.923	3.682	3.571	3.465	3.269	3.092	2.715	2.414	2.168	1.965
11	10.368	9.787	8.760	7.887	7.139	6.495	5.988	5.453	5.234	5.029	4.656	4.327	4.035	3.776	3.656	3.544	3.335	3.147	2.752	2.438	2.185	1.977
12	11.255	10.575	9.385	8.384	7.536	6.814	6.194	5.660	5.421	5.197	4.793	4.439	4.127	3.851	3.725	3.606	3.387	3.190	2.779	2.456	2.196	1.985
13	12.134	11.348	9.986	8.853	7.904	7.103	6.424	5.842	5.583	5.342	4.910	4.533	4.203	3.912	3.780	3.656	3.427	3.223	2.799	2.468	2.204	1.990
14	13.004	12.106	10.563	9.295	8.244	7.367	6.628	6.002	5.724	5.468	5.008	4.611	4.265	3.962	3.824	3.695	3.459	3.249	2.814	2.477	2.210	1.993
15	13.865	12.849	11.118	9.712	8.559	7.606	6.811	6.142	5.847	5.575	5.092	4.675	4.315	4.001	3.859	3.726	3.483	3.268	2.825	2.484	2.214	1.995
16	14.718	13.578	11.652	10.106	8.851	7.824	6.974	6.265	5.954	5.669	5.162	4.730	4.357	4.033	3.887	3.751	3.503	3.283	2.834	2.489	2.216	1.997
17	15.562	14.292	12.166	10.477	9.122	8.022	7.120	6.373	6.047	5.749	5.222	4.775	4.391	4.059	3.910	3.771	3.518	3.295	2.840	2.492	2.218	1.998
18	16.398	14.992	12.659	10.828	9.372	8.201	7.250	6.467	6.128	5.818	5.273	4.812	4.419	4.080	3.928	3.786	3.529	3.304	2.844	2.494	2.219	1.999
19	17.226	15.678	13.134	11.158	9.604	8.365	7.366	6.550	6.198	5.877	5.316	4.844	4.442	4.097	3.942	3.799	3.539	3.311	2.848	2.496	2.220	1.999
20	18.046	16.351	13.590	11.470	9.818	8.514	7.469	6.623	6.259	5.929	5.353	4.870	4.460	4.110	3.954	3.808	3.546	3.316	2.850	2.497	2.221	1.999
21	18.857	17.011	14.029	11.764	10.017	8.649	7.562	6.687	6.312	5.973	5.384	4.891	4.476	4.121	3.963	3.816	3.551	3.320	2.852	2.498	2.221	2.000
22	19.660	17.658	14.451	12.042	10.201	8.772	7.645	6.743	6.359	6.011	5.410	4.909	4.488	4.130	3.970	3.822	3.556	3.323	2.853	2.498	2.222	2.000
23	20.456	18.292	14.857	12.303	10.371	8.883	7.718	6.792	6.399	6.044	5.432	4.925	4.499	4.137	3.976	3.827	3.559	3.325	2.854	2.499	2.222	2.000
24	21.243	18.914	15.247	12.550	10.529	8.985	7.784	6.835	6.434	6.073	5.451	4.937	4.507	4.143	3.981	3.831	3.562	3.327	2.855	2.499	2.222	2.000
25	22.023	19.523	15.622	12.783	10.675	9.077	7.843	6.873	6.464	6.097	5.467	4.948	4.514	4.147	3.985	3.834	3.564	3.329	2.856	2.499	2.222	2.000
26	22.795	20.121	15.983	13.003	10.810	9.161	7.896	6.906	6.491	6.118	5.480	4.956	4.520	4.151	3.988	3.837	3.566	3.330	2.856	2.500	2.222	2.000
27	23.560	20.707	16.330	13.211	10.935	9.237	7.943	6.935	6.514	6.136	5.492	4.964	4.524	4.154	3.990	3.839	3.567	3.331	2.856	2.500	2.222	2.000
28	24.316	21.281	16.663	13.406	11.051	9.307	7.984	6.961	6.534	6.152	5.502	4.970	4.528	4.157	3.992	3.840	3.568	3.331	2.857	2.500	2.222	2.000
29	25.066	21.844	16.984	13.591	11.158	9.370	8.022	6.983	6.551	6.166	5.510	4.975	4.531	4.159	3.994	3.841	3.569	3.332	2.857	2.500	2.222	2.000
30	25.808	22.396	17.292	13.765	11.258	9.427	8.055	7.003	6.566	6.177	5.517	4.979	4.534	4.160	3.995	3.842	3.569	3.332	2.857	2.500	2.222	2.000
40	32.835	27.355	19.793	15.046	11.925	9.779	8.244	7.105	6.642	6.234	5.548	4.997	4.544	4.166	3.999	3.846	3.571	3.333	2.857	2.500	2.222	2.000
50	39.196	31.424	21.482	15.762	12.234	9.915	8.304	7.133	6.661	6.246	5.554	4.999	4.545	4.167	4.000	3.846	3.571	3.333	2.857	2.500	2.222	2.000

REVIEW SUMMARY

1. *Probability analysis* is an application of statistical decision theory that, under certain conditions of uncertainty, leads to more consistent and reliable decisions than single best guesses. As long as the underlying process that generates the decision variable is not expected to change in the future, historical data can be used to model the probability distribution. The *variance* of a probability distribution, σ^2, and the *standard deviation*, which is the square root of the variance and denoted $\sqrt{\sigma}$, are measures of dispersion that are commonly used as measures of risk. The problem of comparing the relative riskiness of alternatives can be resolved by computing the *coefficiency of variation*, a measure that relates the standard deviation of a probability distribution to its expected value:

$$\text{Coefficient of variation} = \frac{\text{Standard deviation } (\sigma)}{\text{Expected value (contribution margin) E(X)}}$$

2. There may be an opportunity to acquire additional information that will be useful in selecting the best decision alternative. The cost of the additional information should be weighted against the increase in the expected value that can be obtained by using the information. The maximum increase in the expected value that could be obtained from additional information is the expected value of *perfect information* and, consequently, the maximum amount one would be willing to pay for additional information.

3. Probabilities should be revised as new information becomes available. One approach to probability revision is an application of Bayes' theorem. Bayes' theorem can be used to revise the original probability estimates for two or more events when new information becomes available about additional events. The revised probability estimate is referred to as *posterior probability*. The estimates made before the new information became available are referred to as *prior probabilities*.

4. A *decision tree* is a graphic representation of the decision points, the alternative actions available to the decision maker, the possible outcomes and the related probabilities for each decision alternative, and the expected values of each event. When possible outcomes can take on any value within a defined range, a *continuous probability distribution* may provide a better description of the nature of the variable and be a better basis for prediction. The *normal distribution* is the most frequently applied continuous distribution because it is symmetrical and it has only one mode. *Monte Carlo simulation* is a computer-oriented procedure that uses statistical sampling techniques to obtain probabilistic approximation of some mathematical or physical problem.

5. One way to evaluate the potential effects of uncertainty on proposed capital expenditures is to consider the effect of the distribution of probable outcomes on the expected cash flows and the relative risk of available capital projects. Probabilistic estimates are most frequently used with the present value method, where the expected value of the net cash flow in each period, rather than the single most likely net cash flow, is discounted to present value. If a probability distribution is not symmetrical, the use of expected values rather than estimates of the most likely events will result in a different net present value.

6. The procedure for computing the variance and the standard deviation for the expected net present value varies, depending upon whether the cash flows in each of the periods are independent, perfectly correlated, or partially independent and partially correlated. If the cash flows in each period are independent, the standard deviation of the expected net present value is computed by taking the square root of the sum of the discounted periodic variances. If the cash flows in each of the periods are perfectly correlated, the standard deviation of the expected net present value is determined by summing the discounted standard deviations for each period over the life of the project. If the period cash flows are neither independent nor perfectly correlated, the cash flows may be treaetd as if they contain a mixture of independent and dependent period cash flows. The expected periodic cash flows are simply divided into the two components, a separate expected value and variance is then computed for each, and finally the standard deviation of the expected net present value is determined by computing the square root of the sum of the variances of the independent cash flows and the dependent cash flows.

7. Once the standard deviation of the expected net present value has been determined, it can be used to evaluate the riskiness of the proposed capital investment. Alternatives with the smallest coefficients of variation are the least risky. Areas of the normal distribution can be related to deviations from the mean expressed in terms of standard deviations to indicate to management the range of return, measured in terms of net present value likely to occur at some level of probability. The reliability of the estimated range for the net present value and the probability of achieving a positive net present value are highly dependent upon the accuracy of the estimates of the expected

values of the annual cash flows and their estimated standard deviations.

8. In capital expenditure analysis as well as differential cost analysis, probability can be used to determine the best strategy under conditions of uncertainty. The first step is to determine the expected value of the annual after-tax net cash inflows. Once the expected value of the annual after-tax net cash inflows has been determined, the expected net present value of each strategy can be determined by discounting the cash inflows for each strategy to present value and subtracting the initial cash outflow. Management must compare net present values and standard deviations for each alternative and determine how much risk it is willing to assume to increase profit.

PART 1

Instructions: *Place a check mark in the appropriate column to indicate whether each of the following statements is True or False.*

	True	False
1. In applying probability distributions to cost studies, the smaller the standard deviation, the smaller the risk that the actual cost will differ from the expected cost.		
2. The value of perfect information is the maximum amount that management would be willing to pay to improve its information.		
3. Decision trees are especially useful when sequential decisions are involved.		
4. Monte Carlo simulation models are computer oriented, because without the speed of the computer they would be impractical to solve.		
5. In practice, most decisions are based on management's best guess of the single most likely result for each period.		
6. Probabilistic estimates are most frequently used with the payback method of capital expenditure evaluation.		
7. If a probability distribution is symmetrical, the use of expected value rather than estimates of the most likely events will result in a different net present value.		
8. The least risky investment is the one with the smallest standard deviation.		
9. Perfectly correlated cash flows might occur if the capital expenditure relates to the production of a new product or entrance into a new market.		
10. Independent cash flows could occur in practice where the capital expenditure relates to the production of an established product, the demand for which is expected to vary in response to temporary changes in consumer tastes.		
11. Investment alternatives with the largest coefficient of variation would be the least risky.		
12. If the expected values of the annual cash flows and their estimated standard deviations are based upon historical data rather than subjective estimates, greater reliance can be placed on the results.		
13. All future events that affect cash flows follow the pattern of random variables drawn from a normal distribution.		
14. If there is dependence among economic variables, computational procedures must be modified by substituting conditional probabilities.		
15. Monte Carlo simulations are especially useful in evaluating problems that contain numerous stochastic variables, because such problems are difficult to evaluate analytically.		

PART 2

Instructions: *In the blank space at the left of each of the following items, place the letter from the right-hand column that identifies the term that best matches the statement in the column on the left. No letter should be used more than once.*

_____ 1. The difference between the average profit under conditions of certainty and the average expected profit using the best strategy under uncertainty.

_____ 2. Based on quantification of the likelihood of the occurrence of possible events.

_____ 3. Provides a numerical measure of the scatter of the possible values around the average value.

_____ 4. Graphic portrayal of alternatives and their expected results.

_____ 5. A procedure that uses statistical sampling techniques in order to obtain a probabilistic approximation of some mathematical or physical problem.

_____ 6. Consider the effect of the distribution of probable outcomes on the expected cash flows and the relative risk of available capital projects.

_____ 7. If a probability distribution is not symmetrical, the use of these rather than estimates of the most likely events will result in a different net present value.

_____ 8. A procedure that is used to revise the original probability estimates for events when new information becomes available.

_____ 9. A measure of the relative variability of a distribution determined by dividing the standard deviation by the expected value.

_____ 10. Situation where the magnitude of cash flows in subsequent periods is not affected by the magnitude of cash flows that occur in earlier periods.

_____ 11. Situation where the magnitude of cash flows in later periods depends upon the magnitude of cash flows in earlier periods.

_____ 12. Situation where the cash flows are neither independent nor perfectly correlated.

_____ 13. Because it is symmetrical and has only one mode, the expected value is not only the mean of the probability of distribution, but is also the mode.

_____ 14. When future events that affect cash flows do not follow a pattern of random variables, it may be necessary to construct this using historical data or subjective estimates based on informed business judgment.

_____ 15. If there is dependence on the variables, computational procedures must be modified by substituting these.

a. value of perfect information
b. probability distribution
c. standard deviation
d. decision tree
e. Monte Carlo simulation
f. Bayes' theorem
g. expected values
h. perfectly correlated cash flows
i. normal distribution
j. mixed cash flows
k. probabilistic estimates
l. nonnormal distribution
m. coefficient of variation
n. independent cash flows
o. conditional variables

PART 3

Instructions: *In the blank space at the left of each of the following items, place the letter of the choice that most correctly completes each item.*

_____ 1. Of the following, the one that is generally viewed as a measure of investment risk is the:
   a. expected value
   b. variance
   c. standard deviation
   d. coefficient of determination
   e. none of the above

_____ 2. These are apt to occur where the capital expenditure relates to the production of a new product or the entrance into a new market:
   a. perfectly correlated cash flows
   b. positive cash flows
   c. independent cash flows
   d. mixed cash flows
   e. none of the above

_____ 3. Because the normal distribution is symmetrical and has only one mode, this is not only the mean of the probability distribtution but it is also the mode.
   a. Coefficient of variance
   b. Standard deviation
   c. Coefficient of determination
   d. Variance
   e. Expected value

_____ 4. This would be the same when a normal probability distribution is used in the analysis as it would when the probability distribution of future cash flows is ignored.
   a. Net present value
   b. Time adjusted rate of return
   c. Payback
   d. Internal rate of return
   e. Accounting rate of return

_____ 5. The standard deviation of the expected net present value is computed by taking the square root of the sum of the discounted periodic variances when the cash flows of each period are:
   a. perfectly correlated
   b. mixed
   c. positive
   d. independent
   e. negative

_____ 6. Not all future events that affect cash flows follow the pattern of random variables drawn from the:
   a. payoff tables
   b. conditional probabilities
   c. normal distribution
   d. nonnormal distribution
   e. none of the above

_____ 7. This is sometimes used to determine the best choice of action in a decision tree analysis:
   a. induction
   b. random scheduling
   c. subjective judgment
   d. backward induction
   e. queuing theory

_____ 8. This technique is especially useful in evaluating problems that contain numerous stochastic variables:
   a. sensitivity analysis
   b. Monte Carlo simulation
   c. queuing theory
   d. linear programming
   e. learning theory

_____ 9. The ARC Radio Company is trying to decide whether to introduce as a new product a wrist "radiowatch" designed for shortwave reception of exact time as broadcast by the National Bureau of Standards. The radiowatch would be priced at $60, which is exactly twice the variable cost per unit to manufacture and sell it. The incremental fixed costs necessitated by introducing this new product would amount to $240,000 per year. A subjective estimate of the expected value of demand for the new product is:
   a. 11,000 units
   b. 10,200 units
   c. 9,000 units
   d. 10,600 units
   e. 9,800 units

(ICMA adapted)

_____ **10.** The ARC Radio Company is trying to decide whether to introduce as a new product a wrist "radiowatch" designed for shortwave reception of exact time as broadcast by the National Bureau of Standards. The radiowatch would be priced at $60, which is exactly twice the variable cost per unit to manufacture and sell it. The incremental fixed costs necessitated by introducing this new product would amount to $240,000 per year. A subjective estimate of the probability that the introduction of this new product will not increase the company's profit is:

a. 0.00

b. 0.04

c. 0.40

d. 0.50

e. 0.60

(ICMA adapted)

PART 4

1. Compute the expected contribution margin for a product of the Silicon Valley Company by completing the schedule below:

Units Demanded	Probability of Unit Demand	Total Contribution Margin of Units Demanded	Expected Contribution Margin
0	.05	-0-	
5	.10	$1,500	
10	.40	3,000	
15	.20	4,500	
20	.15	6,000	
25	.10	7,500	

2. Compute the standard deviation of the expected value.

(1) Contribution Margin (Conditional Value)	(2) Difference from Expected Value	(3) (2) Squared	(4) Probability	(5) (3) × (4)
$	$	$		$

$ _____

Standard deviation =

3. Compute the coefficient of variation.

PART 5

Partridge Inc. is considering an investment in new machinery with a five-year estimated useful life, which has an estimated net present value of $15,000. The cash inflows are expected to be normally distributed; however, 40% of each period's cash inflow is expected to be independent and the remaining 60% is expected to be perfectly correlated. Cash inflows are expected to be $12,000 each period. The independent cash inflows have a standard deviation of $1,000 and the dependent cash inflows have a standard deviation of $2,000. The initial cash outflow has a standard deviation of zero. The corporation's weighted average cost of capital is 10%.

1. Determine the variance of the net present value for the independent cash flows.

(1) Year	(2) Periodic Standard Deviation of Independent Cash Flows	(3) Present Value of $1 at 10%	(4) Periodic Variance (2)^2	(5) Present Value of $1 at 10% Squared (3)^2	(6) Present Value of Variance (4) × (5)
0					
1					
2					
3					
4					
5					

Variance of the net present value for the independent cash flows ...

2. Determine the standard deviation of the net present value for the dependent cash flows.

(1) Year	(2) Periodic Standard Deviation	(3) Present Value of $1 at 10%	(4) Present Value of Standard Deviation (2) × (3)
0			
1			
2			
3			
4			
5			

Standard deviation of the net present value for

dependent cash flows ....

3. Compute the variance of the total net present value of the investment.

Variance of net present value for dependent cash flows ....

Variance of net present value for independent cash flows ....

Variance of total net present value of investment ....

4. Determine the standard deviation of the total net present value of the investment. (Round to the nearest whole dollar.)

PART 6

Racquet Sports Inc. is considering constructing a racquetball facility in a suburb that does not have one. The following data are relevant to the decision.

Annual Demand (Number of One-Hour Time Slots)	Probability of Demand	Annual After-Tax Net Cash Inflows	Cost of Building with Capacity to Meet Demand
60,000	.30	$200,000	$1,500,000
80,000	.40	300,000	2,000,000
100,000	.20	400,000	2,500,000
120,000	.10	500,000	3,000,000

The present value of an annuity of $1 discounted at the company's weighted average cost of capital (10%) over an investment horizon of 20 years is 8.514.

1. Construct a payoff table to determine the expected value of the annual after-tax net cash inflows for each size of racquetball facility.

Potential Action (Racquetball Facility Capacity To Be Built	Annual After-Tax Net Cash Inflows from Different Levels of Demand				Expected Value of After-Tax Net Cash Inflows
	60,000	80,000	100,000	120,000	
60,000					
80,000					
100,000					
120,000					

Probabilities. . .

2. Determine the expected net present value of each alternative racquetball facility size and indicate which size Racquet Sports should build.

(1) Possible Action (Racquetball Facility Capacity To Be Built)	(2) Expected Value of Annual After-Tax Net Cash Inflows	(3) Present Value of 20-Year Annuity of $1 @ 10%	(4) Present Value of Annual After-Tax Net Cash Inflows (2) × (3)	(5) Initial Cash Outflow	(6) Expected Net Present Value (4) – (5)
60,000					
80,000					
100,000					
120,000					

CHAPTER 24
MARKETING EXPENSE AND PROFITABILITY ANALYSIS

REVIEW SUMMARY

1. *Marketing* is the matching of a company's products with markets for the satisfaction of customers at a reasonable profit to the firm. Management requires meaningful marketing expense information in order to determine and analyze the profitability of territories, classes of customers, product lines or brands, and promotional efforts. Control of marketing expenses begins with their assignment to various expense groups such as territories, customers, and products.

2. Major differences between manufacturing expenses and marketing expenses include the following:
   (a) Manufacturing techniques seldom change to any great extent once the factory is set up, whereas changes in market conditions often necessitate changes in channels of distribution.
   (b) Management can control manufacturing factors such as labor cost and number of machines operated, whereas customer resistance is the enigma in marketing expense analysis.
   (c) Factory managers measure their accomplishments in terms of reduced costs per unit, whereas sales managers consider sales the yardstick for measuring their efficiency.
   (d) The effect of manufacturing changes is usually felt quickly, whereas many promotional expenditures are incurred for future results.

3. Marketing expenses may be directly identifiable with functional classifications, although indirectly with respect to other classifications such as territories or products, or vice versa, or the expense may be indirect both as to function as well as to other classifications. Expenses that cannot be assigned directly are recorded in total and then allocated by appropriate bases to various activities.

4. The assignment of functional marketing expenses as percentages of actual sales or manufacturing costs does not offer reliable results. The determination of a functional standard unit costing rate is a more dependable solution. The total expense of each marketing function should be divided by the units of functional service (e.g., number of salespersons' calls, relative media circulation, etc.) to obtain the expense per unit.

5. Recognition of the fixed-variable expense classification is valuable in controlling marketing expenses, and in decision making. Fixed marketing expenses, also called *capacity costs,* include items such as salaries of executive and administrative sales staffs, as well as rent and depreciation marketing facilities. Variable marketing expenses, also called *volume costs,* include the expense of handling, warehousing, and shipping that tends to vary with sales volume.

6. When marketing activities are organized on a territorial basis, each identifiable geographical unit can be charged directly with the expenses incurred within its area, thereby minimizing the proration of expenses. Since the large number of customers makes the allocation and analysis of marketing expenses by customers cumbersome, customers are grouped according to the following characteristics to make the analysis more meaningful: (a) territories, (b) amount of average order, (c) customer-volume groups, or (d) kinds of customers. Just as customers are grouped for purposes of analysis, products sold can be grouped according to product lines or brands possessing common characteristics. To achieve control of salespersons' expenses and to determine the profitability of sales made by salespersons, performance standards and standard costs should be established.

7. A careful analysis of unexpected changes in gross profit is useful to a company's management. Such changes may result from changes in (a) sales prices of products, (b) number of physical units sold, (c) types of products sold, or (d) materials, labor, and overhead costs.

8. Gross profit analysis may be based on a company's sales and cost data. The budgeted sales and costs are accepted as the basis for all comparisons. A sales price variance and a sales volume variance are computed first, followed by a cost price variance and a cost volume variance. The computations are as follows:
   (a) Sales price variance = Actual sales – (Actual unit sales × Budgeted prices)
   (b) Sales volume variance = (Actual unit sales × Budgeted prices) – Budgeted dollar sales
   (c) Cost price variance = Actual cost of goods sold – (Actual unit sales × Budgeted unit costs)
   (d) Cost volume variance = (Actual unit sales × Budgeted unit costs) – Budgeted cost of goods sold

9. The net volume variance is a composite of the sales volume and cost volume variances. It should be analyzed further to determine the sales mix and final sales volume variances. These are computed as follows:
   (a) Sales mix variance = (Actual unit sales × (Budgeted prices – Budgeted costs)) – (Actual unit sales × Budgeted average gross profit per unit)

(b) Final sales volume variance = Budgeted average gross profit per unit × (Actual unit sales – Budgeted unit sales)

10. Gross profit analysis based on budgets and standard costs depicts the weak spots in a period's performance. For example, gains due to higher prices may be more than offset by increased costs, shifts to less profitable products, and decreases in units sold. Planned gross profit is the responsibility of both the marketing and manufacturing functions. The marketing function must explain the changes in sale prices, the shifts in sales mix, and the changes in units sold, whereas the production function must account for changes in costs.

11. For more effective marketing expense analysis, it has been suggested that only the variable manufacturing cost be subtracted from each segment's sales, thus arriving at a figure called "gross contribution margin." Proponents of the contribution margin approach point out that only specific and direct costs, whether fixed or variable, should be assigned to territories, customers, product groups, or salespersons, with a clear distinction as to their fixed and variable characteristics.

12. Under the *profit maximization method* of price setting, the price that yields the largest profit at a certain volume is the price to be charged to a consumer. Some companies set prices based on a *return-on-capital-employed* method, using a formula such as the following:

$$\text{Price} = \frac{\text{Total cost} + (\text{Desired rate of return} \times \text{Total capital employed})}{\text{Sales volume in units}}$$

Conversion cost pricing attempts to direct management's attention to the amount of labor and factory overhead that products require. Using the *contribution margin approach* to pricing, the cost of additional units is accepted as a basis for pricing them, and any price over and above total differential cost is acceptable. The use of *standard costs* for pricing purposes makes cost figures more quickly available and reduces clerical detail.

13. The *Clayton Act* prohibited price discrimination only where it had a serious effect on competition in general, and it contained no other provisions for the control of price discrimination. At the core of the *Robinson-Patman Act* is the provision that differential prices granted must not exceed differences in the cost of serving different customers. To avoid litigation, a firm should establish records that show that price differentials are extended only to the extent justified by allowable cost savings.

PART 1

Instructions: *Place a check mark in the appropriate column to indicate whether each of the following statements is **True** or **False**.*

		True	False
1.	In marketing, the emphasis ordinarily rests on cost control rather than selling.		
2.	A meaningful comparison of the marketing expense of one company with another is not always possible.		
3.	Marketing expense analysis is not easy to perform because the customer is a controlling rather than a controllable factor.		
4.	For marketing expenses, it is easy to identify quantities or units of activity with the cost incurred and results achieved.		
5.	Using budgets, the final sales volume variance may be computed by comparing the budgeted gross profit of actual units sold with the budgeted gross profit.		
6.	Order-filling expenses are the expenses of activities carried on to bring in the sales orders and include selling and advertising.		
7.	To obtain the sales mix variance, the budgeted gross profit of actual units sold is subtracted from the difference between actual sales at budgeted prices and the budgeted cost of actual units sold.		
8.	The number of customers' orders, transactions, or invoice lines would serve as reasonable expense allocation bases for the credit and collection function.		
9.	The number of shipping units, weight, or size of the units would be logical expense allocation bases for the packing and shipping function.		
10.	Another term for fixed marketing expenses, such as salaries, rent, and depreciation, is *capacity costs*.		
11.	Unlike production costs, it is not important to establish flexible budgets and standards for marketing expenses.		
12.	Companies sometimes set minimum dollar values or quantities for orders to eliminate the situation where marketing expenses exceed the gross profit from the order.		
13.	Proponents of the contribution margin approach point out that only specific and direct marketing expenses should be assigned to territories, customers, product groups, or salespersons.		
14.	The Robinson-Patman Act prohibited price discrimination only where it had a serious effect on competition in general.		
15.	The use of standard costs for pricing makes cost figures more difficult to obtain and increases clerical detail.		

PART 2

Instructions: *In the blank space at the left of each of the following items, place the letter from the right-hand column that identifies the term that best matches the statement in the column on the left. No letter should be used more than once.*

_____ 1. Matching of a company's products with markets for the satisfaction of customers at a reasonable profit for the firm.

_____ 2. Those expenses that can be identified with a territory, customer, product, or definite type of sales outlet.

_____ 3. Attempts to direct management's attention to the amount of labor and factory over-head that products require.

_____ 4. Attempts to allocate marketing expenses to territories, customers, products, or sales-persons.

_____ 5. Established by central management at a level considered best for overall company interests.

_____ 6. Approach to pricing in which any price over and above the total differential cost would be acceptable.

_____ 7. Each activity should be a homogeneous unit that can be related to specific items of expense.

_____ 8. Expenses incurred for more than one function or classification and hence must be allocated.

_____ 9. The expense of activities carried on to bring in the sales orders.

_____ 10. The expenses of warehousing, packing and shipping, credit and collection, and general accounting.

_____ 11. Marketing function for which number of customers' orders, transactions, or invoice lines would be appropriate expense allocation bases.

_____ 12. Marketing function for which size, weight, or number of products shipped or handled would be appropriate expense allocation bases.

_____ 13. Marketing function for which quantity of product units sold, relative media circulation, or cost of space directly assignable would be appropriate expense allocation bases.

_____ 14. This has influenced the thinking of the volume-minded sales manager who must recognize that profit is more beneficial than volume.

_____ 15. Another term for fixed marketing expenses that include such items as sales salaries, rent, and depreciation.

_____ 16. Another term for variable marketing expenses that include the expenses of handling, warehousing, and shipping that tend to vary with sales volume.

_____ 17. The difference between actual sales at budgeted prices and at budgeted costs, and actual sales at budgeted average gross profit.

_____ 18. Prohibited discrimination only where it had a serious effect on competition in general.

_____ 19. States that price differentials granted to various customers must not exceed differences in the cost of serving such customers.

_____ 20. Sales mix variance plus or minus final sales volume variance.

a. order-filling expenses
b. direct expenses
c. credit and collection
d. capacity costs
e. Robinson-Patman Act
f. net volume variance
g. Clayton Act
h. marketing function
i. sales mix variance
j. contribution margin pricing
k. contribution margin analysis
l. marketing cost analysis
m. order-getting expenses
n. warehousing
o. marketing
p. volume costs
q. indirect expenses
r. advertising
s. profit maximization pricing
t. conversion cost pricing

PART 3

Instructions: *In the blank space at the left of each of the following items, place the letter of the choice that most correctly completes each item.*

_____ 1. Budgeting or order-getting costs will not be affected by:
  a. policies and actions of competitors
  b. sales promotion policies
  c. general economic conditions
  d. location of distribution warehouses
  e. any of the above

(ICMA adapted)

_____ 2. The control of order-filling costs:
  a. can be accomplished through the use of flexible budget standards
  b. requires a budget that shows budgeted expenses for the average level of activity
  c. is related to pricing decisions, sales promotion, and customer reaction
  d. is not crucial because the order-filling routine is entrenched and external influences are minimal
  e. none of the above

(ICMA adapted)

_____ 3. Radin Company, which sells a single product, provided the following data from its income statement for the calendar years 19X4 and 19X3:

	19X4	19X3 (Base Year)
Sales	$750,000 (150,000 units)	$720,000 (180,000 units)
Cost of goods sold	525,000	575,000
Gross profit	$225,000	$145,000

In an analysis of variation in gross profit between the two years, what would be the effects of changes in sales price and sales volume?

	Sales Price	Sales Volume
a.	$150,000 fav.	$120,000 unfav.
b.	$150,000 unfav.	$120,000 fav.
c.	$180,000 fav.	$150,000 unfav.
d.	$180,000 unfav.	$150,000 fav.

(AICPA adapted)

_____ 4. A single-product company's total cost is $200,000, total capital employed is $500,000, the sales volume is 50,000 units, and the desired rate of return on capital employed is 15%. The product's sales price should be:
  a. $4   b. $10   c. $5.50   d. $7.50   e. none of the above

_____ 5. If capital employed is $10,000,000, the total annual cost is $2,000,000, and the desired rate of return on capital employed is 25%, then the percentage markup on cost should be:
  a. 125%   b. 20%   d. 25%   d. 500%   e. 250%

_____ 6. The Clayton Act provided that:
  a. price discrimination was prohibited only where it had a serious effect on competition in general
  b. price differentials were entirely prohibited
  c. price discrimination that tended to decrease competition was prohibited
  d. pseudo-advertising allowances were prohibited
  e. none of the above

7-10. The standard billing rate per invoice line in the Billing Department was $.40 per line, consisting of $3,000 of fixed expense and $.30 per invoice line of variable expense at a normal capacity of 30,000 invoice lines. Actual sales required 32,000 lines for a month at a total of $12,700.

_____ 7. Based on the above information, the budget allowance for the 32,000 lines billed would be:
  a. $12,700   b. $12,800   c. $12,600   d. $12,500   e. none of the above

8. Based on the above information, the spending variance for the Billing Department would be:
   a. $200 unfavorable
   b. $100 unfavorable
   c. $100 favorable
   d. $200 favorable
   e. none of the above

9. Based on the above information, the idle capacity variance for the Billing Department would be:
   a. $200 unfavorable
   b. $100 unfavorable
   c. $100 favorable
   d. $200 favorable
   e. none of the above

10. The journal entry to record the above variances would include:
    a. a debit to Spending Variance and a debit to Idle Capacity Variance
    b. a credit to Spending Variance and a credit to Idle Capacity Variance
    c. a debit to Spending Variance and a credit to Idle Capacity Variance
    d. a credit to Spending Variance and a debit to Idle Capacity Variance
    e. none of the above

PART 4

Hoosier Company of Indianapolis markets a single product in Indianapolis and Fort Wayne. Marketing expenses for the past year were:

Sales salaries	$108,000
Salespersons' expenses	50,000
Advertising	63,000
Delivery expense	33,000
Credit investigation expense	5,000
Collection expense	12,000
Total	$271,000

Additional information:
(a) The company has six salespersons, two in Fort Wayne and four in Indianapolis, and each is paid the same salary.
(b) The salespersons receive equal allowances for expenses, except that the Fort Wayne salespersons each receive $1,000 per year extra for turnpike toll fees.
(c) All advertising is placed according to the number of subscribers to the Indianapolis and Fort Wayne daily newspapers, 500,000 and 130,000 respectively.
(d) Delivery is made by an outside agency that charges a flat annual fee. The agency made 3,000 deliveries (2,500 in Indianapolis, 500 in Fort Wayne) from a centrally located warehouse.
(e) A total of 500 new customers were obtained: 400 in Indianapolis, 100 in Fort Wayne.
(f) A total of 4,000 new customers' remittances were received: 3,200 from Indianapolis, 800 from Fort Wayne.

Instructions: *Prepare a marketing cost analysis for the two territories, using the schedule below.*

	Total	Territory Indianapolis	Fort Wayne
Sales salaries	$	$	$
Salespersons' expenses			
Advertising			
Delivery expense			
Credit investigation expense			
Collection expense			
Total	$	$	$

PART 5

Silverado Company sells various products through selected retail outlets. Data relative to standard selling costs for one of the company's salespersons show:

Standard sales for the year	$400,000
Standard selling costs for the year	50,000
Sales for June	35,000
Selling costs for June:	
Actual cost	4,100
Budgeted costs for $35,000 sales	4,300

1. Determine the standard selling cost, rounded to the nearest whole dollar, to be charged if the salesperson reported $10,000 sales in the first week of June.

2. Determine the spending variance for the salesperson's June sales.

3. Determine the June idle capacity variance for the salesperson.

PART 6

Genie Electric assembles a large-screen TV that is sold to three classes of customers. The data with respect to these customers are shown below:

Customer Class	Sales	Gross Profit	Number of Sales Calls	Number of Orders	Number of Invoice Lines
Department stores	$ 280,000	$100,000	360	240	1,050
Retail appliance stores....	525,000	200,000	480	1,160	2,300
Wholesalers............	300,000	75,000	600	600	1,650
Total...............	$1,105,000	$375,000	1,440	2,000	5,000

Actual marketing costs for the year are:

Function	Costs	Measure of Activity
Selling	$115,200	Salespersons' calls
Packing and shipping	16,000	Customers' orders
Advertising	50,000	Dollar sales
Credit and Collection	20,000	Invoice lines
General accounting.............	22,000	Customers' orders

Instructions: *Prepare an income statement by customer classes, with functional distribution of marketing expenses. (Round to the nearest dollar.)*

Genie Electric
Income Statement
For the Year Ended December 31, 19–

	Department Stores	Retail Appliance Stores	Wholesalers	Total
Sales	$	$	$	$ $
Cost of goods sold				
Gross profit	$	$	$	$
Less marketing expenses:				
Selling	$	$	$	$
Packing and shipping				
Advertising				
Credit and collection				
General accounting.......				
Total	$	$	$	$
Operating income (loss)	$	$	$	$

PART 7

Fraternity Co. prepared the following income statements by product line:

	Product Delta	Product Gamma	Total
Sales	$550,000	$100,000	$650,000
Cost of goods sold	200,000	62,000	262,000
Gross profit	$350,000	$ 38,000	$388,000
Marketing expenses:			
Advertising	$ 20,000	$ 4,000	$ 24,000
Commissions	25,000	5,000	30,000
Shipping and packing	10,000	10,000	20,000
Administrative sales salaries	8,000	8,000	16,000
Total	$ 63,000	$ 27,000	$ 90,000
General administrative expenses	60,000	12,000	72,000
Total expenses	$123,000	$ 39,000	$162,000
Net income (loss)	$227,000	$ (1,000)	$226,000

Management is considering the elimination of Product Gamma. Additional data for products Delta and Gamma are as follows:

	Product Delta	Product Gamma
Commissions	5% of sales	5% of sales
Variable cost of goods sold	15% of sales	25% of sales
Number of orders processed	1,000	250
Lines of advertising devoted to product	674	–
Variable general and administrative expenses	15% of gross profit	15% of gross profit

All expenses other than those listed above are fixed. Management has determined that the number of orders processed would be a good basis for allocating shipping and packing expenses. Management also notes that advertising has been devoted entirely to promoting Product Delta and is considered variable. Finally, no unallocated fixed cost would be eliminated by dropping Product Gamma.

1. Prepare an income statement showing the contribution by product line, using the schedule below.

	Product Delta	Product Gamma	Total
Sales	$	$	$
Less variable costs and expenses:			
Cost of goods sold	$	$	$
Advertising			
Commissions			
Shipping and packing			
General and administrative expenses			
Total variable costs and expenses	$	$	$
Contribution margin	$	$	$
Fixed costs and expenses:			
Manufacturing costs			
Administrative sales salaries			
General and administrative expenses			
Total fixed costs and expenses			$
Net income			$

2. Compute the change in net income resulting from the elimination of Product Gamma.

PART 8

Actual sales and budget data for 19– for Wilderness Country Equipment Inc. are:

	Product X	Product Y	Total
Actual sales	50,000 units @ $8.00	24,000 units @ $7.00	$568,000
Actual cost of goods sold	50,000 units @ 6.80	24,000 units @ 5.85	480,000
Budgeted sales	40,000 units @ 8.25	25,000 units @ 7.50	$517,500
Budgeted cost of goods sold	40,000 units @ 7.00	25,000 units @ 6.00	430,000

1. Compute the following variances:

(a) Actual sales... $

   Actual sales at budgeted prices:

   X .... $

   Y ....   _____   _____

   Sales price variance .... $ _____

(b) Actual sales at budgeted prices................................ $

   Budgeted sales...   _____

   Sales volume variance..................................... $ _____

(c) Cost of goods sold—actual .... $

   Budgeted cost of actual units sold:

   X .... $

   Y ....   _____   _____

   Cost price variance .... $ _____

(d) Budgeted cost of actual units sold............................. $

   Budgeted cost of budgeted units sold ....   _____

   Cost volume variance .... $ _____

   Sales volume variance..................................... $

   Cost volume variance ....   _____

   Net volume variance .... $ _____

2. Determine the sales mix and final sales volume variances. (Round computations to three decimal places.)

Actual sales at budgeted prices	$
Budgeted cost of actual units sold	_____
Difference..	$
Budgeted gross profit of actual units sold	_____
Sales mix variance	$_____
Budgeted gross profit of actual units sold	$
Budgeted sales .... $	
Budgeted cost of budgeted units sold	_____
Budgeted gross profit	_____
Final sales volume variance	$_____

PART 9

Holly Company is considering changing its sales price of Bopper, presently $25. Increases and decreases of both 10% and 20%, as well as changes in advertising and promotion expenditures, are being considered, with the following estimates results for 19A and 19B:

	Estimated Unit Sales		Estimated Advertising and Promotion Expenditures	
Price	19A	19B	19A	19B
– 20%	225,000	245,000	$ 550,000	$ 600,000
– 10%	210,000	230,000	700,000	725,000
No change	200,000	230,000	750,000	750,000
+ 10%	190,000	210,000	800,000	825,000
+ 20%	175,000	195,000	1,000,000	1,200,000

The company has the necessary flexibility in its production capacity to meet these volume levels. The variable manufacturing cost per unit of Bopper is estimated to be $15 in 19A and $17 in 19B.

Instructions. *Determine the recommended sales price for 19A and 19B, using the schedule provided below:*

Alternative Sales Price	Variable Manufacturing Cost per Unit	Contribution Margin per Unit	Unit Sales	Total Contribution Margin	Additional Advertising and Promotion Expenditures	Contribution to Other Fixed Costs
19A:						
$	$	$		$	$	$
19B:						
$	$	$		$	$	$

PART 10

Plato Inc. sells one of its products at a price of $25 each, with total costs at $20 per unit. The company has $5,000,000 in capital employed. Unit sales amounted to 200,000 units.

1. Determine the return on capital presently employed by the company.

2. Determine the minimum selling price, rounded to the nearest cent, at which the company could sell its product and still maintain the same return on capital, assuming a 10% increase in sales volume, with constant costs and capital employed.

PROFIT PERFORMANCE MEASUREMENTS AND INTRACOMPANY TRANSFER PRICING

REVIEW SUMMARY

1. In equation form, the *rate of return on capital employed* may be expressed as follows:

$$\frac{\text{Profit}}{\text{Sales}} \times \frac{\text{Sales}}{\text{Capital Employed}} = \frac{\text{Rate of Return on}}{\text{Capital Employed}}$$

The *percentage of profit to sales* measures the ability to maintain satisfactory control over costs. The *capital-employed turnover rate* reflects the speed with which committed assets are employed in the operations. There is no single rate of return on capital employed that is satisfactory for all companies.

2. A rate of return on capital employed is computed by using figures from the balance sheet and income statement. Operating income is the preferred profit figure for measuring divisional or departmental performance, because nonoperating items are usually the responsibility of the entire company. Capital employed refers to total assets (the sum of current assets and noncurrent assets). The amount of capital employed should be averaged over the fiscal period, if possible.

3. The determination of divisional return on capital is a matter of relating performance to assets placed at the disposal of divisional management. The best approach is to calculate a rate of return based on sales, costs, and capital employed specific to the division, followed by a rate of return calculation that includes a full allocation of total company sales, costs, and capital employed, so that both rates of return are clearly presented. Divisional return-on-capital-employed measures have been criticized as a motivational tool because a division may seek to maximize relative profits rather than absolute profits. A possible solution is to use a *residual income* figure that emphasizes marginal profit dollars above the cost of capital, rather than the rate of return on capital employed.

4. The real purpose of the return-on-capital-employed ratio is for internal profit measurement and control, with trends more meaningful than single ratios. Executive management of many companies has shown a growing acceptance of the rate-of-return-on-capital-employed concept as a tool in planning, in establishing sales prices, and in measuring operational profitability. Advantages of the use of the rate of return on capital employed are that it (a) focuses management's attention upon earning the best profit possible on the capital available, (b) serves as a yardstick for measuring management's efficiency and effectiveness for the company as a whole and its divisions, (c) ties together the many phases of financial planning, sales objectives, cost control, and the profit goal, (d) affords a comparison of managerial results both internally and externally

(e) develops a keener sense of responsibility and team effort in divisional managers, and (f) aids in detecting weakness with respect to the use or nonuse of individual assets. Limitations of the use of the return-on-capital employed ratio include: (a) the frequent use of a single rate of return for all divisions; (b) the lack of data as to sales, costs, and assets by division; (c) the valuation of assets of different vintages in different divisions might give rise to comparison difficulties; (d) making decisions that are not in the best long-run interest of the firm for the sake of making current period returns look good; and (e) the focus on a single measure of performance may result in the neglect of other activities such as research and development or personnel policies.

5. As long as a segment is not entirely independent and separable, goods and services are generally transferred from one unit to another. When transfers of goods or services are made, a portion of the revenue of one segment becomes a portion of the cost of another, and the price at which transfers are made influences the earnings reported by each profit center. A transfer pricing system must satisfy these three fundamental criteria: (a) allow central management to judge as accurately as possible the performance of the divisional profit center in terms of its separate contribution to the total corporate profit, (b) motivate the division manager to pursue the division's profit goal in a manner conducive to the success of the company as a whole, and (c) stimulate the manager's efficiency without losing the division's autonomy as a profit center.

6. A *cost-based transfer* price may be sufficient in a totally centralized firm or in a firm where there are few intracompany transfers. The *market-based transfer price* is usually identical with the one charged to outside customers. It is the best profitability and performance measurement because it is objective. A *cost-plus transfer price* includes the cost to manufacture plus a normal mark-up and is often used when a market price is not available. A *negotiated transfer price* is sometimes used, because it is felt that the setting of the price by negotiations between buying and selling divisions allows unit managers the greatest degree of authority and control over the profit of their units. An *arbitrary transfer price* is established by central management and is at a level considered best for overall company interests, with neither the buying nor selling units having any control over the final decision. Under a *dual transfer pricing* system, a producing division would have a profit inducement to expand sales and production both internally and externally, but the consuming division's costs would not include an artificial profit.

PART 1

Instructions: *Place a check mark in the appropriate column to indicate whether each of the following statements is **True** or **False**.*

	True	False
1. The rate of return on capital employed may be expressed as the product of two factors: the percentage of profit to sales and the capital-employed turnover rate.	____	____
2. The capital-employed turnover rate reflects the speed with which committed assets are used in the operations.	____	____
3. There is a single rate of return on capital employed that all companies' performances may be measured against.	____	____
4. In measuring divisional performance, operating income is the most appropriate figure to use.	____	____
5. Total assets are the assets included in the capital-employed computation.	____	____
6. The residual income figure emphasizes marginal profit dollars above the cost of capital.	____	____
7. The rate of return on capital employed is not a good measure of profitability for the company as a whole.	____	____
8. An advantage of the use of the rate of return on capital employed is that it focuses management's attention upon earning the best profit possible on the total assets available.	____	____
9. A disadvantage of the use of the rate of return on capital employed is that management may be influenced to make decisions that are not best for the long-run profitability of the firm.	____	____
10. Multiple performance measurement means that different divisions use different standards.	____	____
11. Today, transfer pricing plays a major role in cost control.	____	____
12. A transfer pricing system should stimulate the manager's efficiency without losing the division's autonomy as a profit center.	____	____
13. A cost-based transfer price is most appropriate for use in a totally decentralized firm.	____	____
14. A market-based transfer price is the best profitability and performance measurement because it is objective.	____	____
15. The best thing about an arbitrary transfer price is that it is established by the division involved.	____	____

PART 2

Instructions: *In the blank space at the left of each of the following items, place the letter from the right-hand column that identifies the term that best matches the statement in the column on the left. No letter should be used more than once.*

_____ 1. The percentage of profit to sales times the capital-employed turnover rate.

_____ 2. Sales divided by capital employed.

_____ 3. Measures the degree of success in maintaining satisfactory control over costs.

_____ 4. Provide central management with a more comprehensive picture of divisional performance by considering a wider range of management responsibility.

_____ 5. Sum of current assets and noncurrent assets.

_____ 6. Accountants who favor this method of valuing noncurrent assets argue that it enables the gross assets of one plant to be compared better with those of another plant, where depreciation practices or the age of assets may be different.

_____ 7. Accountants who favor this method of valuing noncurrent assets state that cash built up via a depreciation allowance, if added to gross assets, amounts to overstating the investment.

_____ 8. Accountants who favor this method of valuing noncurrent assets believe that a company receiving a satisfactory return based on book values should recognize the situation as being out of step with actual conditions.

_____ 9. A division's income less an amount representing the company's cost of capital employed by the division.

_____ 10. Established by central management at a level considered best for overall company interests.

_____ 11. A transfer pricing method that has the disadvantage of inflating inventories with intracompany profits that must be eliminated from consolidated financial statements.

_____ 12. A transfer pricing method that is the best profitability and performance measurement because it is objective.

_____ 13. A transfer pricing method that may allow unit managers the greatest degree of authority and control over the profit of their units.

_____ 14. Method of transfer pricing under which a producing division would have a profit inducement to expand sales and production, while the cost to consuming divisions would be the firm's actual costs and would not include an artificial profit.

a. percentage of profit to sales
b. capital employed
c. depreciated cost method
d. residual income
e. capital-employed turnover rate
f. original cost method
g. rate of return on capital employed
h. market-based transfer pricing
i. negotiated transfer pricing
j. dual transfer pricing
k. arbitrary transfer price
l. multiple performance measurement
m. cost-plus transfer pricing
n. inflation accounting method

PART 3

Instructions: *In the blank space at the left of each of the following items, place the letter of the choice that most correctly completes each item.*

_____ 1. A major problem in comparing profitability measures among companies is:
  a. lack of general agreement over which profitability measure is best
  b. differences in the size of the companies
  c. differences in the accounting methods used by the companies
  d. differences in the dividend policies of the companies
  e. effect of interest rates on net income

  (ICMA adapted)

_____ 2. A company's return on ivestment is affected by a change in:

	Capital Turnover	Profit Margin on Sales
a.	Yes	Yes
b.	Yes	No
c.	No	No
d.	No	Yes

  (AICPA adapted)

_____ 3. To evaluate the performance of each department, interdepartmental transfers of a product preferably should be made at prices:
  a. equal to the market price of the department
  b. set by the receiving department
  c. equal to fully allocated costs to the producing department
  d. equal to variable costs to the producing department

  (AICPA adapted)

_____ 4. A management decision may be beneficial for a given profit center, but not for the entire company. From the overall company viewpoint, this decision would lead to action referred to as:
  a. suboptimization
  c. goal congruence
  b. centralization
  d. maximization

  (AICPA adapted)

_____ 5. Mar Company has two decentralized divisions, X and Y. Division X has always purchased certain units from Division Y at $75 per unit. Because Y plans to raise the price to $100 per unit, X wants to purchase these units from outside suppliers for $75 per unit. Y's costs are as follows:

Variable cost per unit .... $ 70
Annual fixed cost $15,000
Annual production of these units for X..................................... 1,000 units

If X buys from an outside supplier, the facilities Y uses to manufacture these units would remain idle. If Mar enforces a transfer price of $100 per unit between Divisions X and Y, the result would be:
  a. suboptimization for the company, because X should buy from outside suppliers for $75 per unit
  b. a lower overall company net income than a transfer price of $75 per unit
  c. a higher overall company net income than a transfer price of $75 per unit
  d. more profitable for the company than allowing X to buy from outside suppliers at $75 per unit

  (AICPA adapted)

_____ 6. Assuming that sales and net income remain the same, a company's return on investment will:
  a. increase if invested capital increases
  b. decrease if invested capital decreases
  c. decrease if the invested capital-employed turnover rate decreases
  d. decrease if the invested capital-employed turnover rate increases
  e. none of the above

  (AICPA adapted)

_____ 7. In a decentralized company in which divisions may buy goods from one another, the transfer pricing system should be designed primarily to:
  a. increase the consolidated value of inventory
  b. prevent division managers from buying from outsiders
  c. minimize the degree of autonomy of division managers
  d. aid in the appraisal and motivation of managerial performance

  (AICPA adapted)

_____ 8. If profits are $25,000, sales are $150,000, and capital employed is $100,000, the rate of return on investment would be:

      a. 16⅔%   b. 150%   c. 66⅔%   d. 25%   e. none of the above

_____ 9. If profits are $10,000, sales are $100,000, and capital employed is $100,000, the capital-employed turnover rate would be:

      a. 1   b. 0.1   c. 10   d. 0   e. none of the above

_____ 10. Residual income is the:

      a. contribution margin of an investment center, less the imputed interest on the invested capital used by the center

      b. contribution margin of an investment center, plus the imputed interest on the invested capital used by the center

      c. income of an investment center, less the imputed interest on the invested capital used by the center

      d. income of an investment center, plus the imputed interest on the invested capital used by the center

      e. none of the above   (AICPA adapted)

PART 4

The management of Wright Brothers Company has been using the return-on-capital-employed method of measuring performance by division and product managers. Recently the management decided to apply the concept to three product groups. The Cost Department assembled the following data from the annual financial statements:

Item	Product 727	Product 747	Product 767
Investment	$ 750,000	$ 500,000	$12,000,000
Sales volume in dollars	1,500,000	1,000,000	6,000,000
Operating profit	75,000	200,000	1,200,000

1. For each product, determine the (1) capital-employed turnover rate, (2) percentage of profit to sales, and (3) rate of return on capital employed.

Product	(1) Capital-Employed Turnover Rate	(2) Percentage of Profit to Sales	(3) Rate of Return on Capital Employed
727			
747			
767			

2. Since 727 and 767 have the same rate of return on capital employed, do they have the same problems? Explain what measures you would take to improve the rate of return for each product.

PART 5

Cannes Chemical Products sells 20,000 gallons of chemical Ennui each year at $30 per gallon. Its plant has a capacity to produce 25,000 gallons per year. Fixed costs related to the plant amount to $200,000 oer year. Variable costs per gallon are $18.

Paris Industrial Products, a subsidiary located in another city, uses Ennui to produce an industrial resin. One-half gallon of Ennui is needed for each 100-pound bag of resin. At present, the resin sells for $50 per bag and costs $40 per bag (all variable costs, including Ennui). The subsidiary sells 10,000 bags per year and at present purchases its Ennui from an outside supplier at $27 per gallon. Cannes Chemical Products asks its subsidiary to buy 5,000 gallons at the $30 market price—an offer which is refused by Paris.

Instructions: *Prepare a comparison of gross profits under the present market-based transfer pricing system for Cannes Chemical Products, its subsidiary,, and the corporation as a whole with the gross profits if the transfer pricing system were based on standard costs for a production level of 25,000 gallons of Ennui, using the schedule below:*

System	Cannes	Paris	Corporation as a Whole
Market-based transfer pricing:			
Sales to outsiders	$	$	$
Cost of goods sold			
Gross profit	$	$	$
Standard costing (using 25,000 gallons as basis for allocating fixed costs):			
Sales to outsiders	$	$	$
Intracompany sales (costs)			
Cost of goods sold			
Gross profit	$	$	$

PART 6

Oslo Co's industrial photo-finishing division, Rho, incurred the following costs and expenses in 1990.

	Variable	Fixed
Direct materials..........................	$200,000	
Direct labor.............................	150,000	
Factory overhead........................	70,000	$42,000
General, selling, and administrative	30,000	48,000
Totals	$450,000	$90,000

During 1990, Rho produced 300,000 units of industrial photo-prints, which were sold for $2.00 each. Oslo's investment in Rho was $500,000 and $700,000 at January 1, 1990, and December 31, 1990, respectively. Oslo normally imputes interest on investments at 15% of average invested capital.

1. Compute Rho's return on average investment for the year ended December 31, 1990.

2. Compute Rho's residual income (loss) for the year ended December 31, 1990.

3. Compute Rho's contribution margin for the year ended December 31, 1990.

SOLUTIONS

CHAPTER 1

Part 1

1. F	6. T	11. T
2. T	7. F	12. T
3. T	8. T	13. T
4. F	9. T	14. F
5. T	10. F	15. T

Part 2

1. a	8. h	15. d
2. p	9. g	16. f
3. o	10. s	17. q
4. n	11. i	18. l
5. m	12. k	19. t
6. c	13. j	20. r
7. e	14. b	

Part 3

1. **c** The operating management group consists of foremen and supervisors; the middle management group consists of department heads, division managers, and branch managers; and the executive management consists of the president, the executive vice-presidents, and the executives in charge of the various functions.

2. **a** Accountability is the reporting of results to higher authority. It is important because it makes possible the measurement of the extent to which objectives have been achieved. Authority is the power to command others to perform or not to perform activities. Responsibility originates particularly in the superior-subordinate relationship because the superior has the authority to require specific work from other people.

3. **d** The line makes decisions and performs the true management function, whereas the staff gives advice and performs technical functions.

4. **e** The human interrelations function directs the company's efforts in relation to the behavior of people inside and outside the company. The resources function involves the acquisition, disposal, and prudent management of a wide variety of resources. The processes function deals with activities such as product design, research and development, and purchasing.

5. **a** Operating managers are primarily concerned with short-range decisions, middle managers with medium-range decisions, and executive managers with long-range decisions.

6. **a** During its existence, the CASB issued a series of Cost Accounting Standards that govern the determination and allocation of specific costs relative to defense contracts.

7. **b** A profit center is the smallest organizationally independent segment of a company that has been charged with profit and loss responsibility.

8. **a** A cost objective is a function, organizational subdivision, contract, or other work unit for which cost data are desired and for which provision is made to accumulate and measure the cost of processes, products, jobs, capitalized projects, etc.

9. **d** Standard costs are predetermined costs for direct materials, direct labor, and factory overhead that are established by using information accumulated from past experience and from scientific research. Budgets should be based on standard costs.

10. **d** A budget is a written expression of management's plans for the future. It aids in: (1) setting goals; (2) informing individuals as to what they must do to contribute to the achievement of these goals; (3) motivating desired performance; (4) evaluating performance; and (5) suggesting corrective action.

Part 4

1. The five tasks are:
   (1) creating and executing plans and budgets for operating under expected competitive and economic conditions
   (2) establishing costing methods and procedures that permit control and, if possible, reductions or improvement of costs
   (3) creating inventory values for costing and pricing purposes, and, at times, controlling physical quantities
   (4) determining company costs and profit for an annual accounting period or a shorter period
   (5) choosing from among two or more alternatives that might increase revenues or decrease costs.

2. The three standards are: CAS 409, which requires contractors to depreciate their assets for contract costing purposes over lives that are based on documenting historical usefulness, irrespective of the lives used for either financial or income tax purposes; CASs 414 and 417, which recognize as a contract cost the imputed cost of capital committed to facilities, thereby overturning the government's long-standing practice of disallowing interest and other financing-type costs.

3. The line-staff concept of management is based on the fundamental assumption that all positions or functional divisions can be categorized into two groups: (1) the line, which makes decisions and performs the true managment functions, and (b) the staff, which gives advice and performs technical functions.

4. Short-range plans, called *budgets*, are prepared through a systematized process, are highly quantified, are expressed in financial terms, and are usually prepared for periods of a quarter or a year. Long-range plans typically extend three to five years into the future, may culminate in a highly summarized set of financial statements or financial targets, and serve as a starting point for each set of short-range plans.

5. Management by exception concentrates on the significant deviation of actual results from predetermined plans.

6. The accountant should go to each superior level of management and to the board of directors, if necessary, until the matter is resolved. The accountant should resign if no internal resolution is achieved.

CHAPTER 2

Part 1

1. T	6. F	11. F
2. F	7. T	12. F
3. T	8. T	13. T
4. T	9. F	14. F
5. F	10. F	15. F

Part 2

1. t	8. f	15. n
2. r	9. d	16. i
3. p	10. b	17. g
4. k	11. s	18. e
5. l	12. q	19. c
6. j	13. o	20. a
7. h	14. m	

Part 3

1. **b** Factory overhead consists of indirect materials, indirect labor, and all other indirect manufacturing costs.

2. **c** The characteristics of fixed costs are: (1) fixed total amount within a relevant output range, (2) decrease in unit cost as volume increases, (3) assignable to departments on the basis of arbitrary cost allocation methods, and (4) controllable by executive management.

3. **a** Only manufacturing costs are inventoriable. Both variable and fixed manufacturing costs must be taken into inventory.

4. **c** Conversion cost represents the cost of converting direct materials into finished products, and consists of direct labor and factory overhead.

5. **e** All four items are fixed costs (i.e., they don't vary with the level of production).

6. **b** Salaries of production executives would remain fixed within a relevant range, whereas the other three costs would vary with the level of production.

7. **b** Power is an indirect factory overhead cost (i.e., it's a manufacturing cost but it can't be identified with specific jobs), whereas the other three items are commercial expenses.

8. **a** Repairs and maintenance would be an example of a semivariable cost because a certain amount of maintenance would be required regardless of the level of activity, although generally the more production that takes place the greater the repairs expense would be.

9. **d** Auditing is a typical administrative expense, whereas the other three items are marketing expenses.

10. **b** Advertising is a typical marketing expense, whereas the other three items are administrative expenses.

Part 4

1. Variable	8. Variable	15. Fixed
2. Variable	9. Fixed	16. Variable
3. Fixed	10. Fixed	17. Variable
4. Variable	11. Semivariable	18. Variable
5. Semivariable	12. Semivariable	19. Semivariable
6. Variable	13. Fixed	20. Semivariable
7. Variable	14. Fixed	

Part 5

1. Adminis. Expenses	8. Market. Expenses	15. Market. Expenses
2. Other Indir. Costs	9. Other Indir. Costs	16. Market. Expenses
3. Indirect Materials	10. Other Indir. Costs	17. Adminis. Expenses
4. Indirect Labor	11. Indirect Labor	18. Adminis. Expenses
5. Adminis. Expenses	12. Indirect Labor	19. Indirect Labor
6. Adminis. Expenses	13. Indirect Materials	20. Indirect Labor
7. Market. Expenses	14. Indirect Materials	

Part 6

1.
Direct labor	$ 6
Variable factory overhead	9
Fixed factory overhead	$15
Conversion cost	$30

2.
Direct material	$25
Direct labor	6
Prime cost	$31

3.
Direct material	$25
Direct labor	6
Variable factory overhead	9
Variable manufacturing cost	$40

4.
Direct material	$25
Direct labor	6
Variable factory overhead	9
Variable marketing	3
Total variable	$43

5. Total Cost = Variable Manufacturing Cost + Variable Marketing Cost + Fixed Cost
= [5,000 × ($25 + $6 + $9)] + (4500 × $3) + [5,000* × ($15 + $5)]
= $200,000 + $13,500 + $100,000 = $313,500

*Because this was the volume level used to compute the unit fixed costs that were given.

CHAPTER 3

Part 1

1. F	6. T	11. F
2. T	7. F	12. T
3. T	8. T	13. F
4. F	9. F	14. T
5. T	10. T	15. T

Part 2

1. i	6. o	11. m
2. c	7. d	12. h
3. f	8. l	13. b
4. a	9. n	14. e
5. k	10. j	15. g

Part 3

1. d Process costing accumulates costs by production process or department. It is used when units are not separately distinguishable from one another during one or more manufacturing processes.

2. b Job order costing would be appropriate for printing because costs would be accumulated per job. The other three processes lend themselves to process costing because they produce units that are not separately distinguishable.

3. b In job order costing, specific materials and labor costs are identified by job, and no averaging occurs.

4. a Factory overhead is usually allocated on the basis of a predetermined rate whether a historical cost system or a standard cost system is used. The other three answers apply only to a standard cost system.

5. d Drug production usually consists of manufacturing long runs of homogeneous products for which process costing is used. The other three industries would utilize job order costing.

6. c Job order costing is used when the products manufactured within a department or cost center are heterogeneous.

7. a Flexible manufacturing systems consist of an integrated collection of automated production processes, automated materials movement, and computerized systems controls.

8. b Fixed automation manufacturing systems are characterized by one kind of product, a large range of viable production volumes, and tightly constrained production quality.

9. a Manual manufacturing systems are characterized by many kinds of products, a substantial learning curve effect, and long lead times.

10. c Flexible manufacturing systems are characterized by several kinds of products, middle-range production volumes, and consistent product quality.

Part 4

1. Direct materials:

Materials inventory, beginning	$20,000	
Purchases	75,000	
Materials available for use	$95,000	
Less raw materials inventory, ending	17,000	
Direct materials consumed		$ 78,000
Direct labor		180,000
Factory overhead		90,000
Total manufacturing costs		$348,000
Add work in process inventory, beginning		55,000
		$403,000
Less work in process inventory, ending		45,000
Cost of goods manufactured		$358,000

2.

Cost of goods manufactured [from (1)]	$358,000
Add finishing goods inventory, beginning	30,000
Cost of goods available for sale	$388,000
Less finishing goods inventory, ending	25,000
Cost of goods sold	$363,000

Part 6

Raw and In Process	162,000	
Accounts Payable		162,000
Finished Goods	165,000	
Raw and In Process		165,000

To backflush material cost from RIP to finished goods. This is a postdeduction. The calculation is:

Material in March 1 RIP balance	20,500
Material received during March	162,000
	182,500
Material in March 31 RIP, per physical count	17,500
Amount to be backflushed	165,000

Cost of Goods Sold	1,100	
Raw and In Process		1,100

Part 5

(a) Materials	70,000	
Accounts Payable		70,000
(b) Work in Process	52,000	
Factory Overhead Control	6,300	
Materials		58,300
(c) Payroll	180,000	
Employees' Income Tax Payable		27,000
FICA Tax Payable		13,500
Accrued Payroll		139,500
(d) Work in Process	75,000	
Factory Overhead Control	40,000	
Marketing Expenses Control	30,000	
Administrative Expenses Control	35,000	
Payroll		180,000
(e) Factory Overhead Control	12,995	
Marketing Expenses Control	3,390	
Administrative Expenses Control	3,955	
FICA Tax Payable		13,500
Federal Unemployment Tax Payable		1,440
State Unemployment Tax Payable		5,400
(f) Factory Overhead Control	27,500	
Accumulated Depreciation		25,000
Prepaid Expenses		2,500
(g) Factory Overhead Control	12,500	
Accounts Payable		12,500
(h) Accounts Payable	76,000	
Accrued Payroll	139,500	
Employees' Income Tax	27,000	
FICA Tax Payable	27,000	
Cash		269,500
(i) Cash	315,000	
Accounts Receivable		315,000
(j) Finished Goods	151,000	
Work in Process		151,000
(k) Accounts Receivable	285,000	
Sales		285,000
Cost of Goods Sold	140,000	
Finished Goods		140,000

CHAPTER 4

Part 1

1. T	6. T	11. F
2. T	7. T	12. F
3. F	8. F	13. T
4. F	9. F	14. F
5. F	10. F	15. T

Part 2

1. o	8. q	15. l
2. k	9. m	16. e
3. h	10. t	17. p
4. c	11. a	18. b
5. s	12. i	19. d
6. j	13. r	20. g
7. f	14. n	

Part 3

1. d The cost of each order produced for a given customer or the cost of each lot to be placed in stock is recorded on a job cost sheet. An invoice is a document used to record the sale of goods or services to a customer. A purchase order is used to order goods from a supplier. A materials requisition sheet is prepared to issue materials from the storeroom to a job.

2. b Payroll taxes are paid up to a certain amount of wages; therefore, since they don't vary in direct proportion to direct labor hours worked, they should be accounted for as factory overhead rather than as direct labor.

3. d Accumulated Depreciation is a general account, whereas the other three are cost accounts and would be a part of a factory ledger if one were maintained.

4. c When completed goods are sold, Cost of Goods Sold is debited and Finished Goods is credited in manufacturing accounting.

5. e

Federal income tax	$15,000
Employees' FICA	7,500
Employer's FICA	7,500
	$30,000

6. b If normal spoilage is caused by exacting specifications, difficult processing, or other unusual and unexpected factors, the spoilage cost should be charged to that order.

7. d Abnormal spoilage is spoilage that is not expected to occur under normal, efficient operating conditions.

8. c Abnormal spoilage is treated as a loss in the period in which it occurs because it is not expected to occur.

9. d Normal spoilage is included in the cost of the good units produced because it is expected to occur.

10. e

Total production cost	$2,200
Reduction for abnormal spoilage:	
20 units × $\left(\dfrac{\$2,200}{550}\right)$	80
	$2,120

Part 4
Direct Materials

Date	Department	Req. No.	Cost	Total
3/12	Cutting	6281	$3,600	
3/12	Assembly	6288	240	
3/19	Cutting	6299	1,800	
3/19	Assembly	6308	360	$6,000

Direct Labor

Date	Department	Hours	Hourly Rate	Cost	Total
3/12	Cutting	400	$10.80	$4,320	
3/12	Assembly	200	9.50	1,900	
3/19	Cutting	220	10.80	2,376	
3/19	Assembly	300	9.50	2,850	$11,446

Factory Overhead Applied

Date	Department	Rate of Application	Hours	Cost	Total
3/12	Cutting	$7.50 per machine hour	300	$2,250	
3/12	Assembly	$6.00 per direct labor hour	200	1,200	
3/19	Cutting	$7.50 per machine hour	160	1,200	
3/19	Assembly	$6.00 per direct labor hour	300	1,800	$6,450

Direct materials	$ 6,000	Sales price	$50,000
Direct labor	11,446	Factory cost	$23,896
Factory overhead applied	6,450	Marketing and administrative expenses	9,558
Total factory cost	$23,896	Cost to make and sell	33,454
		Profit	$16,546

Part 5

Work in Process

March 1 Bal.:		To finished goods......	100,000
No. 101	15,000		
No. 103	5,300		
Materials	25,000		
Direct labor	30,000		
Factory overhead	30,000		
	105,300		
March 31 Bal.:			
No. 110	5,300		

Finished Goods

From work in process ..	100,000	To cost of goods sold...	91,000
March 31 Bal.:			
No. 107	9,000		

Cost of Goods Sold

From finished goods ...	91,000	
	1,500	
	92,500	

Factory Overhead Control

31,500	30,000
	1,500
	31,500

Applied Factory Overhead

30,000	30,000

Part 6

Account	Subsidiary Record	Debit	Credit
1. Materials		25,000	
Accounts Payable			25,000
2. Payroll		33,000	
Employees' Income Tax Payable			4,950
FICA Tax Payable			2,475
Accrued Payroll			25,575
3. Accrued Payroll		25,575	
Cash			25,575
4. Factory Overhead Control		5,500	
Indirect Labor	5,500		
Work in Process		27,500	
Job 101	7,500		
Job 102	12,000		
Job 103	8,000		
Payroll			33,000
5. Factory Overhead Control		4,059	
Payroll Taxes	4,059		
FICA Tax Payable			2,475
State Unemployment Tax Payable			264
Federal Unemployment Tax Payable			1,320
6. Factory Overhead Control		2,500	
Supplies	2,500		
Work in Process		29,000	
Job 101	9,000		
Job 102	12,000		
Job 103	8,000		
Materials			31,500
7. Factory Overhead Control		1,000	
Depreciation	1,000		
Accumulated Depreciation			1,000
8. Factory Overhead Control		10,000	
Other Factory Overhead Costs	10,000		
Accounts Payable			10,000
9. Work in Process		27,500	
Job 101	7,500		
Job 102	12,000		
Job 103	8,000		
Applied Factory Overhead			27,500
10. Finished Goods		52,000	
Job 101	28,000		
Job 103	24,000		
Work in Process			52,000
11. Cash		40,000	
Sales			40,000
12. Cost of Goods Sold		28,000	
Finished Goods			28,000
13. Applied Factory Overhead		27,500	
Factory Overhead Control			27,500
14. Factory Overhead Control		4,441	
Cost of Goods Sold			4,441

Part 7

Account	Subsidiary Record	Debit	Credit
1. Factory Overhead Control ($25 × 50)		1,250	
Defective Work	1,250		
Materials			250
Payroll			500
Applied Factory Overhead			500
Finished Goods (1,000 × $60)		60,000	
Work in Process			60,000
2. Work in Process		1,250	
Materials			250
Payroll			500
Applied Factory Overhead			500
Finished Goods		61,250	
Work in Process			61,250

CHAPTER 5

Part 1

1. T	6. F	11. T
2. F	7. T	12. T
3. F	8. F	13. F
4. T	9. T	14. T
5. F	10. F	15. F

Part 2

1. m	8. o	15. l
2. q	9. k	16. r
3. t	10. s	17. b
4. d	11. p	18. n
5. i	12. j	19. c
6. g	13. f	20. e
7. a	14. h	

Part 3

1. **a** The equivalent unit computation would include only the good units transferred out plus the work done on the units still in process at the end of the period.

2. **b** If the lost units occur at the end of the process (e.g., at the time of final inspection), then the units still in process should not bear any of the lost unit cost.

3. **d** All of the statements in a through c are features of process costing.

4. **b** The cost per job would appear on a job order cost sheet. Answers a, b, and c would appear on a cost production report.

5. **d** The cost of normal shrinkage and scrap is a product cost that attaches to the inventory rather than a period cost that is expensed when it occurs.

6. **a** Answer a is a characteristic of process costing; b and c relate to job order costing; and d would not be true for either standard or job order costing.

7. **c** If the percentage of completion of the ending work in process inventory were overstated, then the equivalent units would also be overstated. If equivalent units were overstated, then the cost per unit would be understated. If the cost per unit were understated, then the total cost of the completed goods would also be understated.

8. **b** Transferred-in cost is the cost of the production of a previous internal process that is subsequently used in a succeeding internal process.

9. **e** The correct answer is: 12,000 + 6,000 = 18,000.

10. **d** The correct answer is: Let X = units started during the month:

$$3,000 + X = 10,000 + 4,000$$
$$X + 11,000$$

Part 4

1. Quantity schedule:

Units received from Department A		80,000
Units transferred to finished goods.............................	50,000	
Units still in process	30,000	80,000

2. Equivalent production:

	Transferred in from Department A	Materials	Conversion
Transferred to finished goods..............	50,000	50,000	50,000
Ending inventory	30,000	30,000	7,500
	80,000	80,000	57,500

3. Department B

    Cost per equivalent unit
      for materials cost ($40,000 ÷ 80,000) = $.50
      for conversion cost ($115,000 ÷ 57,500) = $2.00

Part 5

Reina Inc.
Department B
Cost of Production Report
For the Month of June, 19–

Quantity Schedule

Units received from preceding department		15,000
Units transferred to next department	13,125	
Units still in process	1,875	15,000

Cost Charged to the Department:	Total Cost	Unit Cost
Cost from preceding department:		
Transferred in during the month	$ 90,000	$ 6.00
Cost added by department:		
Materials	$ 57,500	$ 4.00
Labor................................	68,750	5.00
Factory overhead	34,375	2.50
Total cost added	$ 160,625	$ 11.50
Total cost to be accounted for..........	$ 250,625	$ 17.50

Cost Accounted for as Follows

Transferred to next department		229,688
Work in process—ending inventory:		
Cost from preceding department	$ 11,250	
Materials	5,000	
Labor.............................	3,125	
Factory overhead	1,562	20,937
Total cost accounted for		$ 250,625

Additional Computations:
Equivalent production:
Materials = 13,125 + (1,875 × ⅔) = 14,375
Labor and factory overhead = 13,125 + (1,875 × ⅓) = 13,750

Part 6

Zabricki Industries, Inc.
Department B
Cost of Production Report
For the Month of May, 19–

Quantity Schedule

Units received from preceding department		20,000
Units transferred to next department	16,000	
Units still in process (50% labor and overhead) .	3,000	
Units lost in process	1,000	20,000

Cost Charged to the Department	Total Cost	Unit Cost
Cost from preceding department:		
Transferred in during the month	$ 247,000	$ 12.35
Adjusted cost from preceding department:		
$247,000 ÷ (20,000 – 1,000 lost units)		$ 13.00
Cost added by department:		
Labor...............................	105,000	$ 6.00
Factory overhead	78,750	4.50
Total cost added	$ 183,750	$ 10.50
Total cost to be accounted for..........	$ 430,750	$ 23.50

Cost Accounted for as Follows

Transferred to next department		$ 376,000
Work in process—ending inventory:		
Cost from preceding department	$ 39,000	
Labor...............................	9,000	
Factory overhead	6,750	54,750
Total cost accounted for		$ 430,750

Additional Computations:
Equivalent production:
Labor and factory overhead = 16,000 + (3,000 × .50) = 17,500

Part 7

1.

Cooking Department
Cost of Production Report
For the Month of July, 19–

Quantity Schedule

Units received from preceding department		16,000
Units transferred to next department	12,000	
Units still in process (all materials—½ labor and factory overhead)	3,000	
Units lost in process (abnormal—½ materials, labor, and factory overhead)...............	1,000	16,000

Cost Charged to the Department	Total Cost	Unit Cost
Cost from preceding department:		
Transferred in during the month (16,000 units)	$ 80,000	$ 5.00
Cost added by department:		
Materials	$ 27,900	$ 1.80
Labor...............................	84,000	$ 6.00
Factory overhead	56,000	4.00
Total cost added	$ 167,900	$ 11.80
Total cost to be accounted for..........	$ 247,900	$ 16.80

Cost Accounted for as Follows

Transferred to next department (12,000 × $16.80).............................		$ 201,600
Transferred to factory overhead:		
From preceding department (1,000 × $5)	$ 5,000	
Materials (1,000 × ½ × $1.80).............	900	
Labor (1,000 × ½ × $6.00)	3,000	
Factory overhead (1,000 × ½ × $4.00)	2,000	10,900
Work in process—ending inventory:		
From preceding department (3,000 × $5.00) ..	$ 15,000	
Materials (3,000 × $1.80)	5,400	
Labor (3,000 × ½ × $6.00)	9,000	
Factory overhead (3,000 × ½ × $4.00)	6,000	35,400
Total cost accounted for		$ 247,900

Additional Computations:
Equivalent production:
Materials = 12,000 + 3,000 + (1,000 × ½) = 15,500
Labor and factory overhead = 12,000 + (3,000 × ½) + (1,000 × ½) = 14,000
Unit costs:
Materials = $27,900 ÷ 15,500 = $1.80
Labor = $84,900 ÷ 14,000 = $6
Factory overhead = $56,000 ÷ 14,000 = $4

2.
Factory Overhead Control	10,900	
Work in Process—Cooking Department......		10,900

CHAPTER 6

Part 1

1. T	6. F	11. T
2. T	7. F	12. T
3. F	8. F	13. T
4. T	9. F	14. F
5. F	10. T	15. T

Part 2

1. a Under the fifo method, the degree of completion of the beginning work in process must be stated in order to compute completed unit costs; average costing does not require the degree of completion of the beginning work in process.

2. c Equivalent units of production under fifo = percent of work required to complete beginning inventory + units started and completed during period + percent of work performed on ending inventory.

3. b Since the cost of the beginning inventory is kept separate from the cost of the goods started and completed during the period under fifo but not under average costing, the cost of goods manufactured would be the same under both methods when there is no beginning inventory.

4. c $18,000 + (5,000 \times 60\%) = 21,000$

5. b
$(\$12,000 + \$29,000) \div (12,000 + 8,000) = \$2.05$
$(\$ 2,500 + \$ 5,500) \div (12,000 + 8,000) = .40$
$(\$ 1,000 + \$ 5,000) \div (12,000 + 6,000) = \underline{.33}$
$\overline{\$2.78}$

6. a $90,000 \times \$.44$ . . . . $\$39,600$ goods completed
$10,000 \times \$.24$ . . . . . . $\$2,400$
$5,000 \times \$.20$ . . . . . . $\underline{1,000}$ $\$ 3,400$ work in process, ending

7. e Quantity schedule:

Work in process, October 1	6,000
Units started	50,000
	56,000
Transferred out	44,000
Work in process, October 31	12,000
	56,000

Materials cost of work in process, October 31:
$$\frac{\$3,000 + \$25,560}{56,000} = \$.51 \times 12,000 = \$6,120$$

8. a $12,000 + 7,000 = 19,000$

9. e Process costing is concerned with charging costs to departments rather than to jobs.

10. c $14,000 + (80\% \times 7,000) = 19,600$

Part 3

1.

	Materials Units	Conversion Units
Department A:		
Transferred out	2,500	2,500
Ending inventory	1,000	250
Equivalent production	3,500	2,750

	Units from Preceding Dept.	Conversion Units
Department B:		
Transferred out	2,600	2,600
Ending inventory	500	250
Equivalent production	3,100	2,850

2.

	Materials Units	Conversion Units
Department A:		
Transferred out	2,500	2,500
Less beginning inventory (all units)	500	500
Started and finished this period .	2,000	2,000
Add beginning inventory (work this period)	0	125
Add ending inventory (work this period)	1,000	250
Equivalent production	3,000	2,375

	Units from Preceding Dept.	Conversion Units
Department B:		
Transferred out	2,600	2,600
Less beginning inventory (all units)	600	600
Started and finished this period .	2,000	2,000
Add beginning inventory (work this period)	0	300
Add ending inventory (work this period)	500	250
Equivalent production	2,500	2,550

Part 4

1.

Materials (7,500 × $3)	$22,500
Labor (3,750 × $2.30)	8,625
Overhead (3,750 × $2.30)	8,625
Work in process inventory	$39,750

Computations:

Materials: $\dfrac{\$7,500 + \$120,000}{35,000 + (15,000 \times .50)} = \$3.00$

Labor and overhead: $\dfrac{\$9,125 + \$80,000}{35,000 + (15,000 \times .25)} = \$2.30$

2.

Materials (7,500 × $1.714)	$12,855.00
Labor (3,750 × $1.185)	4,443.75
Overhead (3,750 × $1.185)	4,443.75
Work in process inventory	$21,742.50

Computations:
Materials:

$$\frac{\$120,000}{35,000 - 10,000 + (10,000 \times .25) + (15,000 \times .50)} = \$3.428$$

Labor and overhead:

$$\frac{\$80,000}{35,000 - 10,000 + (10,000 \times .50) + (15,000 \times .25)} = \$2.37$$

Part 5

Palm Springs Supply Company
Department B
Cost of Production Report
For the Month of June, 19–

Quantity Schedule

Units in process at beginning	5,000	
Units received from preceding department	45,000	50,000
Units transferred to next department	38,000	
Units completed and on hand	2,000	
Units still in process	8,000	
Units lost in process	2,000	50,000

Cost Charged to the Department	Total Cost	Unit Cost
Cost from preceding department:		
Work in process—beginning inventory	$ 30,000	
Transferred in during period	225,000	
Total	$255,000	$5.100
Adjusted cost from preceding department		$5.313
Cost added by department:		
Work in process—beginning inventory:		
Labor	$ 2,000	
Factory overhead	1,000	
Cost added during period:		
Labor	25,000	$ .613
Factory overhead	12,500	.307
Total cost added	$ 40,500	$ .920
Total cost to be accounted for	$295,500	$6.233

Cost Accounted for as Follows

Transferred to next department (38,000 × $6.233)		$236,854
Work in process—ending inventory:		
Completed and on hand (2,000 × $6.233)		12,466
Still in process:		
Cost from preceding department (8,000 × $5.313)		42,504
Labor (4,000 × $.613)		2,452
Factory overhead (4,000 × $.307)		1,228
Total cost accounted for		$295,504*

*Rounding difference

Additional Computations:

Equivalent production—labor and overhead:

Units transferred to next department	38,000
Units completed and on hand	2,000
Units in process (8,000 × ½)	4,000
	44,000

Part 6

Chomyszak Chemical Company
Refining Department
Cost of Production Report
For the Month of May, 19–

Quantity Schedule

Units in process at beginning (½ labor and factory overhead)	10,000	
Units received from preceding department	37,000	47,000
Units transferred to next department	40,000	
Units still in process (¾ labor and factory overhead)	5,000	
Units lost in process	2,000	47,000

Cost Charged to the Department	Total Cost	Unit Cost
Work in process—beginning inventory	$ 10,000	
Cost from preceding department:		
Transferred in during the month (37,000 units)	$120,000	$3.243
Adjusted cost from preceding department		$3.429
Cost added by the department:		
Labor	$ 50,000	$1.290
Factory overhead	40,000	1.032
Total cost added	$ 90,000	$2.322
Total cost to be accounted for	$220,000	$5.751

Cost Accounted for as Follows

Transferred to next department—			
From beginning inventory:			
Inventory cost	$10,000		
Labor added (10,000 × ½ × $1.29)	6,450		
Factory overhead added (10,000 × ½ × $1.032)	5,160	$ 21,610	
From current production:			
Units started and finished (30,000 × $5.751*)		172,537	$194,147
Work in process—ending inventory:			
Adjusted cost from preceding department (5,000 × $3.429)		$ 17,145	
Labor (5,000 × ¾ × $1.290)		4,838	
Factory overhead (5,000 × ¾ × $1.032)		3,870	25,853
Total cost accounted for			$220,000

*30,000 units × $5.751 = $172,530. To avoid a decimal discrepancy, the cost transferred from current production is computed as follows: $220,000 − ($21,610 + $25,853) = $172,537.

Additional Computations:

Equivalent production:	Labor and Factory Overhead
Transferred out	40,000
Less beginning inventory (all units) . . .	10,000
Started and finished this period	30,000
Add beginning inventory (work this period)	5,000
Add ending inventory (work this period)	3,750
	38,750 units

CHAPTER 7

Part 1				Part 2		
1. F	6. T	11. F		1. k	6. b	11. c
2. T	7. F	12. T		2. f	7. l	12. e
3. F	8. T	13. T		3. d	8. i	13. g
4. T	9. T	14. F		4. n	9. a	14. m
5. T	10. T	15. F		5. h	10. j	15. o

Part 3

1. a The relative sales value method enjoys great popularity because of the argument that the market value of any product is a manifestation of the cost incurred in its production.

2. a Whenever two or more different joint products or by-products are created from a single cost factor, a joint cost results. By-products and joint products are difficult to cost because a true joint cost is indivisible.

3. d This method is called the market value (reversal cost) method and it reduces the manufacturing cost of the main product by an estimate of the by-product's value at the time of recovery. The by-product account is charged with this estimated amount and the manufacturing cost of the main product is credited. Any additional costs of materials, labor, or factory overhead incurred after the by-product is separated from the main product are charged to the by-product.

4. a All manufacturing costs (materials, labor, and overhead) should be allocable as joint costs.

5. a Joint costs should be allocated in a manner that assigns a proportionate amount of the total cost to each product by means of a quantitative basis such as the market or sales value method, the quantitative or physical unit method, the average unit cost method, or the weighted average method.

6. e Answers a, b, c, and d are all methods of allocating joint costs.

7. d $\dfrac{\$75,000}{\$75,000 + \$50,000} \times \$60,000 = \$36,000$

8. e Erin: $\dfrac{\$9,000 - \$3,000}{\$15,000 - \$6,000} \times \$6,600 = \$4,400$

Braugh: $\dfrac{\$6,000 - \$3,000}{\$15,000 - \$6,000} \times \$6,600 = \$2,200$

9. c

Product	Market Value at Split-Off (Per Gallon)	Gallons	Market Value at Split-Off	Apportionment of Joint Production Cost
A	$10	500	$ 5,000	$1,200
B	14	1,000	14,000	3,360
			$19,000	$4,560

$3,360 + $2,000 = $5,360 cost to produce 1,000 gallons of B

10. b

	Segment No. 1
Sales...	$900,000
Traceable cost.....................................	$400,000
Common cost ($600,000 × .40)......................	240,000
Total cost...	$640,000
Operating profit	$260,000

Part 4

1.

Sales.....................................		$15,000
Cost of goods sold:		
Beginning inventory.........................	$ 3,750	
Total production cost.......................	6,750	
Cost of goods available for sale...............	$10,500	
Ending inventory (4,000 units × $.75)...........	3,000	7,500
(a) Gross profit.............................		$ 7,500
Marketing and administrative expense..........		3,000
Operating income		$ 4,500
Revenue from sale of by-product..............		750
(b) Income before income tax...................		$ 5,250

2. (a) $7,500 + $750 = $8,250

  (b) $8,250 - $3,000 = $5,250

3. (a) $15,000 - $6,750 = $8,250

  (b) $8,250 - $3,000 = $5,250

4.

(a) Beginning inventory...........................		$3,750
Total production cost.........................	$6,750	
Less revenue from by-product...................	750	6,000
Cost of goods available for sale.................		$9,750

New average unit cost for main product: $9,750 ÷ 14,000 = $.696

  (b) 4,000 units × $.696 = $2,784

Part 5

Labreque Laminators Inc.
Income Statement
For the Month of July, 19–

	Main Product	By-Product Lam	By-Product Nate	Total
Sales	$80,000	$12,000	$6,000	$98,000
Cost of goods sold:				
Manufacturing cost before separation:				
Costs assigned:				
Operating profit		$ 3,000	$1,200	
Marketing and administrative expense		2,000	750	
Manufacturing cost after separation		5,000	2,500	
Total		$10,000	$4,450	
Cost before separation	$36,450*	$ 2,000	$1,550	$40,000
Manufacturing cost after separation	15,000	5,000	2,500	22,500
Cost of goods sold	$51,450	$ 7,000	$4,050	$62,500
Gross profit	$28,550	$ 5,000	$1,950	$35,500
Marketing and administrative expense...........................	8,000	2,000	750	10,750
Operating profit..	$20,550	$ 3,000	$1,200	$24,750

* $40,000 – $2,000 – $1,550 = $36,450

Part 6

Grimm Chemicals Inc.
Allocation of Joint Cost
For January, 19–

	Units Produced (1)	Units Sold	Units in Ending Inventory	Unit Sales Price (2)	Market Value of Production	Joint Cost Allocated (3)	Cost of Sales (4)	Ending Inventory
Inkin........	2,000	1,500	500	$10	$ 20,000	$ 15,000	$11,250	$ 3,750
Blinkin	6,000	5,000	1,000	12	72,000	54,000	45,000	9,000
Nodd	10,000	8,000	2,000	7	70,000	52,500	42,000	10,500
					$162,000	$121,500	$98,250	$23,250

Computations

(1) Inkin: 1/5 × 10,000 = 2,000
    Blinkin: 3/5 × 10,000 = 6,000
    Nodd: 5/5 × 10,000 = 10,000

(2) Inkin: $15,000 ÷ 1,500 = $10
    Blinkin: $60,000 ÷ 5,000 = $12
    Nodd: $56,000 ÷ 8,000 = $7

(3) $\dfrac{\text{Joint processing cost}}{\text{Market value of production}} = \dfrac{\$60.75 \times (10,000 \div 5)}{\$162,000} = \dfrac{\$121,500}{\$162,000} = \$.75$

    Inkin: $20,000 × .75 = $15,000
    Blinkin: $72,000 × .75 = $54,000
    Nodd: $70,000 × .75 = $52,500

(4) Inkin: 1,500 × $10 × .75 = $11,250
    Blinkin: 5,500 × $12 × .75 = $45,000
    Nodd: 8,000 × $7 × .75 = $42,000

Part 7

1.

Celestial Products Inc.
Quantitative Unit Method
For April, 19–

	Units Produced and Sold	Joint Cost Allocated*	Unit Market Value	Unit Cost of Sales	Unit Gross Profit
Darth	225,000	$ 759,375	$10	$3.375	$ 6.625
Vader	75,000	253,125	5	3.375	11.625
	300,000	$1,012,500			

Computations:

*Darth: $\frac{225,000}{300,000} \times \$1,012,500 = \$759,375$ Vader: $\frac{75,000}{300,000} \times \$1,012,500 = \$253,125$

2.

Celestial Products Inc.
Relative Sales Value Method
For April 19,–

	Units Produced and Sold	Unit Market Value	Total Market Value	Joint Cost Allocation*	Unit Cost of Sales	Unit Gross Profit
Darth	225,000	$10	$2,250,000	$ 675,000	$3.00	$ 7.00
Vader	75,000	15	1,125,000	337,500	4.50	10.50
	300,000		$3,375,000	$1,012,500		

Computations:

$* \ \frac{\text{Cost of sales}}{\text{Total market value}} = \frac{\$1,012,500}{\$3,375,000} = .30$

Darth: $2,250,000 \times .30 = \$675,000$
Vader: $1,125,000 \times .30 = \$337,500$

CHAPTER 8

Part 1

1. T	6. F	11. T
2. T	7. T	12. F
3. F	8. T	13. T
4. T	9. T	14. F
5. T	10. T	15. T

Part 2

1. o	8. b	15. n
2. k	9. i	16. c
3. a	10. q	17. l
4. j	11. f	18. r
5. t	12. e	19. d
6. g	13. p	20. m
7. s	14. h	

Part 3

1. c $\frac{360}{60 - 10} \times 2\% = 14.4\%$

2. d According to the AICPA, market should not exceed the net realizable value, which is the estimated selling price in the ordinary course of business, less reasonably predictable costs of completion and disposal.

3. b If normal spoilage is caused by exacting specifications, difficult processing, or other unusual and unexpected factors, the spoilage cost should be charged to that order.

4. d Since under fifo the earliest goods purchased are the first goods considered to be sold, the latest purchased merchandise would be assignable to inventory.

5. d All withdrawals of materials from the storeroom are evidenced by a materials requisition form and result in debits to Work in Process, Factory Overhead, or Marketing and Administration Expense.

6. c As used in the phrase "lower of cost or market," the term "market" means current replacement cost, except that it should not exceed the expected sales price less a deduction for costs yet to be incurred in making the sale, and it should not be less than the expected amount to be realized in the sale of the goods, reduced by a normal profit margin.

7. c Choices a, b, and d are all valid reasons in favor of using the lifo method. Statement c, however, is more typical of the fifo method, in that the earliest goods purchased by a business are usually the first ones sold.

8. d Answers a, b, and c are all correct. Answer d, however, is incorrect because the "floor" provides for the normal profit margin of $12.

9. d Answers a, b, and c are all correct. Answer d, however, is incorrect in that it is lifo not fifo that permits some control by management over the amount of income for a period through controlled purchases.

10. b If the inventory cost on the balance sheet was lower using fifo than lifo, the most recent purchases (which would appear on the balance sheet under fifo) were less expensive than the earlier purchases (which would appear on the balance sheet using lifo).

Part 4

1. First-in, first-out costing

Date	Received			Issued			Balance			
	Quantity	Unit Cost	Amount	Quantity	Unit Cost	Amount	Quantity	Unit Cost	Amount	
July 2	200	$4.50	$ 900				200	$4.50	$ 900	
8	60	5.00	300				60	5.00	300	$1,200
18				100	$4.50	$450	100	4.50	450	
							60	5.00	300	750
24	240	6.00	1,440				240	6.00	1,440	2,190
31				100	4.50	450	200	6.00	1,200	
				60	5.00	300				
				40	6.00	240				

Cost of materials consumed . . . . $1,440   Cost assigned to inventory $1,200

2. Last-in, first-out costing

Date	Received			Issued			Balance			
	Quantity	Unit Cost	Amount	Quantity	Unit Cost	Amount	Quantity	Unit Cost	Amount	
July 2	200	$4.50	$ 900				200	$4.50	$ 900	
8	60	5.00	300				60	5.00	300	
18				60	$5.00	$ 300	160	4.50	720	
				40	4.50	180				
24	240	6.00	1,440				240	6.00	1,440	2,160
31				200	6.00	1,200	160	4.50	720	
							40	6.00	240	960

Cost of materials consumed . . . . $1,680   Cost assigned to inventory $960

3. Average costing

Date	Received			Issued			Balance		
	Quantity	Unit Cost	Amount	Quantity	Unit Cost	Amount	Quantity	Unit Cost	Amount
July 2	200	$4.50	$ 900				200	$4.50	$ 900.00
8	60	5.00	300				260	4.615	1,200.00
18				100	$4.615	$ 461.50	160	4.615	738.40
24	240	6.00	1,440				400	5.445	2,178.00
31				200	5.445	1,089	200	5.445	1,089.00

Cost of materials consumed . . . . $1,550.50   Cost assigned to inventory $1,089

Part 5

1.

Case	Cost	Replacement Cost	Floor	Ceiling	Market	Lower of Cost or Market
A	$4.00	$5.00	$6.00	$7.50	$6.00	$4.00
B	7.00	6.50	6.00	7.50	6.50	6.50
C	6.50	5.50	6.00	7.50	6.00	6.00
D	5.00	5.50	6.00	7.50	6.00	5.00
E	6.50	8.25	6.00	7.50	7.50	6.50
F	7.25	7.50	6.00	7.50	7.50	7.25

Account	Subsidiary Record	Debit	Credit
2. Cost of Goods Sold (or Factory Overhead Control)		500	
Inventory Adjustment–Lower of Cost or Market	500		
Materials–Allowance for Inventory Decline to Market			500

Part 6

Account	Subsidiary Record	Debit	Credit
1. Factory Overhead Control ($25 × 50)		1,250	
Defective Work	1,250		
Materials			250
Payroll			500
Applied Factory Overhead			500
Finished Goods (1,000 × $60)		60,000	
Work in Process			60,000
2. Work in Process		1,250	
Materials			250
Payroll			500
Applied Factory Overhead			500
Finished Goods (1,000 × $61.25)		61,250	
Work in Process			61,250

CHAPTER 9

Part 1

1. T	6. T	11. F
2. T	7. F	12. T
3. F	8. F	13. F
4. T	9. F	14. T
5. T	10. T	15. T

Part 2

1. q	8. j	15. p
2. k	9. f	16. e
3. t	10. m	17. r
4. h	11. s	18. c
5. a	12. b	19. n
6. d	13. i	20. l
7. o	14. g	

Part 3

1. d $\sqrt{\dfrac{2 \times RU \times CO}{CU \times CC}} = \sqrt{\dfrac{2 \times 40{,}000 \times \$60}{\$10}} = \sqrt{480{,}000} = 693$

2. a $EOQ = \sqrt{\dfrac{2 \times RU \times CO}{CU \times CC}}$

$200 = \sqrt{\dfrac{2 \times 6{,}000 \times \text{Setup cost}}{\$.60}}$

$\$.60\,(40{,}000) = (2 \times 6{,}000 \times \text{Setup cost})$
$\$24{,}000 = 12{,}000\,(\text{Setup cost})$
Setup cost = $2

3. e 10,000 ÷ 250 = 40 units, daily usage
40 units daily usage × 90 days = 3,600

4. c In determining EOQ, only the variable ordering costs, such as preparing the purchase order, handling the income shipment, and preparing the receiving report, should be considered.

5. a The three items needed to compute the EOQ are the annual demand, the cost of placing an order, and the annual cost of carrying one unit in stock.

6. c The EOQ is that point where carrying costs equal ordering costs. If a quantity greater than the EOQ is ordered, carrying costs will exceed ordering costs.

7. c The more uncertainty that management is willing to accept regarding an out-of-stock condition, the smaller will be the amount of safety stock carried, and vice versa.

8. a 25% + 50% = 75% probability at 225 units.

9. a The economic order quantity is that point where ordering costs and carrying costs are minimized.

10. c If safety stocks are ignored, the only factor relevant for determining the order point would be the anticipated demand during the lead time.

Part 4

1.
January	10,000	
February	13,500	
March	14,800	
	38,300	
Reserve or safety stock	7,500	
Total needed		45,800
Jan. 1 inventory	8,000	
Jan. delivery	12,000	
Feb. delivery	13,000	
Total scheduled supply	33,000	
Quantity to order for March delivery		12,800

2.
(a) Jan. 1 inventory		8,000
On order for January and February delivery		25,000
		33,000
Forecase usage, Jan. and Feb.		23,500
March 1 inventory		9,500
(b) To order for March delivery		12,800
		22,300
Forecast usage, March		14,800
March 31 inventory		7,500

Part 5

$$\text{EOQ} = \sqrt{\frac{2 \times \text{RU} \times \text{CO}}{\text{CU} \times \text{CC}}} = \sqrt{\frac{2 \times 180{,}000 \times \$80}{\$400 \times .20}} = \sqrt{360{,}000} = 600$$

$$\frac{\text{RU} \times \text{CO}}{\text{EOQ}} = \frac{180{,}000 \times \$80}{600} = \$24{,}000 \text{ Order cost}$$

$$\frac{\text{CU} \times \text{CC} \times \text{EOQ}}{2} = \frac{\$400 \times .20 \times 600}{2} = \$24{,}000 \text{ Carrying Cost}$$

Part 6

Safety Stock Level	Expected Annual Stockouts	Total Stockout Cost	Total Carrying Cost	Total Stockout and Carrying Cost
0	50	$5,000	–0–	$5,000
200	30	3,000	$400	3,400
400	10	1,000	800	1,800
800	5	500	1,600	2,100

The optimum level of safety stock is 400 units, because that is the level at which total stockout cost and carrying cost are minimized.

Part 7

1. $\text{EOQ} = \sqrt{\dfrac{2 \times (250 \times 100) \times \$25}{\$5}} = \sqrt{250{,}000} = 500$

2.
Maximum use per day	150 units
Normal use per day	100
Safety stock (maximum)	50 units × 10 days lead time = 500 units

3.
Normal use per day (100) × days of lead time (10)	1,000 units
Safety stock	500
Order point	1,500 units

4.
Order point	1,500 units
Normal use during lead time (100 × 10)	1,000
On hand at time order received	500 units
Quantity ordered	500
Normal maximum delivery	1,000 units

5.
Order point	1,500 units
Minimum use during lead time (50 × 10)	500
On hand at time order received	1,000 units
Quantity ordered	500
Absolute maximum inventory	1,500 units

5.
Economic order quantity ÷ 2	250 units
Safety stock	500
Average inventory, assuming normal lead time and usage	750 units

Part 8

Item	Units	% of Total	Unit Cost	Total Cost	% of Total
H	100	1	$200.00	$20,000	40
D	200	2	55.00	11,000	22
I	300	3	16.70	5,010	10
G	500	5	9.60	4,800	9.6
B	600	6	8.00	4,800	9.6
F	750	7.5	2.40	1,800	3.6
C	1,500	15	.50	750	1.5
J	1,750	17.5	.40	700	1.4
A	3,000	30	.21	630	1.3
E	1,300	13	.40	520	1
	10,000	100		$50,010	100

2.

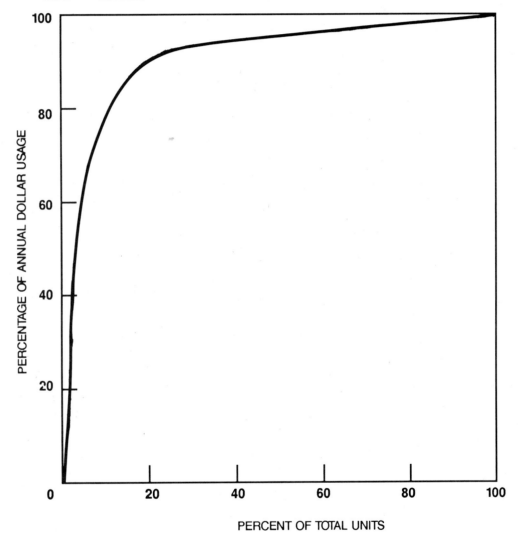

Part 9

1. The safety stock:

$$\sqrt{\frac{5,000}{9-1}} = \sqrt{\frac{5,000}{8}} = \sqrt{625} = 25; \ (1.860)(25)(\sqrt{1}\ ) = 47$$

2. The order point:
   250 + 47 = 297

3. The safety stock if lead time is 4 months:

$$(1.860)(25)(\sqrt{4}\ ) = 93$$

CHAPTER 10

Part 1

1. T	6. T	11. T
2. T	7. F	12. T
3. F	8. F	13. T
4. T	9. T	14. T
5. T	10. F	15. F

Part 2

1. o	8. j	15. h
2. t	9. c	16. p
3. k	10. i	17. g
4. a	11. b	18. n
5. s	12. d	19. l
6. q	13. r	20. m
7. f	14. e	

Part 3

1. d Before the daily time tickets are sent to the payroll department, the total time reported on each time ticket is compared with the total hours on each employee's time clock card. If there is any difference, an adjustment is made after having identified the reasons for the difference.

2. c

Times	Cumulative Average Required Labor Hours per Time
1	100 minutes
2	80 (100 × .8)
4	64 (80 × .8)

3. d 4 × 64 = 256

4. c The clock card (or time card) is needed to provide evidence of the employee's presence in the plant from the time of entry to departure.

5. d In the 100% group bonus plan, each worker in the group receives an hourly rate for production up to the standard output. Units produced in excess of the standard are regarded as time saved by the group, and each worker is in effect paid a bonus for time saved.

6. a The pace at which an observed employee is working is referred to as a rating or performance rating.

7. d Fringe costs form a substantial element of labor cost and include such items as the employer portion of the FICA tax, holiday pay, overtime premium pay, and pension costs.

8. d The employee performance report—significant adverse changes shows significant differences between a worker's usual efficiency and the efficiency attained in the current report.

9. a To curtail the wage-price spiral requires increases that do not exceed the unit cost reduction resulting from increased productivity.

10. c The cost department is responsible for recording the direct and indirect labor costs on the job cost sheets and departmental expense analysis sheets, respectively.

Part 4

Worker	Hours Worked	Output Units	Standard Units	Efficiency Ratio	Base Rate	Base × Efficiency Ratio	Total Earned	Labor Cost per Unit	Overhead per Hour	Overhead per Unit	Conversion Cost per Unit
Adams	40	840	800	1.05	$15.00	$15.75	$630.00	$.75	$20.00	$ .96	$1.71
Burley	40	800	800	1.00	15.00	15.00	600.00	.75	20.00	1.00	1.75
Condon	40	880	800	1.10	15.00	16.50	660.00	.75	20.00	.90	1.65
Dow	36	750	720	1.04	10.00	10.40	374.40	.50	20.00	1.06	1.56
Evert	40	720	800	.90	7.50	–	300.00	.42	20.00	1.12	1.54

Part 5

Day	Units Produced	Daily Earnings	Labor Cost per Unit Produced Each Day
Monday	30	$ 96.00	$3.20
Tuesday	32	96.00	3.00
Wednesday	46	138.00	3.00
Thursday	28	96.00	3.43
Friday	34	102.00	3.00

Part 6

1.

Cumulative Lots	×	Cumulative Average Time (Lots)	=	Cumulative Time (Total Hours)
1		150.00		150.00
2		120.00 (150 × .8)		240.00 (120 × 2)
4		96.00 (120 × .8)		384.00 (96 × 4)
8		76.80 (96 × .8)		614.40 (76.80 × 8)

2. 614.40 × $20 = $12,288

3.
$12,288	cost of eight lots
–3,000	cost of first lot
$ 9,288	cost of lots 2–8

CHAPTER 11

Part 1

1. F	6. T	11. F
2. T	7. F	12. F
3. F	8. T	13. T
4. F	9. T	14. T
5. T	10. T	15. T

Part 2

1. s	8. t	15. i
2. c	9. m	16. e
3. d	10. p	17. n
4. f	11. a	18. g
5. q	12. r	19. h
6. j	13. b	20. k
7. 1	14. o	

Part 3

1. b Payroll taxes are treated as an indirect manufacturing cost and are debited to Factory Overhead when the payroll is recorded.

2. d In determining whether overtime premium should be charged to a specific job or spread over all jobs via the factory overhead rate, the key consideration is whether the job was worked on during the overtime period because it was a rush order or merely as a result of random scheduling.

3. d $\dfrac{\$600 \times 4 \text{ weeks}}{48 \text{ weeks}} = \$50$

4. a Capitalizing the costs of acquiring an employee requires collecting the costs of acquiring, hiring, and training an employee and is sometimes used in professional sports.

5. d The stochastic rewards valuation model involves a stochastic process defined as a natural system that changes in time in accordance with the laws of probability.

6. d Under the Pension Reform Act of 1974, employers must currently contribute the normal cost of the plan for the plan years plus a level funding, including interest, of past service costs and certain other costs.

7. c Income taxes are withheld from each wage payment in accordance with the amount of the employee's earnings and exemptions claimed on form W-4.

8. b To spread the bonus cost over production throughout the year via the predetermined factory overhead rate, the weekly entry would include a debit to Factory Overhead Control for the ratable portion of the bonus pay.

9. c Answers a, b, and d are all factors that affect the ultimate cost of a company pension plan. Answer c is correct because the law, not management discretion, determines when employees will be vested.

10. c The annual earnings base on which the employer pays unemployment insurance tax is $7,000. Answers a, b, and d are not bases.

Part 4

1.

	Connolly	Lueke	Maxie	Maier	Total
Hours worked	40	40	46	40	
Piecework	780	–	–	–	
Rate (hourly / piece)	$ .50	$ 7.00	$ 8.80	$ 15.00	
Direct labor	$ 390.00	–	$ 404.80	–	$ 794.80
Indirect labor	–	$ 280.00	–	$ 600.00	880.00
Overtime premium	–	–	26.40	–	26.40
Gross pay	$ 390.00	$ 280.00	$ 431.20	$ 600.00	$1,701.20
Income tax (15%)	$ 58.50	$ 42.00	$ 64.68	$ 90.00	255.18
FICA tax (7.5%)	29.25	21.00	30.36	45.00	125.61
Health insurance (5%)	19.50	14.00	21.56	30.00	85.06
Total deductions	$ 107.25	$ 77.00	$ 116.60	$ 165.00	$ 465.85
Net pay	$ 282.75	$ 203.00	$ 314.60	$ 435.00	$1,235.35

2.

Account	Subsidiary Record	Debit	Credit
(a) Payroll		1,701.20	
Accrued Payroll			1,235.35
Employees' Income Tax Payable			255.18
FICA Tax Payable			125.61
Health Insurance			85.06
(b) Accrued Payroll		1,235.35	
Cash			1,235.35
(c) Work in Process		794.80	
Factory Overhead Control		1,137.48	
Indirect Labor	880.00		
Overtime Premium	26.40		
FICA Tax	125.61		
Federal Unemployment Tax	13.61		
State Unemployment Tax	91.86		
Payroll			1,701.20
FICA Tax Payable			125.61
Federal Unemployment Tax Payable			13.61
State Unemployment Tax Payable			91.86

Part 5

1. Work in Process	770			2. Work in Process	700	
Payroll		770		Factory Overhead Control	70	
				Payroll		770

Part 6

Account	Subsidiary Record	Debit	Credit
Work in Process		3,300	
Factory Overhead Control		300	
Bonus Pay ($3,300 ÷ 11)	300		
Vacation Pay ($3,300 ÷ 11)	300		
Accrued Payroll			3,300
Liability for Bonus			300
Liability for Vacation Pay			300

CHAPTER 12

Part 1

1. F	6. T	11. T
2. T	7. T	12. F
3. T	8. T	13. T
4. T	9. F	14. F
5. F	10. F	15. T

Part 2

1. r	8. a	15. p
2. q	9. l	16. k
3. b	10. t	17. j
4. i	11. g	18. e
5. d	12. n	19. f
6. o	13. s	20. h
7. m	14. c	

Part 3

1. b Fixed costs remain the same, in total, within a relevant range of activity.

2. a The statistical scattergraph is used for analyzing semivariable expenses by plotting various costs (e.g., electricity expense) on the y axis and measurement figures (e.g., direct labor dollars) on the x axis, and then fitting a line to the data points by visual inspection.

3. b A variable expense is expected to increase or decrease proportionally, in total, to an increase or decrease in activity, and to remain constant on a per-unit basis within a relevant range.

4. b Simple regression analysis involves the use of two variables: (1) an independent variable representing a measure of activity, such as machine hours, and (2) a dependent variable representing expense, such as repairs and maintenance.

5. b

6. d Fixed costs change in total over time due to price changes, and they also change when the level of activity is outside the relevant range.

7. c When $r = 0$, there is no correlation, and when $r = +1$, the correlation is perfect. As r approaches $+1$, the correlation is positive, and as r approaches -1, the correlation is negative.

8. e $480 + $.50(20,000) = $10,480$

9. c Fixed expenses, such as depreciation or a long-term lease agreement, commit management for a long period of time; therefore they are called "committed fixed costs."

10. c The least squares method is the alternative that most precisely separates fixed and variable costs.

Part 4

1.	Production costs:		
	Direct labor		$250,000
	Direct materials		300,000
	Overhead to be incurred:		
	Supervision [$4,000 + ($2 × 10,000 units)]	$24,000	
	Power [$1,000 + ($1 × 10,000 units) + ($2 × 1,000 machine hours)]	13,000	
	Factory supplies [$1,750 + ($.50 × 10,000 units)]	6,750	
	Depreciation—equipment	7,000	
	Depreciation—building	80,000	130,750
	Total production cost		$680,750
2.	Overhead applied ($13 × 10,000 units)	$130,000	
	Overhead to be incurred	130,750	
	Underapplied overhead	$ (750)	

Part 5

1. (a)

	Repairs and Maintenance	Machine Hours			High	Low
High	$1,667	350		Total Repairs and Maintenance	$1,667	$1,405
Low	1,405	241		Variable cost	841	579
Difference	$ 262	109		Fixed cost	$ 826	$ 826

Variable rate .... $\dfrac{\$262}{109}$ = $2.404 per machine hour

(b)

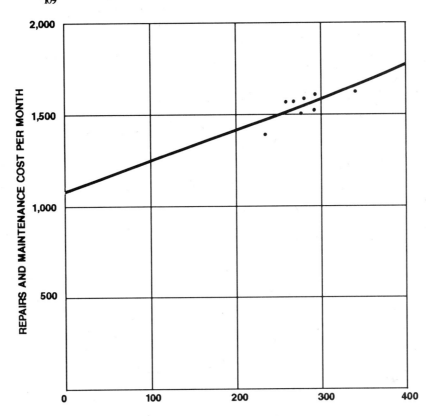

Average cost ($12,602 ÷ 8) $1,575
Less fixed cost 1,050
Variable cost .... $ 525

Variable cost per machine hour: $\dfrac{\$525}{2,294 \div 8}$ = $1.831

(c)

Month	(1) Machine Hours	(2) Difference from Average Hours	(3) Repairs and Maintenance Cost	(4) Difference from Average of Repairs and Maintenance Cost	(5) (2) Squared	(6) (2) × (4)	(7) (4) Squared
January	297	10	$ 1,548	$ (27)	100	$ (270)	$ 729
February	350	63	1,667	92	3,969	5,796	8,464
March	241	(46)	1,405	(170)	2,116	$ 7,820	28,900
April	280	(7)	1,534	(41)	49	287	1,681
May	274	(13)	1,600	25	169	(325)	625
June	266	(21)	1,600	25	441	(525)	625
July	285	(2)	1,613	38	4	(76)	1,444
August	301	14	1,635	60	196	840	3,600
Total	2,294	(2)*	$12,602	$ 2*	7,044	$13,547	$46,068

* Rounding difference

Average machine hours (x): $\dfrac{2,294}{8}$ = 287

Average repairs and maintenance cost (y): $\dfrac{\$12,602}{8}$ = $1,575

Variable rate (b): $\dfrac{\$13,547}{7,044}$ = $1.923

Fixed cost per month: $y = a + bx$
$1,575 = a + (\$1.923 \times 287)$
$a = \$1,575 - \$552 = \$1,023$

2.

Month	(1) Machine Hours	(2) Repairs and Maintenance Cost	(3) Predicted Repairs and Maintenance Cost*	(4) Prediction Error (2) – (3)	(5) Prediction Error Squared [(4) Squared]
January	297	$ 1,548	$ 1,594	$(46)	$ 2,116
February	350	1,667	1,696	(29)	841
March	241	1,405	1,486	(81)	6,561
April	280	1,534	1,561	(27)	729
May	274	1,600	1,550	50	2,500
June	266	1,600	1,535	65	4,225
July	285	1,613	1,571	42	1,764
August	301	1,635	1,602	33	1,089
Total	2,294	$12,602	$12,595	$ 7	$19,825

$$\sqrt{\frac{\Sigma (y_i - y_i^1)^2}{n-2}} = \sqrt{\frac{Col.\ 5}{8-2}} = \sqrt{\frac{\$19,825}{6}} = \sqrt{\$3,304} = \$57.48$$

* $1.923x + 1,023$

3. $y_1 = t_{95\%}\ s^1 \sqrt{1 + \frac{1}{n} + \frac{(x_i - \bar{x})^2}{\Sigma(x_i - \bar{x})^2}} = \$1,600 \pm (2.477)(\$57.58)(1.149)^{**}$

$= \$1,600 \pm \$162$

$^{**} \sqrt{1 + \frac{1}{8} + \frac{(300 - 287)^2}{7,044}} = 1.149$

4. $r = \frac{\Sigma(x - \bar{x})(v - \bar{y})}{\sqrt{\Sigma(x - \bar{x})^2(v - \bar{y})^2}} = \frac{13,547}{\sqrt{(7,044)(46,068)}} = .7520$

$r^2 = .5655$

CHAPTER 13

Part 1

1. F	6. F	11. T
2. F	7. T	12. T
3. F	8. F	13. F
4. T	9. F	14. T
5. T	10. T	15. T

Part 2

1. f	8. n	15. t
2. l	9. g	16. a
3. b	10. h	17. q
4. m	11. p	18. o
5. e	12. s	19. i
6. c	13. j	20. d
7. r	14. k	

Part 3

1. d When the overhead applied to jobs or products during the period is more than the actual overhead incurred, overhead is said to be overapplied.

2. a Since the normal capacity concept is based on the average utilization of the physical plant over a period long enough to level out the highs and lows in every business venture, the differences over a period of time between actual factory overhead and applied factory overhead will usually be minimal when the predetermined overhead rate is based on it.

3. c The fixed cost per-unit would be more because the same dollar amount of fixed cost is being spread over fewer units. The per-unit variable cost should be unchanged because the fewer units produced should result in less variable cost.

4. c The spending variance is a result of the prices paid for overhead items or the quantities used of overhead items being more or less than was budgeted for a given level of production.

5. a There should be a high correlation between the base being used and the type of overhead cost incurred. Answers b through d are examples of bases that are frequently used.

6. e If factory overhead is overapplied, the actual costs incurred during the period were less than the costs applied to products.

7. a If factory overhead costs are mostly variable, changes in the level of production should have little effect on the amount of overhead cost applied to products.

8. a The direct labor hour method is considered the most accurate method of applying overhead when the overhead cost is comprised predominantly of labor-related costs.

9. d Internal Revenue Service regulations require that inventories include an allocated portion of significant annual overhead variances.

10. a The idle capacity variance is due to volume or activity factors and results from the under- or overutilization of plant and equipment.

Part 4

1. $20 per unit
   $10 per direct labor hour
   125% of direct labor cost
   $50 per machine hour

2. $20 per hour variable
   $30 per hour fixed
   $50 per hour

3. Work in Process 500,000
   Applied Factory Overhead 500,000
       or Factory Overhead Control

4. Factory Overhead Control

5. (a)
Work in Process		Factory Overhead Control	
520,000		550,000	520,000

   (b) Underapplied
       $30,000

   (c)
Overhead Rate	March Overhead Applied
$ 4	$208,000
6	312,000
10	520,000

Part 5

Factory Expense Category	Budget Rate	Level of Activity (Direct Labor Hours)			
		45,000	50,000	55,000	60,000
Variable costs (per direct labor hour):					
Indirect labor	$2.00	$ 90,000	$100,000	$110,000	$120,000
Indirect materials	.80	36,000	40,000	44,000	48,000
Repairs	.60	27,000	30,000	33,000	36,000
Total variable cost	$3.40	$153,000	$170,000	$187,000	$204,000
Fixed costs (total):					
Depreciation—factory and machinery	$200,000	$200,000	$200,000	$200,000	$200,000
Insurance—factory and machinery	50,000	50,000	50,000	50,000	50,000
Total fixed cost	$250,000	$250,000	$250,000	$250,000	$250,000
Total overhead budget		$403,000	$420,000	$437,000	$454,000
Factory overhead rate per hour		$8.96	$8.40	$7.95	$7.57
Fixed overhead rate per hour		$5.56	$5.00	$4.55	$4.17

Part 6

1. Actual factory overhead $200,000
   Applied factory overhead [7.50 × (120% of 20,000)] 180,000
   Over- or underapplied factory overhead .... $ 20,000 underapplied

2. Actual factory overhead $200,000
   Overhead for capacity attained:
       Fixed factory overhead .... $ 50,000
       Variable factory overhead (120% × $100,000) 120,000   170,000
   Spending variance .... $ 30,000 unfav.

   Factory overhead for capacity attained...................... $170,000
   Factory overhead applied 180,000
   Idle capacity variance.................................. $ (10,000) fav.

CHAPTER 14

Part 1		
1. F	6. T	11. T
2. F	7. T	12. F
3. T	8. F	13. T
4. T	9. F	14. T
5. T	10. F	15. T

Part 2		
1. j	8. i	15. p
2. s	9. t	16. r
3. m	10. a	17. e
4. o	11. k	18. n
5. q	12. l	19. c
6. d	13. b	20. h
7. g	14. f	

Part 3

1. b A producing department renders a service that contributes directly to the manufacture of the product by changing the shape, form, or nature of the material that is converted into the finished product.

2. b All of the other departments listed are service departments.

3. d All of the other departments listed are producing departments.

4. c

	P1	P2	S1	S2*
Beginning	$400,000	$300,000	$52,640	$105,280
Allocation of S2: 30%	31,584			
50%		52,640		
20%			21,056	(105,280)
			$73,696	0
Allocation of S1: 4/7	42,112			
3/7		31,584	(73,696)	
Ending	$473,696	$384,224	0	

*Note that S2 is distributed before S1 because it has higher costs to be distributed.

5. a To charge each department with its fair share of an expense, a base using some factor common to all departments must be found. Therefore, the number of employees would be a good basis to use for charging supervision.

6. d The direct labor method allocates service department costs to producing departments only.

7. a

Direct labor	$ 10,000
Other	190,000
	$200,000
Percentage of employees	× .25
Payroll Department costs chargeable to Department B	$ 50,000

8. c All of the items listed except for the number of employees in each department are factors to be considered.

9. a All of the items listed are direct departmental overhead costs except for the expenses associated with the factory building, which would have to be allocated to the individual departments.

10. c A better case for allocating telephone and telegraph expense would be the number of employees or the number of telephones.

Part 4

1. Using the step method of allocation:

		Service Departments		Producing Departments		Total
	X	Y	Z	A	B	
Total	$40,000	$30,000	$25,000	$100,000	$150,000	$345,000
Dept. X distribution	($40,000)	16,000	12,000	8,000	4,000	
Dept. Y distribution		($46,000)	18,400	16,100	11,500	
Dept Z distribution			($55,400)	38,780	16,620	
Total				$162,880	$182,120	$345,000

2. Using the direct method of allocation:

		Service Departments		Producing Departments		Total
	X	Y	Z	A	B	
Total	$40,000	$30,000	$25,000	$100,000	$150,000	$345,000
Dept. X distribution	($40,000)	—	—	26,667	13,333	
Dept. Y distribution		($30,000)	—	17,500	12,500	
Dept Z distribution			($25,000)	17,500	7,500	
Total				$161,667	$183,333	$345,000

Part 5

	Total	Producing Departments						Service Departments							
		Preparation		Mixing		Packaging		Utilities		Maintenance		Materials Handling		Factory Office	
Distribution of service departments:															
Utilities:															
70% metered hours		(30%)	1,512	(36%)	1,814	(14%)	706	(5,040)	(10%)	504	(6%)	302	(4%)	202	
30% sq. footage		(36%)	778	(26%)	562	(24%)	518	(2,160)	(4%)	86	(2%)	43	(8%)	173	
								$ 7,200		$4,790					
Maintenance		(50%)	2,395	(25%)	1,198	(10%)	479			$(4,790)	(10%)	479	(5%)	239	
												$3,699		$3,189	
Materials Handling		(45%)	1,664	(35%)	1,295	(20%)	740					($3,699)			
Factory Office		(40%)	1,276	(40%)	1,276	(20%)	637							$(3,189)	
	$35,500		$13,625		$11,845		$10,030								
Bases:															
Pounds handled		300,000		500,000											
Direct labor cost						$20,000									
Rates		$.0454 per pound handled		$.0237 per pound handled		50.15% of direct labor cost									

Part 6

1. Equations:　Utilities = $25,000 + 25\%$ Maintenance
　　　　　　　　Maintenance = $40,000 + 10\%$ Utilities

　Substitutions:　　U = $25,000 + .25 ($40,000 + .10U)$
　　　　　　　　　U = $25,000 + $10,000 + .25U$
　　　　　　.975 U = $35,000
　　　　　　　　U = $\underline{\underline{35,987}}$

　　　　　　　　M = $40,000 + .10 ($35,897)$
　　　　　　　　M = $\underline{\underline{$43,593}}$

2.

	Total	Milling	Planing	Utilities	Maintenance
Primary Overhead	$215,000	$90,000	$60,000	$ 25,000	$ 40,000
Distribution of:					
Utilities		17,948	14,359	(35,897)	3,593
Maintenance		17,437	15,258	10,897	(43,593)
	$215,000*	$125,385*	$89,617*	-0-	-0-

*Rounding difference

CHAPTER 15

Part 1

1. T	6. F	11. T
2. T	7. T	12. F
3. T	8. T	13. F
4. T	9. F	14. T
5. T	10. T	15. T

Part 2

1. s	8. e	15. p
2. o	9. t	16. i
3. h	10. k	17. n
4. q	11. m	18. c
5. a	12. r	19. l
6. g	13. b	20. d
7. f	14. j	

Part 3

1. c Since the department manager did not have the authority to make the decision regarding his or her compensation, he or she should not be held accountable for the related salary charges.

2. c Any overhead charges shown on a responsibility report should be limited to those expenses over which the supervisor has control.

3. d Management by exception as related to cost accounting would involve management's concern for those actual expenses that had significant unfavorable variances from the budgeted amounts.

4. c A cost should be assigned to a responsibility center if its incurrence is controllable by the manager of that center.

5. b An indirect cost should be assigned to a product on the basis of the amount of cost that was incurred due to the production of that product.

6. a The department manager should be measured on the basis of the revenue generated by the department, less the department expenses over which the manager had control.

7. a Responsibility accounting is based on a classification of managerial responsibilities at every level in the organization for the purpose of establishing a budget for each.

8. d If both controllable and uncontrollable costs are to appear on a performance report, a clear distinction should be made between them.

9. b The costs would be controllable by the production vice-president who decided to lease the production equipment.

10. d Inefficiencies in a service department should not be allocated to producing departments, but rather should be reported on the service department's performance report as an unfavorable variance from budget.

Part 4

1. Budgeted variable cost at capacity / Capacity available =
　$48,000 / 150 000 kwh = $.32

2. Fixed cost distribution:

	Matching	Finishing
$25,000 × (100 000/150 000)	$16,667	
$25,000 × (50 000/150 000)		$ 8,333
Variable cost distribution:		
$.32 × 85 000 kwh	27,200	
$.32 × 45 000 kwh		14,400
Total cost distributed	$43,867	$22,733

3. Total variable cost ....

	Matching	Finishing
Total variable cost		$40,000
Cost distributed:		
Machining	$27,200	
Finishing	14,400	41,600
Overdistributed cost		$ 1,600

Part 5

1. General Maintenance: $100,000 / 10,000 hours = $10 per service hour
   Machine Repairs: $40,000 / 2,000 hours = $20 per service hour

2.

	Department			
	Machining	Assembling	Finishing	Total
General Maintenance	$46,000	$25,000	$16,000	$ 87,000
Machine Repairs	26,000	13,000	5,000	44,000
Total	$72,000	$38,000	$21,000	$131,000

3.

	Monthly Budget	Fixed Cost Percentage	Fixed Cost	Variable Cost	Variable Rate Per Hour
General Maintenance	$100,000	75%	$75,000	$25,000	$2.50
Machine Repairs	$ 40,000	60%	24,000	16,000	8.00

	General Maintenance		Machine Repairs	
Actual Overhead		$94,000		$45,000
Budget Allowance:				
Fixed Overhead	$ 75,000		$ 24,000	
Variable Overhead:				
($2.50 × 8,700 hrs.)	21,750	96,750		
($8.00 × 2,200 hrs.			17,600	41,600
Spending Variance		$(2,750) Fav.		$ 3,400 Unfav.

4.

	General Maintenance	Machine Repairs
Budget Allowance	$96,750	$41,600
Costs Charged Out:		
($10 × 8,700 hrs.)	$87,000	
($20 × 2,200 hrs.)		44,000
Idle Capacity Variance	$ 9,750 Unfav.	$(2,400) Fav.

CHAPTER 16

Part 1

1. F	6. T	11. T
2. T	7. F	12. T
3. T	8. T	13. T
4. T	9. T	14. F
5. F	10. F	15. T

Part 2

1. s	8. t	15. j
2. m	9. i	16. c
3. a	10. q	17. n
4. k	11. d	18. f
5. o	12. p	19. l
6. b	13. e	20. g
7. r	14. h	

Part 3

1. **a** Some organizations use a continuous budget, by which a month or quarter in the future is added as the month or quarter just ended is dropped, and the budget for the entire period is revised and updated as needed.

2. **d** Both probability analysis and sensitivity analysis evaluate the probability of different outcomes.

3. **a** In the *a priori* method, the profit objectives take precedence over the planning process. In the *a posteriori* method, the profit objectives emerge as the product of the planning process. In the pragmatic method, management uses a profit standard that has been tested empirically and sanctioned by experience.

4. **d**

5. **a** Market trends and economic factors, inflation, population growth, personal consumption expenditures, and indexes of industrial production form the background for long-range planning.

6. **c** The principal functions of the budget committee are to (1) decide on general policies, (2) request, receive, and review individual budget estimates, (3) suggest revisions to budget estimates, (4) approve budgets and later revisions, (5) receive and analyze budget reports, and (6) recommend actions designed to improve efficiency where necessary.

7. **d** The budgeted balance sheet discloses unfavorable ratios and serves as a check on the accuracy of all other budgets.

8. **b** All of the items in a through c are limitations of profit planning.

9. **a** The sales variable is usually the most difficult to predict, because the demand for an entity's products or services normally depends on forces and factors largely beyond the scope of management's control.

10. **e** Production = Sales + Ending Inventory - Beginning Inventory
    54,000 = 60,000 + 12,000 - 18,000

Part 4

1.

VCR Model No.	Predicted Unit Sales	Less: Beginning Inventory	Plus: Ending Inventory	Production Required
007	500	40	25	485
2525	800	20	40	820
1984	1,300	110	65	1,255

2.

VCR Model No.	Unit Sales	Unit Price	Total Sales
007	500	$500	$ 250,000
2525	800	450	360,000
1984	1,300	400	520,000
Total sales			$1,130,000

3.

VCR Model No.	Units Produced	Production Cost
007	485	$145,500 (485 × $500 × .60)
2525	820	$221,400 (820 × $450 × .60)
1984	1,255	$301,200 (1255 × $400 × .60)
Total production cost		$668,100

Working capital required: $668,100 × 20% = $133,620

Part 5

	Napoli	Roma	Venezia
1.			
Units required to meet sales budget	40,000	20,000	50,000
Add desired ending inventories	3,000	1,000	4,000
Total units required	43,000	21,000	54,000
Less estimated beginning inventories	2,500	2,000	5,000
Planned production	40,500	19,000	49,000

2.

	Pasta	Salsa
Napoli	40,500 × 4 lbs. = 162,000	40,500 × 2 lbs. = 81,000
Roma	19,000 × 5 lbs. = 95,000	-0-
Venezia	-0-	49,000 × 3 lbs. = 147,000
	257,000	228,000
Add desired ending inventories	6,000	7,500
	263,000	235,500
Less estimated beginning inventories	5,000	6,000
Budgeted quantities of materials purchased ..	258,000	229,500
Budgeted purchase price per pound	$.50	$1.00
Budgeted dollar amounts of materials purchased	$129,000	$229,500

3.

	Napoli	Roma	Venezia	Total
Materials:				
Pasta: 40,500 × 4 × 4 × $.50	$ 81,000			$ 81,000
19,000 × 5× $.50....................................		$ 47,500		47,500
Salsa: 40,500 × 2 × $1.00	81,000			81,000
49,000 × 3 × $1.00			$147,000	147,000
	$162,000	$ 47,500	$147,000	$ 356,500
Direct labor:				
40.5 × 200 × $20.........................	$162,000			$ 162,000
19 × 400 × $20		$152,000		152,000
49 × 50 × $20			$ 49,000	49,000
	$162,000	$152,000	$ 49,000	$ 363,000
Factory overhead—variable				
40.5 × 200 × $10.........................	$ 81,000			$ 81,000
19 × 400 × $10		$ 76,000		76,000
49 × 50 × $10			$ 24,500	24,500
	$ 81,000	$ 76,000	$ 24,500	$ 181,500
Total variable manufacturing cost	$405,000	$275,500	$220,500	$ 901,000
Fixed manufacturing cost				100,000
Total manufacturing cost				$1,001,000

Part 6

1.
B.J. Hastings Company
Budgeted Cost of Goods Manufactured and Sold Statement
For the Year Ending December 31, 19C

Materials:
Beginning inventory	$ 87,500	
Add purchases	568,663	
Total goods available for use	$ 656,163	
Less ending inventory	107,125	
Cost of materials used		$ 549,038
Direct labor		2,161,680
Factory overhead		226,503
Total manufacturing cost		$2,937,221
Add beginning inventory of finished goods		84,745
Cost of goods available for sale		$3,021,966
Less ending inventory of finished goods		60,895
Cost of goods sold		$2,961,071

2.
B.J. Hastings Company
Budgeted Income Statement
For the Year Ending December 31, 19C

	Amount	% of Sales
Sales	$3,650,000	100.0%
Cost of goods sold	2,961,071	81.1
Gross profit	$ 688,929	18.9%
Commercial expenses:		
Marketing expenses......$300,000 (8.2%)		
Administrative expenses...............200,000 (5.5%)	500,000	13.7
Income from operations	$ 188,929	5.2%
Other (income) expense	(25,000)	.7
Income before income tax	$ 213,929	5.9%
Less provision for income tax	64,179	1.8
Net income	$ 149,750	4.1%

Part 7

1.
Lozado Corporation
Projected Statement of Income and Retained Earnings
For Year Ending December 31, 19D
(000s omitted)

Revenue:			
Sales		$900,000	
Other income		15,000	$915,000
Cost of goods manufactured and sold:			
Materials	$225,000		
Direct labor	270,000		
Variable factory overhead	140,000		
Fixed factory overhead	24,000		
	$659,000		
Beginning inventory	60,000		
	$719,000		
Ending inventory	98,850*	$620,150	
Marketing:			
Salaries	$ 21,000		
Commissions	25,000		
Promotion and advertising	55,000	$101,000	
General and administrative:			
Salaries	$ 25,000		
Travel	4,000		
Office costs	11,000	$ 40,000	761,150
Income before income tax			$153,850
Income tax			46,155
Net income			$107,695
Beginning retained earnings			197,900
Subtotal			$305,595
Less dividends			7,500
Ending retained earnings			$298,095

*Inventory
Units:	
Beginning inventory	50,000
Subtracted from inventory (500,000 – 475,000)	25,000
Ending inventory	75,000
Cost:	
19D Manufacturing costs	$659,000
Units manufactured	500,000
Cost per unit	$ 1.318
Ending units	75,000
Cost of ending inventory	$ 98,850

2.
Lozado Corporation
Budgeted Balance Sheet
December 31, 19D   (000s omitted)

Assets			Liabilities and Shareholders' Equity		
Current assets:			Current liabilities:		
Cash	$ 2,400		Accounts payable	$ 65,000	
Accounts receivable	120,000		Accrued payables	40,000	
Inventory	98,850	$221,250	Income tax payable	26,905	
Plant and equipment	$480,000		Notes payable	75,000	$206,905
Less accumulated depreciation	82,000	398,000	Shareholders' equity:		
Total assets		$619,250	Common stock	$ 95,000	
			Retained earnings	298,095	393,095
			Total liabilities and shareholders' equity		$600,000

CHAPTER 17

Part 1

1. T	6. F	11. T
2. T	7. T	12. F
3. T	8. F	13. T
4. F	9. F	14. T
5. T	10. F	15. T

Part 2

1. i	8. b	15. h
2. q	9. n	16. j
3. d	10. r	17. o
4. a	11. s	18. e
5. l	12. c	19. g
6. k	13. t	20. f
7. p	14. m	

Part 3

1. **c** PPBS (Planning, Programming, Budgeting System) is an analytical tool that is closely related to cost-benefit analysis, focusing on the final results rather than the initial dollars expended.

2. **d** The longest path through a network is known as the critical path.

3. **b** Cash flows are budgeted based on projected sales.

4. **d** ZBB requires managers to start over each budget period and to justify each proposed expenditure.

5. **c** The major burden of PERT is the determination of the longest time duration for the completion of an entire project.

6. **c** $120,000 - $35,000 - $25,000 + $65,000 + $80,000 + $45,000 = $250,000

7. **c**

Estimated cost of goods sold for November	$ 900,000
Estimated inventories at end of November	160,000
	$1,060,000
Estimated inventories at beginning of November	180,000
Estimated November purchases	$ 880,000
Estimated percentage of payments in November for purchases in November	× 80%
Estimated payments in November for purchases in November	$ 704,000
Estimated payments in November for purchases prior to November	210,000
Estimated cash disbursements for inventories in November	$ 914,000

8. **c** $t_e = \dfrac{t_o + 4t_n + t_p}{6} = \dfrac{4 + 4(8) + 18}{6} = 9$

9. **e** $1,350,000 - $1,200,000 - $90,000 - $400,000 + $500,000 + $100,000 - $50,000 = $210,000

10. **a** The purpose of a flexible budget is to provide a budget that is adjusted to actual volume.

Part 4

Knutson Nut Company
Cash Budget
For March – June, 19–

	March	April	May	June
Receipts from:				
Cash sales	$20,000	$12,000	$16,000	$ 22,000
January credit sales (35% × $24,000)	8,400	–	–	–
February credit sales:				
60% × $18,000	10,800	–	–	–
35% × $18,000	–	6,300	–	–
March credit sales	–	6,000	3,500	–
April credit sales	–	–	2,400	1,400
May credit sales	–	–	–	7,200
Total receipts	$39,200	$24,300	$21,900	$ 30,600
Disbursements for:				
Payroll	$ 4,000	$ 3,000	$ 5,000	$ 6,000
Other expenses	5,000	4,800	5,200	5,600
February purchases (50% × $10,000)	5,000	–	–	–
March purchases	3,000	3,000	–	–
April purchases	–	2,600	2,600	–
May purchases	–	–	2,800	2,800
June purchases	–	–	–	4,000
Tax payment	–	–	–	35,000
Total disbursements	$17,000	$13,400	$15,600	$ 53,400
Net increase (decrease) in cash:				
Receipts less disbursements	$22,000	$10,900	$ 6,300	$(22,800)
Cash balances:				
Beginning	5,000	27,200	38,100	44,400
Ending	$27,200	$38,100	$44,400	$21,600

Part 5

1.

Activity	t_e	
A-B	$\dfrac{4 + 4(6) + 8}{6}$	= 6
A-C	$\dfrac{16 + 4(18) + 20}{6}$	= 18
A-D	$\dfrac{6 + 4(9) + 12}{6}$	= 9
B-E	$\dfrac{6 + 4(10) + 14}{6}$	= 10
C-F	$\dfrac{5 + 4(9) + 19}{6}$	= 10

D-F	$\dfrac{3 + 4(5) + 7}{6}$	= 5
E-H	$\dfrac{10 + 4(16) + 22}{6}$	= 16
F-E	$\dfrac{3 + 4(7) + 11}{6}$	= 7
F-G	$\dfrac{4 + 4(6) + 14}{6}$	= 7
G-H	$\dfrac{7 + 4(11) + 15}{6}$	= 11

2.

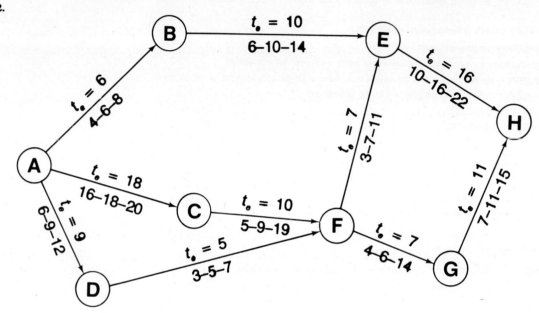

3. Path

1	$6 + 10 + 16 = 32$
2	$18 + 10 + 7 + 16 = 51$ ← Critical Path
3	$18 + 10 + 7 + 11 = 46$
4	$9 + 5 + 7 + 16 = 37$
5	$9 + 5 + 7 + 11 = 32$

Part 6

	60% of Normal Capacity	80% of Normal Capacity	100% of Normal Capacity
Units	300,000	400,000	500,000
Direct labor hours	2,880	3,840	4,800
Direct materials	$12,000	$16,000	$ 20,000
Direct labor	34,560	46,080	57,600
Supplies	1,440	1,920	2,400
Indirect labor	8,640	11,520	14,400
Other charges	2,880	3,840	4,800
Fixed factory overhead	2,500	2,500	2,500
Total manufacturing cost	$62,020	$81,860	$101,700
Manufacturing cost per unit	$.2067	$.2047	$.2034
Factory overhead rate per direct labor hour	$5.37	$5.15	$5.02

CHAPTER 18

Part 1				**Part 2**		
1. T	6. F	11. T		1. c	8. b	15. l
2. F	7. T	12. F		2. g	9. j	16. k
3. T	8. T	13. T		3. e	10. d	17. s
4. T	9. T	14. T		4. i	11. t	18. q
5. T	10. T	15. T		5. a	12. n	19. o
				6. h	13. r	20. m
				7. f	14. p	

Part 3

1. **c** Normal standards are set for a normal level of operation and efficiency, intended to represent challenging yet attainable results. Theoretical standards are set for an ideal or maximum level of operation and efficiency. Expected actual standards are set for an expected level of operation and efficiency. Practical capacity is theoretical capacity less allowance for unavoidable interruptions.

2. **d** The volume variance indicates the cost of capacity available but not utilized.

3. **c**

Actual factory overhead		$220,000
Budget allowance based on standard hours allowed:		
Fixed overhead budgeted	$ 66,000	
Variable overhead (32,000 standard hours allowed × $5 variable overhead rate)	160,000	226,000
Controllable variance		$ 6,000

4. **a** Labor rate variance = Actual hours (Actual rate – Standard rate)

5. **e** Standard rate × (Actual quantity – Standard rate) = $1.30 × [5800 – (1,000 × 6)] = $260 favorable

6. **b** Total factory overhead variance = Actual factory overhead ($86,000) – Standard applied factory overhead ($80,000) = $6,000 unfavorable

7. **d** $\frac{\$40,000}{20,000 \text{ units}} = \$2$

$2.20 – $2.10 = $.10 × 20,000 units = ($2,000) unfavorable

8. **c** If actual materials used exceeds standard materials, then the usage variance must be unfavorable. If actual cost is less than standard cost, however, the favorable materials price variance must more than offset the unfavorable materials usage variance.

9. **a** If the materials price variance is isolated at the time of use, it is known as the materials price usage variance.

10. **a** The higher paid, more experienced workers had a higher wage rate, but they were more efficient.

Part 4

1.	Pounds	Unit Cost		Amount	
Actual quantity used	29,200	$ 1.10	Actual	$ 32,120	
Actual quantity used	29,200	1.00	Standard	29,200	
Materials price usage variance		.10		$ 2,920	unfav.
Actual quantity used	29,200	$ 1.00	Standard	$ 29,200	
Standard quantity allowed	28,500	1.00	Standard	28,500	
Materials quantity variance	700			$ 700	unfav.

2.	Time	Rate		Amount	
Actual hours worked	19,500	$14.50	Actual	$282,750	
Actual hours worled	19,500	15.00	Standard	292,500	
Labor rate variance		$(.50)		$(9,750)	favorable
Actual hours worked	19,500	$15.00	Standard	$292,500	
Standard hours allowed	19,000	15.00	Standard	285,000	
Labor time variance	500			$ 7,500	unfav.

3.			
Actual factory overhead			$118,000
Budget allowance based on standard hours allowed:			
Fixed overhead budgeted		$20,000	
Variable overhead (9,500 × 2 × $5)		95,000	115,000
Controllable variance			$ 3,000 unfav.
Budget allowance based on standard hours allowed			$115,000
Overhead charged to production (9,500 ×2) ($1 fixed + $5 variable)			114,000
Volume variance			$ 1,000 unfav.

4. Actual factory overhead $118,00
Budget allowance based on actual hours
worked:
 Fixed overhead budgeted $20,000
 Variable overhead (19,500 ×$5) 97,500   117,500
 Spending variance .... $ 500 unfav.
Budget allowance based on actual hours
worked $117,500
Actual hours × standard overhead rate
 (19,500 × $6)......................   117,000
 Idle capacity variance............... $ 500 unfav.
Actual hours × standard overhead rate.... $117,000
Overhead charged to production   114,000
 Efficiency variance................. $ 3,000 unfav.

5. Actual factory overhead $118,000
Budget allowance based on actual hours
worked   117,500
 Spending variance .... $ 500 unfav.
Budget allowance based on actual hours
worked $117,500
Budget allowance based on standard
hours allowed   115,000
 Variable efficiency variance .... $ 2,500 unfav.
Actual hours × fixed overhead rate ...... $ 19,500
Standard hours allowed × fixed overhead
rate   19,000
 Fixed efficiency variance .... $ 500 unfav.
Normal capacity hours × fixed overhead
rate (20,000 × $1) .... $ 20,000
Actual hours worked × fixed overhead
rate (19,500 ×$1)   19,500
 Idle capacity variance............... $ 500 unfav.

Part 5

1.

Material	Pounds	Actual Cost per Pound	Amount	
X	220,000	2.00	440,00	
Y	60,000	1.00	60,000	
Z	170,000	3.00	510,000	$1,010,000

Material	Pounds	Standard Price per Pound	Amount	
X	220,000	1.75	385,000	
Y	60,000	.85	51,000	
Z	170,000	3.25	552,500	988,500

Materials price usage variance .... $ 21,500 unfav.

2. Actual quantities at standard .... $ 988,500
Actual quantities at standard materials cost
 (450,000 × $2.20) 990,000
Materials mix variance .... $ (1,500) fav.

3. Actual input quantities at standard materials cost . $ 990,000
Actual output quantity at standard materials cost . 1,031,250
Materials yield variance .... $ 41,250 fav.

CHAPTER 19

Part 1				Part 2		
1. T	6. T	11. T		1. h	6. i	11. o
2. T	7. F	12. F		2. b	7. c	12. k
3. F	8. T	13. T		3. j	8. d	13. n
4. T	9. F	14. F		4. f	9. g	14. l
5. T	10. T	15. F		5. a	10. e	15. m

Part 3

1. a Unfavorable variances are recorded as debits and favorable variances as credits.

2. b Materials price variances indicate the difference between the purchase price and the standard price. If they are isolated at the time of purchase, they are known as materials purchase price variances.

3. b If significant variances exist, inventory and cost of goods sold figures are not stated at actual cost in a standard cost system unless these variances are allocated prior to the preparation of the financial statements.

4. c Immaterial variances appear as part of Cost of Goods Sold on the income statement in the period in which they arose.

5. b A credit balance in Labor Efficiency Variance indicates that direct labor was overapplied because the standard hours allowed were greater than the actual hours worked.

6. b Current IRS regulations require that significant standard cost variances be included in inventory. Also, the taxpayer must treat both favorable and unfavorable variances consistently.

7. b Actual rate $ 7.00 ($241,500 ÷ 34,500)
   Standard rate   6.40 ($3,200 ÷ 500)
               $ .60
              ×34,500 hours
   Rate variance $20,700 unfavorable

8. d The three-variance method is used because there is a factory overhead efficiency variance, and the variance is unfavorable because it is recorded as a debit.

9. d The materials mix variance must be favorable because it was recorded as a credit.

10. d If the new standard costs reflect conditions that affected the actual cost of the goods in the ending inventory, most firms adjust the ending inventory to the new standard cost. Ending inventories are costed at the old standards if the new standards have not affected costs in the past period.

Part 4

Materials	90,000		Factory Overhead Control	60,000	
Materials Purchase Price Variance		900	Various Credits		60,000
Accounts Payable		89,100	Work in Process	59,750	
Materials Purchase Price Variance	750		Factory Overhead Control		59,750
Materials Price Usage Variance		750	Idle Capacity Variance	1,500	
Work in Process	81,600		Efficiency Variance		750
Labor Efficiency Variance......................		1,000	Spending Variance		500
Labor Rate Variance		600	Factory Overhead Control		250
Payroll		80,000			

Part 5

1.

	Square Yards	Unit Cost		Amount	
Actual quantity purchased	15,000	$ 5.20	Actual	$78,000	
Actual quantity purchased	15,000	4.95	Standard	74,250	
Materials purchase price variance	15,000	$ .25		$ 3,750	unfav.
Actual quantity used	12,500	$ 4.95	Standard	$61,875	
Standard quantity allowed	12,000	4.95	Standard	59,400	
Materials quantity variance	500			$ 2,475	unfav.

	Time	Rate		Amount	
Actual hours worked	8,500	$ 8.25	Actual	$70,125	
Actual hours worked	8,500	8.00	Standard	68,000	
Labor rate variance	8,500	$ .25		$ 2,125	unfav.
Actual hours worked	8,500	$ 8.00	Standard	$68,000	
Standard hours allowed	8,000	8.00	Standard	64,000	
Labor efficiency variance	500			$ 4,000	unfav.

Actual factory overhead		$32,100
Budget allowance based on actual hours worked:		
Fixed overhead budgeted	$20,000	
Variable overhead	12,750	32,750
Spending variance		$ (650) fav.
Budget allowance based on actual hours worked..................................		$32,750
Budget allowance based on standard hours allowed:		
Fixed overhead budgeted	$20,000	
Variable overhead (8,000 hours × $1.50)..	12,000	32,000
Variable efficiency variance		$ 750 unfav.
Actual hours × fixed overhead rate (8,500 × $2)		$17,000
Standard hours allowed × fixed overhead rate (8,000 × $2)		16,000
Fixed efficiency variance		$ 1,000 unfav.
Budget allowance based on actual hours worked		$32,750
Actual hours worked × factory overhead rate (8,500 × $3.50)		29,750
Idle capacity variance...		$ 3,000 unfav.

2.

Materials	74,250		Finished Goods	151,400	
Materials Purchase Price Variance	3,750		Work in Process		151,400
Accounts Payable........................		78,000	Accounts Receivable	150,000	
Work in Process	59,400		Sales		150,000
Materials Quantity Variance	2,475		Cost of Goods Sold...........................	113,550	
Materials		61,875	Finished Goods		113,550
Payroll...................................	70,125		Cost of Goods Sold..........................	16,450	
Accrued Payroll		70,125	Factory Overhead Spending Variance	650	
Work in Process	64,000		Materials Quantity Variance		2,475
Labor Rate Variance	2,125		Labor Rate Variance		2,125
Labor Efficiency Variance	4,000		Factory Overhead Idle Capacity Variance		3,000
Payroll		70,125	Materials Purchase Price Variance		3,750
Factory Overhead Control....................	32,100		Labor Efficiency Variance		4,000
Various Credits		32,100	Factory Overhead Variable Efficiency Variance		750
Work in Process	28,000		Factory Overhead Fixed Efficiency Variance		1,000
Factory Overhead Control		28,000			
Factory Overhead Idle Capacity Variance	3,000				
Factory Overhead Variable Efficiency Variance ...	750				
Factory Overhead Fixed Efficiency Variance	1,000				
Factory Overhead Spending Variance		650			
Factory Overhead Control		4,100			

Part 6

1. Materials—Id (900 lbs. @ $3) 2,700.00
   Materials—Ego (2,000 lbs. @ $1.50) 3,000.00
   Materials Purchase Price Variance—Id [900 lbs. × ($3.20 – $3)] 180.00
      Accounts Payable 5,580.00
      Materials Purchase Price Variance—Ego [2,000 lbs. × ($1.50 –$1.35)] 300.00
2. Work in Process. 3,937.50
   Materials Mix Variance . . . .   412.50[1]
      Materials. 4,350.00
   Finished Goods—Materials. 4,725.00
      Work in Process 3,937.50
      Materials Yield Variance . . . .   787.50[2]

[1]Actual quantity × standard price:

800 lbs. × $3	$2,400	
1,300 lbs. × $1.50	1,950	$4,350.00

Actual quantity × weighted average of standard mix cost

(input) (2,100 lbs. × $1.875*)		3,937.50
Materials mix variance		$ 412.50 unfav.
Id	60 lbs. @ $3	$180
Ego	180 lbs. @ $1.50	270
	240 lbs.	$450

*$450 ÷ 240 lbs. = $1.875 per lb. weighted average standard mix cost (input)

[2]Standard finished cost (output): $\frac{\$450}{200 \text{ lbs.}}$ = $2.25 per lb.

Actual quantity × standard cost (input) (from above)	$3,937.50
Finished product × standard finished cost (output) (2,100 lbs.	
@ $2.25).	4,725.00
Materials yield variance	$ (787.50) fav.

Part 7

1. Materials purchase price variance to:

Materials	$\frac{\$25,000}{\$400,000}$ × $	(7,000)=	$ (437.50)
Work in Process	$\frac{\$40,000}{\$400,000}$ × $	(7,000)=	(700.00)
Finished Goods	$\frac{\$35,000}{\$400,000}$ × $	(7,000)=	(612.50)
Cost of Goods Sold	$\frac{\$300,000}{\$400,000}$ × $	(7,000)=	(5,250.00)
Total			$ (7,000.00)

Materials price usage variance to:

Work in Process	$\frac{\$40,000}{\$375,000}$ × $	9,240 =	$ 985.60
Finished Goods	$\frac{\$35,000}{\$375,000}$ × $	9,240 =	862.40
Cost of Goods Sold	$\frac{\$300,000}{\$375,000}$ × $	9,240 =	$ (7,392.00)
Total			$ (9,240.00)

Labor rate variance to:

Work in Process	$\frac{\$35,000}{\$750,000}$ ×	$(12,160)=	$ (567.47)
Finished Goods	$\frac{\$35,000}{\$750,000}$ ×	$(12,160)=	(567.47)
Cost of Goods Sold	$\frac{\$680,000}{\$750,000}$ ×	$(12,160)=	(11,025.06)
Total			$(12,160.00)

Labor efficiency variance to:

Work in Process	$\frac{\$35,000}{\$750,000}$ × $	6,340 =	$ 295.87
Finished Goods	$\frac{\$35,000}{\$750,000}$ × $	6,340 =	295.87
Cost of Goods Sold	$\frac{\$680,000}{\$750,000}$ × $	6,340 =	5,748.26
Total			$ 6,340.00

Overhead variances to:

Work in Process	$\frac{\$62,000}{\$600,000}$ × $	9,790 =	$ 1,011.63
Finished Goods	$\frac{\$88,000}{\$600,000}$ × $	9,790 =	1,435.87
Cost of Goods Sold	$\frac{\$450,000}{\$600,000}$ × $	9,790 =	7,342.50
Total			$ 9,790.00

2. Standard:

Materials	$	300,000
Labor		680,000
Overhead		450,000
	$	1,430,000
Add unfavorable variances:		
Material price usage variance	7,392.00	
Labor efficiency variance	5,748.26	
Overhead variances	7,342.50	20,482.76
		1,450,482.76
Less favorable variances:		
Materials purchase price variance	(5,250.00)	
Labor rate variance	(11,025.06)	(16,257.06)
Cost of Goods Sold		$1,434,207.70

CHAPTER 20

<table>
<tr><td colspan="3" align="center">Part 1</td><td colspan="3" align="center">Part 2</td></tr>
<tr><td>1. T</td><td>8. T</td><td>15. T</td><td>1. c</td><td>8. j</td><td>15. m</td></tr>
<tr><td>2. T</td><td>9. F</td><td>16. T</td><td>2. a</td><td>9. n</td><td>16. l</td></tr>
<tr><td>3. T</td><td>10. T</td><td>17. F</td><td>3. e</td><td>10. p</td><td>17. i</td></tr>
<tr><td>4. T</td><td>11. F</td><td>18. F</td><td>4. b</td><td>11. q</td><td>18. t</td></tr>
<tr><td>5. F</td><td>12. T</td><td>19. T</td><td>5. d</td><td>12. f</td><td>19. s</td></tr>
<tr><td>6. T</td><td>13. F</td><td>20. T</td><td>6. k</td><td>13. o</td><td>20. r</td></tr>
<tr><td>7. F</td><td>14. T</td><td></td><td>7. h</td><td>14. g</td><td></td></tr>
</table>

Part 3

1. **a** The use of direct costing for financial reporting is not accepted by the accounting profession, the IRS, or the SEC. The position of these groups is generally based on their opposition to excluding fixed costs from inventories.

2. **d** Proponents of direct costing argue that period costs, such as depreciation, property taxes, and insurance, are a function of time rather than of production and should be excluded from the cost of the product.

3. **d** In absorption costing, fixed manufacturing expenses form part of the predetermined factory overhead rate and are included in inventories. The exclusion of this overhead from inventories under direct costing and its offsetting effect on periodic income determination has been criticized by opponents of direct costing.

4. **e** Since direct costing excludes fixed manufacturing costs from inventory, the differences would be
400 units × $2 fixed manufacturing cost per unit = $800 decrease in inventory

5. **d**
Operating income (direct costing)	$50,000
Cost released in inventory decline (5,000 units × $4)	− 20,000
Operating income (absorption costing)	$30,000

6. **b**
Break-even sales	$400,000
Sales beyond break-even:	
Operating income for 19A ($200,000) ÷ contribution margin (40%)	500,000
Total sales for 19A	$900,000

7. **c** Unit selling price = $8,000,000 ÷ 160,000 = $50
Unit variable cost = $2,000,000 ÷ 160,000 = $12.50 ∴
$$\text{Break-even units} = \frac{\$3,000,000}{\$50 - \$12.50} = \$80,000$$

8. **c** Contribution margin per unit:
Y = $120 − $70 = $50
Z = $500 − $200 = $300 ∴
$$\text{Break-even units} = \frac{\$300,000}{(.6 \times \$50) + (.4 \times \$300)} = 2,000$$

9. **a** The contribution margin as a percentage of sales will decrease because the variable cost as a percentage of sales increases. If the fixed cost increases and the contribution margin ratio decreases, both of these factors will cause the break-even point to increase.

10. **d** The contribution per unit is needed to compute break-even sales units; it is obtained by subtracting the variable cost per unit from the sales price per unit.

Part 4

1. Ending inventory: 5,000 × $15 = $75,000

2.
Fixed manufacturing cost ($60,000 total ÷ 30,000)	$ 2
Variable manufacturing cost per unit	15
Total cost per unit	$17

Ending inventory: 5,000 × $17 = $85,000

3.
Variable manufacturing cost (25,000 × $15)	$375,000
Variable administrative cost (30,000 × $5)	150,000
Total	$525,000

4.
Fixed manufacturing cost (25,000 × $2)	$50,000
Fixed marketing and administrative expenses	25,000
Total	$75,000

5.
Fixed manufacturing cost	$60,000
Fixed marketing and administrative expense	25,000
Total	$85,000

Sergio Corporation
Income Statement—Absorption Costing
For Quarter Ended June 30, 19–

1.

Sales			$1,000,000
Cost of goods manufactured:			
Materials	$100,000		
Direct labor	250,000		
Factory overhead—variable	125,000		
Factory overhead—fixed	150,000		
Cost of goods manufactured		$625,000	
Finished goods inventory			
(10,000 × $12.50)		125,000	
Cost of goods sold			500,000
Gross profit			$ 500,000
Marketing and administrative			
expenses			350,000
Operating income			$ 150,000

Sergio Corporation
Income Statement—Direct Costing
For Quarter Ended June 30, 19–

2.

Sales			$1,000,000
Variable cost of goods manufactured:			
Materials	$100,000		
Direct labor	250,000		
Factory overhead—variable	125,000		
Variable cost of goods			
manufactured		$475,000	
Finished goods inventory			
(10,000 × $9.50)		95,000	
Variable cost of goods sold			380,000
Contribution margin			$ 620,000
Fixed expenses:			
Factory overhead	$150,000		
Marketing and administrative			
expenses	350,000		500,000
Operating income			$ 120,000

Part 6

1.

	Oct.	Nov.	Dec.
Sales	$5,000	$2,000	$20,000
Beginning inventory	-0-	$1,500	$ 3,900
Variable cost of goods manufactured (variable costs)	3,000	3,000	3,000
Variable cost of goods available for sale	$3,000	$4,500	$ 6,900
Ending inventory (ending units × $3 variable cost/unit)	1,500	3,900	900
Variable cost of goods sold	$1,500	$ 600	$ 6,000
Gross contribution margin	$3,500	$1,400	$14,000
Less fixed factory overhead	2,000	2,000	2,000
Gross profit (loss)	$1,500	$ (600)	$12,000

2.

	Oct.	Nov.	Dec.
Gross profit—absorption costing	$2,500	$1,000	$10,000
Gross profit—direct costing	1,500	(600)	12,000
Difference	$1,000	$1,600	$ (2,000)
Inventory change—absorption costing	$2,500	$4,000	$ (5,000)
Less inventory change—direct costing	1,500	2,400	(3,000)
Difference	$1,000	$1,600	$ (2,000)

Part 7

1. $\dfrac{\$80,000}{1 - \dfrac{90}{150}} = \dfrac{\$80,000}{.40} = \$200,000$

2. $\dfrac{\$80,000}{(\$150 - \$90)} = 1,333 \text{ units}$

3.

Part 8

1. $\dfrac{\$600,000}{1 - \dfrac{\$140}{\$400}} = \dfrac{\$600,000}{1 - .35} = \dfrac{\$600,000}{.65} = \$923,077$

   (b) $\dfrac{\$600,000}{\$400 - \$140} = 2,308$ units

   (c) $\dfrac{2,308}{3,000} = 76.93\%$

2. (a) $\$1,200,000 - \$923,077 = \$276,923$

   (b) $\dfrac{\$1,200,000 - \$923,077}{\$1,200,000} = 23.08\%$

3. $\dfrac{\$600,000}{1 - \dfrac{140}{350}} = \dfrac{\$600,000}{.6} = \$1,000,000$

4. (a) $\dfrac{\$600,000 + \$100,000}{.65} = \$1,076,923$

   (b) $\dfrac{\$600,000 + \$100,000}{.60} = \$1,166,667$

5.
Sales (3,000 units × $400)	$1,200,000
Variable cost (3,000 units × $140)	420,000
Contribution margin	$ 780,000
Fixed cost	600,000
Expected profit	$ 180,000*

or

C/M × M/S × Budgeted Sales =
65% × 23.08% × $1,200,000 = $180,024*

*Rounding difference

Part 9

1.
	Woofers	Tweeters
Selling price	$11	$15
Variable cost	$ 6	$ 4
Fixed cost	3	1
Total cost	$ 9	$ 5
Profit	$11	$10

2. Woofers $\dfrac{\$11}{\$20} = 55\%$

   Tweeters $\dfrac{\$10}{\$15} = 66.67\%$

3.
	Woofers	Tweeters
Selling price	$20	$15
Variable cost	6	4
Contribution margin	$14	$11

4. Woofers $\dfrac{\$14}{\$20} = 70\%$

   Tweeters $\dfrac{\$11}{\$15} = 73.33\%$

5. Woofers $14 × 50 units per hour = $700
   Tweeters $11 × 70 units per hour = $770

6. Produce all Tweeters because its contribution margin per limiting or critical factor (hours available) is greater than Woofers'. Note that it is not the contribution margin per unit, Part (3), but rather the contribution margin per hour, Part (5), that is the determining factor.

Part 10

Composite break-even point in dollars $= \dfrac{\$2,500,000}{1 - \dfrac{\$ 80}{\$166.25}} = \dfrac{\$2,500,000}{1 - .48} = \dfrac{\$2,500,000}{.52} = \$4,807,692$

Method of Payment	Patient Mix	Average Daily Reimbursement Rate	Weighted Daily Reimbursement Rate
Self-pay	20%	$200	$40.00
Private insurance	25	200	50.00
Medicare	30	150	45.00
Medicaid	25	125	31.25
			$166.25 or $166

Composite break-even point in inpatient days $= \dfrac{\$4,807,692}{\$166} = 28,962$ days

CHAPTER 21

Part 1

1. F	6. T	11. T
2. T	7. F	12. T
3. F	8. T	13. T
4. T	9. T	14. F
5. T	10. F	15. F

Part 2

1. e	6. d	11. o
2. a	7. b	12. k
3. c	8. h	13. n
4. g	9. j	14. m
5. f	10. i	15. l

Part 3

1. e The opportunity cost is zero when there is no alternative use of the facility.

2. c Because sunk costs are past costs, they are not relevant to an alternative choice decision problem.

3. d Imputed costs include interest on invested capital, rental value of company-owned properties, and salaries of owner-operators of proprietorships and partnerships. These costs are not considered in a company's regular cost and profit calculations, but they are relevant in deciding between alternative courses of action.

4. b Depreciation is a fixed factory overhead cost that will be incurred whether or not the idle capacity is used. Direct materials, direct labor, and variable factory overhead are variable costs that will not be incurred unless the capacity is used.

5. b
Selling price			$18
Less:			
Variable costs		$16	
Overtime		3	19
Loss			$(1) × 40,000 units = $(40,000)

6. a
Variable costs	$6
Income ($10,000 ÷ 10,000)	1
Selling price	$7

7. b
Direct materials	$ 2
Direct labor	8
Variable overhead	4
Applied fixed overhead that would not continue (⅓ × $6)	2
	$16

$16 × 5,000 units = $80,000

8. b Differential cost, also known as marginal cost or incremental cost, is the added cost incurred when a project or an undertaking is extended beyond its originally intended goal.

9. e Contribution margin:
  Product q: $20 − $13 = $7
  Product p: $17 − $12 = $5
  Contribution margin maximization objective function is 7q + 5p.

10. c The constraints are the types of branches, the available capital, and the maximum number of employees to be hired. Choices a, b, and d all relate to those constraints.

Part 4

1. The company should accept the special order because the proposed $9.50 sales price more than covers all variable manufacturing costs per unit, which are:

Direct materials	$4.00
Direct labor	2.50
Variable factory overhead	2.00
Total	$8.50

Note: Even if the variable marketing expense of $.50 per unit is incurred for this order, there will still be a positive contribution margin of $.50 per unit.

2. The company would be willing to pay an outside supplier as much as the variable manufacturing cost of $8.50 per unit plus the $.25 per unit of fixed cost that would be saved, or $8.75 per unit.

Part 5

Variable cost to make [($5 + $17 + $10) × 1,000]	$32,000
Fixed factory overhead eliminated ($8 × 1,000)	8,000
Savings from alternate use of facilities	10,000
	$50,000
Cost to buy ($45 × 1,000)	45,000
Savings from buying	$ 5,000

Part 6

1. $\dfrac{\text{Added cost}}{\text{Units produced}} = \dfrac{\$10,000}{5,000} = \$2.00$ per unit

2.
	Chi	Phi	Kappa
Sales value if processed further	$90,000	$72,000	$58,000
Sales value at split-off	75,000	60,000	43,000
Added sales value	$15,000	$12,000	$15,000
Added cost	15,000	20,000	10,000
Difference in favor (against) processing further	$ –0–	$ (8,000)	$ 5,000

Part 7

1.
	Micro	Macro
Sales price per unit	$25	$26
Standard cost per unit	17	28
Profit (loss) per unit	$ 8	$(2)
Total profit (loss)	$400,000	$(50,000)

2. Both products have a positive contribution margin and should be continued unless there is a more profitable alternative.

3.
	Macro	Macro Plus
Sales price	$26	$50
Variable cost per unit	18	20
Contribution margin per unit	$ 8	$30
Total contribution margin	$200,000	$375,000

4. The opportunity cost of Macro is the $200,000 in contribution margin that will be forgone if Macro Plus is produced.

Part 8

1. Department	Hours Available	Hours Required		Maximum Units	
		Per Apollo	Per Lunar	Apollo	Lunar
Mixing	80	2	1	$\frac{80}{2} = 40$	$\frac{80}{1} = 80$
Molding	60	.5	1	$\frac{60}{.5} = 120$	$\frac{60}{1} = 60$

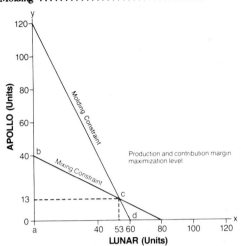

2. a(Apollo = 0; Lunar = 0); $100,000(0) + $80,000(0) = $0 CM
    b(Apollo = 40; Lunar = 0); $100,000(40) + $80,000(0) = $4,000,000 CM
  * c(Apollo = 13; Lunar = 53); $100,000(13) + $80,000(53) = $5,540,000 CM
    d(Apollo = 0; Lunar = 60); $100,000(0) + $80,000(60) = $4,800,000 CM
    13 units of Apollo and 53 units of Lunar maximize the CM with $5,540,000
    * Corner point "c" values:

$$\begin{array}{r} 1x + 2y = 80 \\ \underline{-1x - .5y = -60} \\ 1.5y = \overline{20} \\ y = 13.33, \text{ or } 13 \end{array}$$

$$\begin{array}{l} 1\,x + 2y = 80 \\ 1x + 2(13.333) = 80 \\ 1x + 26.67 = 80 \\ x = 53.33 \text{ or } 53 \end{array}$$

Part 9

6,000 ravioli and 6,000 ziti packages

Mixing	$(3 \times 6,000) + (4 \times 6,000) = 42,000$
Stuffing	$(4 \times 6,000) + (3 \times 6,000) = 42,000$
Cooking	$(3 \times 6,000) + (2 \times 6,000) = 30,000$

No constraints are violated;
  CM = $1(6,000) + $.50(6,000) = $9,000

7,200 ravioli and 4,800 ziti packages

Mixing	$(3 \times 7,200) + (4 \times 4,800) = 40,800$
Stuffing	$(4 \times 7,200) + (3 \times 4,800) = 43,200$
Cooking	$(3 \times 7,200) + (2 \times 4,800) = 31,200$

No constraints are violated;
  CM = $1(7,200) + $.50(4,800) = $9,600

8,400 ravioli and 3,600 ziti packages

Mixing	$(3 \times 8,400) + (4 \times 3,600) = 39,600$
Stuffing	$(4 \times 8,400) + (3 \times 3,600) = 44,400$
Cooking	$(3 \times 8,400) + (2 \times 3,600) = 32,400$

No constraints are violated;
  CM = $1(8,400) + $.50(3,600) = $10,200

9,600 ravioli and 2,400 ziti packages

Mixing	$(3 \times 9,600) + (4 \times 2,400) = 38,400$
Stuffing	$(4 \times 9,600) + (3 \times 2,400) = 45,600$
Cooking	$(3 \times 9,600) + (2 \times 2,400) = 33,600$

The Stuffing Department constraint is violated; therefore, this is not a feasible solution.

Conclusion: The feasible solution that will maximize the contribution margin is 8,400 ravioli and 3,600 ziti packages.

CHAPTER 22

Part 1

1. T	6. F	11. T
2. F	7. T	12. F
3. T	8. T	13. F
4. F	9. T	14. F
5. F	10. T	15. T

Part 2

1. h	6. j	11. c
2. b	7. n	12. i
3. f	8. m	13. d
4. k	9. a	14. g
5. o	10. l	15. e

Part 3

1. c Future costs that differ between alternatives are the relevant costs. Historical costs are not relevant costs, and b and d are incorrect because variable costs alone or fixed costs alone are not relevant costs.

2. d The cost of capital represents the expected return that investors demand for a given level of risk; a, b, and c are capital expenditure evaluation techniques.

3. a Payback is the point where cumulative net cash inflow equals the cost of the investment.

$2,000 × 3 yrs. = $ 6,000
$3,000 × 3 yrs. = 9,000
                  $15,000

4. b Advantages of using the payback method include: (1) it is simple to compute and easy to understand, (2) it may be used to select those investments yielding a quick return of cash, (3) it permits a company to determine the length of time required to recapture its original investment, and (4) it is a widely used method that is an improvement over an intuitive method.

5. b The advantages of the net present value method and discounted cash flow rate of return methods include: (1) consideration of the time value of money and (2) consideration of cash flows over the entire life of the project.

6. c The time adjusted rate of return is the rate at which the sum of positive present values (inflows) exactly equals the sum of negative present values (outflows):

$843,000 = $800,000 + $43,000

7. a Let x = original investment.
NPV = PV of cash flows – Investment
$2,000 = ($8,000 × .91) + ($9,000 × .83) + ($10,000 × .75) – x
x = $20,250

8. a Disadvantages of the present value method include: (1) it is difficult to compute and to understand, (2) management must determine a discount rate to be used, (3) it does not consider the relative size of competing investments, and (4) it does not account for differences due to projects having unequal lives.

9. d $\dfrac{\text{Net cash inflow – depreciation}}{\text{Initial investment}}$ = Accounting rate of return

$\dfrac{\text{Net cash inflow} - (\$28,000/8)}{\$28,000}$ = 15%

Net cash inflow – $3,500 = $4,200
Net cash inflow = $7,700

10. a The answer is the interest rate that causes the present value of the cash flows to equal the amount of the investment; in this case, $497.

Part 4

Funds—Source	Proportion of Funds	After-Tax Cost	Weighted Cost
Bonds [15% × (1 – 30% tax rate)]	.333	.105	.0350
Preferred stock	.167	.125[1]	.0209
Common stock and retained earnings	.500	.162[2]	.0810
	1.00		.1369 or 13.69%

[1] (12% × $100 par) ÷ $96 = .125
[2] ($121,500 ÷ 50,000) ÷ $15 = .162

Part 5

1.

Year	Cash Benefit	Annual Depreciation*	Taxable Income	Federal Income Tax	Net After-Tax Cash Inflow
1	$45,000	$20,000	$25,000	$7,500	$ 37,500
2	50,000	32,000	18,000	5,400	44,600
3	44,000	19,200	24,800	7,440	36,560
4	38,000	11,500	26,500	7,950	30,050
5	34,000	11,500	22,500	6,750	27,250
6	10,000	5,800	4,200	1,260	8,740
					$184,700

*Year	Depreciable Base	MACRS Rate	Annual Depreciation
1	$100,000	20.0%	$20,000
2	100,000	32.0	32,000
3	100,000	19.2	19,200
4	100,000	11.5	11,500
5	100,000	11.5	11,500
6	100,000	5.8	5,800

2. (a)

Year	Cash Flow	Needed	Balance	Payback Years Required
1	$37,500	$100,000	$62,500	1.00
2	44,600	62,500	17,900	1.00
3	36,560	17,900	17,900	.49
4	–	–	–	–
5	–	–	–	–
6	–	–	–	–
Total payback period in years				2.49

(b) The average annual return on original investment = $\dfrac{\text{Net income}}{\text{Economic life}}$ ÷ Original investment = $\dfrac{\$84,700*}{6 \text{ yrs.}}$ ÷ $100,000 = 14.1%

* Net after-tax cash inflow	$184,700
Less depreciation	100,000
Net income	$ 84,700

(c) The average annual return on average investment = $\dfrac{\text{Net income}}{\text{Economic life}} \div \text{Average investment} = \dfrac{\$84,700}{6 \text{ yrs.}} \div \$50,000^* = \underline{\underline{28.2\%}}$

* Original investment	$100,000
Investment at end of life	—0—
Average investment ($100,000 ÷ 2) .	$ 50,000

(d) The net present value.

Year	Cash (Outflow) Inflow	Present Value of $1 at 12%	Net Present Value of Cash Flow
0.....................	$(100,000)	1.000	$(100,000)
1.....................	37,500	.893	33,488
2.....................	44,600	.797	35,546
3.....................	36,560	.712	26,031
4.....................	30,050	.636	19,112
5.....................	27,250	.567	15,451
6.....................	8,740	.507	4,431
Net present value			$ 34,059

(e) The discounted cash flow rate of return.

Year	Cash (Outflow) Inflow	Present Value of $1 at 25%	Net Present Value of Cash Flow	Present Value of $1 at 26%	Net Present Value of Cash Flow
0.....................	$(100,000)	1.000	$(100,000)	1.000	$(100,000)
1.....................	37,500	.800	30,000	.794	29,775
2.....................	44,600	.640	28,544	.630	28,098
3.....................	36,560	.512	18,719	.500	18,280
4.....................	30,050	.410	12,321	.397	11,930
5.....................	27,250	.328	8,938	.315	8,584
6.....................	8,740	.262	2,290	.250	2,185
			$ 812		$ (1,148)

Discounted cash flow rate of return: $25\% + (1\% \times \dfrac{812}{1,960}) = 25.41\%$

Part 6

1. (a) Purchase:

Investment			$(300,000)
Annual net cash inflow..	$100,000	$100,000	
Less depreciation	30,000		
Taxable income	$ 70,000		
Income tax		28,000	
Annual net cash inflow, after income tax		$ 72,000	
Present value of annual after-tax cash inflow			$406,800[1]
Present value of salvage value			9,660[2]
Net present value			$116,460

[1]$72,000 × 5.650 = $406,800
[2]$30,000 × .322 = $9,660

(b) Lease:

Annual net cash inflow, before lease payment	$ 100,000
Less annual lease payment	70,000
Annual net cash inflow	$ 30,000
Income tax	12,000
Annual net cash inflow, after income tax	$ 18,000
Net present value	$ 101,700*

*$18,000 × 5.650 = $101,700

2. Decision: The purchase alternative is preferable by $14,760.

CHAPTER 23

Part 1

1. F	6. F	11. F
2. T	7. F	12. T
3. T	8. T	13. F
4. T	9. T	14. T
5. T	10. T	15. T

Part 2

1. a	6. k	11. h
2. b	7. g	12. j
3. c	8. f	13. i
4. d	9. m	14. l
5. e	10. n	15. o

Part 3

1. c In capital budgeting analysis, the standard deviation is generally viewed as a measure of investment risk.

2. a Perfectly correlated cash flows might occur because consumer acceptance of the product in one period might have a direct bearing on the level of sales in the following period.

3. e Because the normal distribution is symmetrical and has only one mode, the expected value is not only the mean of the probability distribution but it is also the mode.

4. a The net present value of the expected cash flows would be the same when a normal probability distribution is used in capital expenditure analysis as it would when the probability distribution of future cash flows is ignored.

5. d If the cash flows in each period are independent, the standard deviation of the expected net present value is computed by taking the square root of the sum of the discounted period variances.

6. c Sometimes it may be necessary to construct a nonnormal probability distribution because not all future events that affect cash flows follow the pattern of random variables drawn from a normal distribution.

7. d In decision tree analysis, a process referred to as "backward induction" is used to determine the best course of action.

8. b Monte Carlo simulations are especially valuable in evaluating problems that contain numerous stochastic variables because such problems are difficult to evaluate analytically.

9. b

6,000 × .2 =	1,200
8,000 × .2 =	1,600
10,000 × .2 =	2,000
12,000 × .2 =	2,400
14,000 × .1 =	1,400
16,000 × .1 =	1,600
Expected value	10,200

10. c Break-even dollars $= \dfrac{\text{Fixed costs}}{1 - \dfrac{\text{Variable costs}}{\text{Sales}}} = \dfrac{\$240,000}{1 - \dfrac{\$30}{\$60}} = \dfrac{\$240,000}{1 - .5} = \$480,000$

Break-even units $= \dfrac{\$480,000}{\$60} = 8,000$ units $\therefore$

40% chance, .2 (at 6,000) + .2 (at 8,000) or .4 that this new product will not increase company profit.

Part 4

1.

Expected Contribution Margin
0
$ 150
1,200
900
900
750
$3,9- 00

2.

(1) Contribution Margin (Conditional Value)	(2) Difference From Expected Value ($3,900)	(3) (2) Squared	(4) Probability	(5) (3) × (4)
—0—	− 3,900	15,210,000	.05	$ 760,500
$1,500	− 2,400	5,760,000	.10	576,000
$3,000	− 900	810,000	.40	324,000
$4,500	+ 600	360,000	.20	72,000
$6,000	+ 2,100	4,410,000	.15	661,500
$7,500	+ 3,600	12,960,000	.10	1,296,000
				$3,690,000

Standard deviation $= \sqrt{\$3,690,000} = \$1,921$

3. Coefficient of variation $= \dfrac{\text{Standard deviation}}{\text{Expected contribution margin}} = \dfrac{\$1,921}{\$3,900} = .4926$

Part 5

1.

(1) Year	(2) Periodic Standard Deviation of Independent Cash Flows	(3) Present Value of $1 at 10%	(4) Periodic Variance $(2)^2$	(5) Present Value of $1 at 10% Squared $(3)^2$	(6) Present Value of Variance (4) × (5)
0	$ 0	1,000	0	1.000000	$ 0
1	1,000	.909	$1,000,000	.826281	826,281
2	1,000	.826	1,000,000	.682276	682,276
3	1,000	.751	1,000,000	.564001	564,001
4	1,000	.683	1,000,000	.466489	466,489
5	1,000	.621	1,000,000	.385641	385,641
Variance of the net present value for the independent cash flows					$2,924,688

2.

(1) Year	(2) Periodic Standard Deviation	(3) Present Value of $1 at 10%	(4) Present Value of Standard Deviation (2) × (3)
0	$ 0	1.000	0
1	2,000	.909	$1,818
2	2,000	.826	1,652
3	2,000	.751	1,502
4	2,000	.683	1,366
5	2,000	.621	1,242
Standard deviation of the net present value for dependent cash flows			$7,580

3. Variance of net present value for dependent cash flows ($7,580^2) $57,456,400

Variance of net present value for independent cash flows 2,924,688

Variance of total net present value of investment $60,381,088

4. $\sqrt{60,381,088} = \$7771$

Part 6

1.

Potential Action (Racquetball Facility Capacity to Be Built)	Annual After-Tax Net Cash Inflows from Different Levels of Demand				Expected Value of After-Tax Net Cash Inflows
	60,000	80,000	100,000	120,000	
60,000	$200,000	$200,000	$200,000	$200,000	$200,000
80,000	200,000	300,000	300,000	300,000	270,000
100,000	200,000	300,000	400,000	400,000	300,000
120,000	200,000	300,000	400,000	500,000	310,000
Probabilities	.30	.40	.20	.10	

2.

(1) Possible Action (Racquetball Facility Capacity To Be Built)	(2) Expected Value of Annual After-Tax Net Cash Inflows	(3) Present Value of 20-Year Annuity of $1 @ 10%	(4) Present Value of Annual After-Tax Net Cash Inflows (2) × (3)	(5) Initial Cash Outflow	(6) Expected Net Present Value (4) – (5)
60,000	$200,000	8.514	$1,702,800	$1,500,000	$202,800
80,000	270,000	8.514	2,298,780	2,000,000	298,780
100,000	300,000	8.514	2,554,200	2,500,000	54,200
120,000	310,000	8.514	2,639,340	3,000,000	(360,660)

Racquet Sports should build the the racquetball facility with the 80,000 one-hour time slot capacity because it has the largest net present value.

CHAPTER 24

Part 1

1. F	6. F	11. F
2. T	7. T	12. T
3. T	8. T	13. T
4. F	9. T	14. F
5. T	10. T	15. F

Part 2

1. o	8. q	15. d
2. b	9. m	16. p
3. t	10. a	17. i
4. l	11. c	18. g
5. s	12. n	19. e
6. j	13. r	20. f
7. h	14. k	

Part 3

1. d Order-getting costs are the costs of activities carried on to bring in the sales orders, whereas warehousing is an order-filling cost.

2. a Flexible budgets should be used for the control of marketing costs, such as order-filling costs, because a comparison of actual costs with predetermined *fixed* budget figures does not always give a fair evaluation of the activities of a function, due to the influence of volume and capacity.

3. a
Actual 19X4 sales	$ 750,000
19X4 sales at 19X3 prices (150,000 × $4)	600,000
Favorable sales price variance	$(150,000)
Actual 19X4 sales at 19X3 prices	$ 600,000
Total 19X3 sales	720,000
Unfavorable sales volume variance	$ 120,000

4. c Price = $\dfrac{\text{Total cost} + (\text{Desired rate of return} \times \text{Total capital employed})}{\text{Sales volume in units}}$

$= \dfrac{\$200,000 + (15\% \times \$500,000)}{50,000 \text{ units}} = \dfrac{\$275,000}{50,000 \text{ units}} = \$5.50$

5. a Return on capital employed = $\dfrac{\text{Profit}}{\text{Capital employed}}$

$.25 = \dfrac{\text{Profit}}{\$10,000,000}$

Profit = $.25 \times \$10,000,000 = \$2,500,000$

$\dfrac{\text{Profit}}{\text{Cost}} = \dfrac{\$2,500,000}{\$2,000,000} = 125\%$

6. a The Clayton Act prohibited price discrimination only where it had a serious effect on competition in general and did not contain any other provisions for the control of price discrimination.

7. c Budget allowance:
Fixed overhead budget	$ 3,000
Variable overhead ($.30 × 32,000 invoice lines)	9,600
	$12,600

8. b Spending variance:
Actual expenses	$12,700
Budget allowance	12,600
Unfavorable spending variance	$ 100

9. d Idle capacity variance:
Budget allowance	$12,600
Standard cost charged in ($.40 × 32,000 lines)	12,800
Favorable idle capacity variance	$ (200)

10. c The journal entry to record the variances would be:
Applied Billing Expense	12,800	
Billing Expense—Spending Variance	100	
Billing Expense—Idle Capacity Variance		200
Actual Billing Expense		12,700

Part 4

	Total	Indianapolis	Fort Wayne
		Territory	
Sales salaries	$108,000	$ 72,000	$36,000
Salespersons' expenses	50,000	32,000	18,000
Advertising	63,000	50,000	13,000
Delivery expense	33,000	27,500	5,500
Credit investigation expense	5,000	4,000	1,000
Collection expense	12,000	9,600	2,400
Total	$271,000	$195,100	$75,900

Part 5

1. $50,000 ÷ $400,000 = .125
$10,000 × .125 = $1,250.

2.
Actual cost	$4,100
Budget allowance	4,300
Spending variance	$ (200) fav.

3.
Budget allowance	$4,300
Standard selling cost ($35,000 × .125)	4,375
Idle capacity variance	$ (75) fav.

Part 6

Genie Electric
Income Statement
For the Year Ended December 31, 19–

	Department Stores	Retail Appliance Stores	Wholesalers	Total
Sales	$280,000	$525,000	$300,000	$1,105,000
Cost of goods sold	180,000	325,000	225,000	730,000
Gross profit	$100,000	$200,000	$ 75,000	$ 375,000
Less marketing expenses:				
Selling	$ 28,800	$ 38,400	$ 48,000	$ 115,200
Packing and shipping	1,920	9,280	4,800	16,000
Advertising	12,670	23,756	13,574	50,000
Credit and collection	4,200	9,200	6,600	20,000
General accounting	2,640	12,760	6,600	22,000
Total	$ 50,230	$ 93,396	$ 79,574	$ 223,200
Operating income (loss)	$ 49,770	$106,604	$ (4,574)	$ 151,800

Part 7

1.

	Product Delta	Product Gamma	Total
Sales	$550,000	$100,000	$650,000
Less variable costs and expenses:			
Cost of goods sold (at 15%)	$ 75,000	$ –	$ 75,000
(at 25%)	–	25,000	25,000
Advertising	24,000	–	24,000
Commissions (at 5%)	25,000	5,000	30,000
Shipping and packing	16,000	4,000	20,000
General and administrative expenses (15% of gross profit)	45,000	5,700	50,700
Total variable costs and expenses	$185,000	$ 39,700	$224,700
Contribution margin	$365,000	$ 60,300	$425,300
Fixed costs and expenses (not allocated):			
Manufacturing costs			$162,000
Administrative sales salaries			16,000
General and administrative expenses			21,300
Total fixed costs and expenses			$199,300
Net income			$226,000

2. Net income would decrease by $60,300 with the elimination of Product Gamma, since Product Gamma's contribution margin would be eliminated and the fixed costs allocated to Product Gamma in the original income statements would continue if Product Gamma were not produced.

Additional Computations:

Allocation of shipping and packing costs–

$$\frac{\text{Shipping and packing expenses}}{\text{Number of orders processed}} = \frac{\$20,000}{1,250} = \$16 \text{ per order}$$

To Product Delta . . . . 1,000 orders × $16 = $16,000
To Product Gamma . . . . 250 orders × $16 = $4,000

Fixed costs and expenses:

Manufacturing costs = Total costs – Variable costs
= $262,000 – $75,000 – 25,000
= $162,000

Marketing costs = Administrative sales salaries
= $16,000

General and administrative expenses = Total costs – Variable costs
= $72,000 – $50,700
= $21,300

Part 8

1. (a) Actual sales $568,000
Actual sales at budgeted prices:
X $412,500
Y 180,000   592,500
Sales price variance . . . . $ 24,500 unfav.

(b) Actual sales at budgeted prices $592,500
Budgeted sales 517,500
Sales volume variance . . . . $ 75,000 fav.

(c) Cost of goods sold—actual $480,000
Budgeted cost of actual units sold:
X $350,000
Y 144,000   494,000
Cost price variance . . . . $ 14,000 fav.

(d) Budgeted cost of actual units sold $494,000
Budgeted cost of budgeted units sold . . 430,000
Cost volume variance . . . . $ 64,000 unfav.

Sales volume variance . . . . $ 75,000 fav.
Cost volume variance . . . . 64,000 unfav.
Net volume variance . . . . $ 11,000 fav.

2. Actual sales at budgeted prices $592,500
Budgeted cost of actual units sold 494,000
Difference 98,500
Budgeted gross profit of actual units sold
[($517,500 – $430,000) ÷ 65,000]
× 74,000 99,615
Sales mix variance . . . . $ 1,115 unfav.

Budgeted gross profit of actual units sold . 99,615
Budgeted sales $517,500
Budgeted cost of budgeted units sold 430,000
Budgeted gross profit 87,500
Final sales volume variance . . . . $ 12,115 fav.

Part 9

Alternative Sales Price	Variable Manufacturing Cost per Unit	Contribution Margin per Unit	Unit Sales	Total Contribution Margin	Additional Advertising and Promotion Expenditures	Contribution to Other Fixed Costs
19A:						
$20.00	$-					
	15	$ 5.00	225,000	$1,125,000	$ 550,000	$ 575,000
22.50	15	7.50	210,000	1,575,000	700,000	875,000
25.00	15	10.00	200,000	2,000,000	750,000	1,250,000
27.50	15	12.50	190,000	2,375,000	800,000	1,575,000
30.00	15	15.00	175,000	2,625,000	1,000,000	1,625,000

The recommended sales price would be $30.

19B:						
$20.00	$-					
	17	$ 3.00	245,000	$ 735,000	$ 600,000	$ 135,000
22.50	17	5.50	230,000	1,265,000	725,000	540,000
25.00	17	8.00	220,000	1,760,000	750,000	1,010,000
27.50	17	10.50	210,000	2,205,000	825,000	1,380,000
30.00	17	13.00	195,000	2,535,000	1,200,000	1,335,000

The recommended sales price would be $27.50.

Part 10

1.
$$\text{Price} = \frac{\text{Total cost} + (\text{Desired rate of return} \times \text{Total capital employed})}{\text{Sales volume in units}}$$

$$\$25 = \frac{(\$20 \times 200{,}000) + (\text{Desired rate of return} \times \$5{,}000{,}000)}{200{,}000}$$

$\$5{,}000{,}000 = \$4{,}000{,}000 + \$5{,}000{,}000 \times \text{Desired rate of return}$

Desired rate of return $= 20\%$

2.
$$\text{Price} = \frac{(\$20 \times 220{,}000) + (.20 \times \$5{,}000{,}000)}{220{,}000} = \$24.55$$

CHAPTER 25

Part 1

1. T	6. T	11. T
2. T	7. F	12. T
3. F	8. T	13. F
4. T	9. T	14. T
5. T	10. F	15. F

Part 2

1. g	6. f	11. m
2. e	7. c	12. h
3. a	8. n	13. i
4. l	9. d	14. j
5. b	10. k	

Part 3

1. c The use of different accounting methods by companies makes comparisons without first adjusting the financial statements difficult.

2. a Return on investment = Capital turnover rate × Profit margin on sales

3. a Market-based transfer prices are the best transfer prices to use for evaluating departmental performance.

4. a Suboptimization means that the decision made by the individual segment manager did not maximize the profits for the company as a whole.

5. d If Y's facilities would otherwise remain idle, it would be more profitable for X to buy inside because there would be a positive contribution margin of $5 per unit ($75 – $70) to contribute to the recovery of the fixed costs of $15,000.

6. c ROI is affected by both profit as a percentage of sales and by capital turnover. If one decreases while the other remains the same, ROI will decrease.

7. d In a decentralized company, the transfer pricing system should be designed so that division managers have the freedom to sell/buy outside if it enhances division profit. The appraisal of managerial performance is meaningful only if division managers are given this autonomy.

8. d Rate of return on capital employed $= \dfrac{\text{Profit}}{\text{Capital employed}} = \dfrac{\$25{,}000}{\$100{,}000} = 25\%$

9. a Capital-employed turnover rate $= \dfrac{\text{Sales}}{\text{Capital employed}} = \dfrac{\$100{,}000}{\$100{,}000} = 1$

10. c Residual Income = Income – (Capital Charge × Assets Employed)

Part 4

1. Product	Capital-Employed Turnover Rate	Percentage of Profit to Sales	Rate of Return on Capital Employed
727	$\dfrac{\$1,500,000}{\$\ 750,000} = 2$	$\dfrac{\$\ \ \ 75,000}{\$1,500,000} = 5\%$	$5\% \times 2 = 10\%$
747	$\dfrac{\$1,000,000}{\$\ 500,000} = 2$	$\dfrac{\$\ 200,000}{\$1,000,000} = 20\%$	$20\% \times 2 = 40\%$
767	$\dfrac{\$\ 6,000,000}{\$12,000,000} = .5$	$\dfrac{\$1,200,000}{\$6,000,000} = 20\%$	$20\% \times .5 = 10\%$

2. No, they do not have the same problems. 727's profit as a percentage of sales is too low, whereas 767's capital-employed turnover rate is too low. Assuming that sales are currently maximized, 727 must concentrate on cost-cutting measures, while 767 must reduce its investment in assets such as receivables, inventory, and property, plant and equipment.

Part 5

System	Cannes	Paris	Corporation as a Whole
Market-based transfer pricing:			
Sales to outsiders	$ 600,000	$ 500,000	$1,100,000
Cost of goods sold	560,000 [1]	400,000	960,000
Gross profit	$ 40,000	$ 100,000	$ 140,000
Standard cost (using 25,000 gallons as basis for allocating fixed costs):			
Sales to customers	$ 600,000	$ 500,000	$1,100,000
Intracompany sales (costs)	130,000	(130,000) [3]	—
Cost of goods sold	(650,000) [2]	(265,000) [4]	(915,000)
Gross profit	$ 80,000	$ 105,000	$ 185,000

[1]($18 \times 20,000$ gals.) + \$200,000 = \$560,000

[2]($18 \times 25,000$ gals.) + \$200,000 = \$650,000

[3]$\left(\$18 + \dfrac{\$200,000}{25,000} \right) \times 5,000$ gals. = \$130,000

[4]$\left(\$40 - \dfrac{\$27}{2} \right) \times 10,000$ bags = \$265,000

Part 6

1. Average invested capital = $\dfrac{\$500,000 + \$700,000}{2} = \$600,000$

Net income:

Sales	$600,000
Less: Variable costs	450,000
Contribution margin	$150,000
Less: Fixed costs	90,000
Operating income	$ 60,000

Return on investment = $\dfrac{\$60,000}{\$600,000} = 10\%$

2. Residual income (loss) = $60,000 − (15% × $600,000) = ($30,000)

3.

Sales	$600,000
Less: Variable costs	450,000
Contribution margin	$150,000